the Love and Glory of God

Images of the mosaic iconography on the front [Theotokos Platytera] and back covers [border and scroll work] of this book are the work of Mosaic Iconographer Robert Andrews in the Church of the Transfiguration of Our Lord and Saviour Jesus Christ in Lowell, Massachusetts, USA.

Cover photographs by Jean Butler, Westford, Massachusetts, USA   http://jeanbutlerphotography.com/about.html

Mary
for the Love and Glory of God

Essays on Mary and Ecumenism
given at the International Congress of the
Ecumenical Society of the Blessed Virgin Mary,
USA at Pittsburgh, Pennsylvania (2008)

edited by

Maura Hearden
and
Virginia M. Kimball

with a Foreword by
William McLoughlin, OSM
Hon. Gen. Sec.

Page Editing ... Susan Lillian Fall

authorHOUSE®

AuthorHouse™
1663 Liberty Drive
Bloomington, IN 47403
www.authorhouse.com
Phone: 1-800-839-8640

First published by AuthorHouse 3/24/2011

ISBN: 978-1-4567-5667-3 (sc)
ISBN: 978-1-4567-5668-0 (e)

Library of Congress Control Number: 2011904359

Printed in the United States of America

Contents

Notes on Contributors

Very Rev. John Behr is Dean of St. Vladimir's Seminary in Crestwood, New York, and Professor of Patristics there, teaching courses in Patristics, Dogmatics and Scriptural Exegesis, and also is the Distinguished Lecturer in Patristics at Fordham University in New York City. Among his voluminous published works are: *The Mystery: Life in Death; The Way to Nicea* vol. 1; *The Nicene Faith*, vol. 2; and *Asceticism and Anthropology in Irenaeus and Clement*. Fr. Behr is a priest of the Orthodox Church in America (OCA). He has been a member of the Lutheran-Orthodox Dialogue, USA, from 2000 to the present.

Dr. Robert L. Fastiggi is Professor of Systematic Theology at Sacred Heart Major Seminary in Detroit, Michigan. He is a member of the Mariological Society of America and one of the editors of the *New Catholic Encyclopedia*.

Sr. Nonna Verna Harrison is an Eastern Orthodox nun and a professor of Church History. She is a specialist in Patristics and Orthodox Theology, author of many scholarly articles and books, including *St. Basil the Great: On the Human Condition, St. Gregory of Nazianzus: Festal Orations,* and *God's Many-Splendored Image: Theological Anthropology for Christian Formation.*

Dr. Maura Hearden is Roman Catholic and a professor of Theology at De Sales University, Center Valley, Pennsylvania. She holds a doctorate in Theology from Marquette University and centers her research and interests in Mariology, inter-religious dialogue and ecumenism. She serves as a member on the board of the Ecumenical Society of the Blessed Virgin Mary, USA.

Rev. Jennifer Mary Kimball is pastor of the First Congregational Church, United Church of Christ, of Walton, New York. She is a board member of ESBVM, USA. Annually, Rev. Kimball and her church present an Intergenerational Day for Women and Daughters on Mary, called "A Day of Reflection on Mary," now in its fourth year and in conjunction with ESBVM, USA.

Dr. Virginia M. Kimball is an Eastern Orthodox theologian and adjunct professor at Assumption College in Worcester, Massachusetts. She holds a Doctorate in Marian Theology from the International Marian Institute in Dayton, Ohio. Dr. Kimball is president of the Ecumenical Society of the Blessed Virgin Mary, USA branch, and former president of the Mariological Society of America. She was a contributor to *Mary for Time and Eternity*, a collection of essays on Mary and ecumenism published by ESBVM, Gracewing Publications, 2007; *Theological Illuminations: Discovering Received Tradition in the Eastern Orthros of the Feasts of the Theotokos;* has contributed journal articles to *Marian Studies;* and poetry and articles to the Mary Page and other online websites.

Rev. Dr. Donald Charles Lacy is a United Methodist pastor and well-known ecumenist, author and lecturer, long-time Mariologist, and member of the board the ESBVM, USA. He is a tireless promoter of the importance of the Virgin Mary among Protestants. He is author of the popular *Collected Works of Donald Charles Lacy, Fast Food for the Soul, More Fast Food for the Soul, Paul's Pastoral Passages of Promise, With an Attitude of Gratitude* and numerous articles.

Father Bill M. McLoughlin, OSM is a Servite friar, currently serving as Catholic Chaplain at the University of Bath and Bath Spa University in the UK. He is also Parish Priest of Saints Peter & Paul Church - one of the City of Bath parishes, serves as a Hospital Chaplain, and is the Honorary General Secretary of the ESBVM.

Sr. Barbara Jean Mihalchick, OSBM, is a Byzantine Catholic who holds an M.A. in Christian Spirituality. She is vocation director of the Uniontown, Pennsylvania, Province of the Sisters of the Order of St. Basil the Great and Program Director of the Mount St. Macrina House of Prayer, and serves as retreat leader and spiritual director.

Sr. Mary Catherine Nolan, OP, is a Roman Catholic, Dominican sister, theologian, Mariologist, author, lecturer and retreat director. She holds an S.T.D. from the International Marian Research Institute in Dayton, Ohio. Currently, she is a board member of the Mariological Society of America and is actively researching the role of the Virgin Mary in Islam. She is the author of *Mary's Song: Living the Timeless Prayer.*

Rev. Dr. Edward J. Ondrako, OFM Conv, is Scholar in Residence at the Franciscan International Study Centre in Canterbury, Kent, England. He is the author of *Progressive Illuminations: A Journey with John Henry Cardinal Newman, 1980-2005,* published in 2006. He is an active member in the ESBVM.

The Rev. Dr. Paul Snowden Russell III is an Anglican priest and Dean of St. Joseph of Arimathea Anglican Theological College in Berkeley, California. He is a noted Syriac scholar, author of numerous articles and books, is a distinguished member of the North American Syriac Symposium. He specializes in research on St. Ephraem the Syrian.

Foreword

Thirty years ago, Dr. Eric Kemp, Executive Co-Chairmen of the ESBVM and also Anglican Bishop of Chichester at that time, along with Dr. Gordon Wakefield, Principal of Queen's College, Birmingham, UK, both gone to God, and the surviving Dr. Mervyn Alexander, Roman Catholic Bishop Emeritus of Clifton, UK offered recognition of the work of the ESBVM as a serious discussion on the place of Mary which should not be merely a peripheral subject, but treated with care as it was in the ESBVM. They pointed out that, "In the course of our meetings all the central Christian doctrines come under scrutiny. We have also been led into many highways and byways of art, history, literature and science! More than ever we are convinced that Mary represents a way forward in ecumenical relations."

This claim can be made of ESBVM efforts of recent time as well and very much for the essays furnished in this collection. If the ESBVM is faithful to its task, it moves away from the mere criticism of excess that particular traditions had once made, albeit as a desire for correction, while lamentably often losing sight of the purpose of renewal, which was to recover the value then at risk and not, as sometimes happened, totally to discard it. These papers once again endeavor to help all look afresh at sources of strength and insight in various traditions that sometimes have been reduced to a silence about the Blessed Virgin Mary, that was often mistaken and self-impoverishing, but also to that transition in devotion to the Mother of God from East to West that Newman saw as an enrichment that came gradually and later.

The historic first holding of our International ESBVM Congress in the United States of America was a remarkable moment. We hope without hubris that we might say that the long tradition of international congresses presented by our society has been a rich contribution to the particular work of Ecumenism in which we are engaged as an international society

11

now in our 43rd year. The fact that the 16th Congress broke new ground in being held in the USA was the culmination of a long standing participation from its inception by members of the society in the States, including distinguished ecumenists, to mention but a few, such as Dr. Donald Dawes, Rev. Ross McKenzie, Fr. Fred Jelly, OP and Fr. Eamon Carroll, OCarm., some now gone to Lord, who were generous travelers to the early congresses held in the UK and Ireland and enthusiastic encouragers of ecumenical exchange in groundbreaking times. New and equally distinguished contributors are emerging today and a fresh impetus to efforts in the USA and in Europe can rightly be expected.

A wonderful fare of reflection and prayer emerged at the 2008 ESBVM Congress as is evidenced in the following pages, and the whole of our Society will undoubtedly benefit from its having taken place. The appearance of the papers in published form will now benefit a wider audience, too, which is one of the key purposes of holding the international congresses.

The task of achieving publication of papers is often a daunting one, and the indefatigable efforts of the editors in this case in the face of not a few difficulties are to be more than commended. The papers brought together in this volume are wide-ranging. The original topic of the congress dealt with 'Daughter of Zion: Mother of the New Creation' with which the *'glory'* part of the collection's title resonates and various presenters touched a thread dealing with 'mediation' echoed in the *'love of God'* part of the title.

The focus of the ten contributors whose material is included ranges from ecumenism per se and its history within certain traditions to recent Mariological work in which the writers had been engaged, and crucially much of this has been usefully ecumenical too. The representation of Christian traditions reflecting the membership of the ESBVM and an awakening interest across the Christian communities is evidenced in the material at hand, and the readiness to discuss issues with freshness and new insights demonstrates the value of drawing together on these occasions of exchange.

The Constitution of The Ecumenical Society of the Blessed Virgin Mary indicates that it exists to advance the study at various levels of the place of the Blessed Virgin in the Church under Christ, and of related theological questions; and in the light of such study to promote ecumenical devotion. Over this past decade and earlier, various dialogues have taken up the question of Mary, and we see that greater understanding with regard to the place of Mary in the Church has resulted. The papers brought together in the 16th International Congress stand well in that continuing effort and foster that wish that the Blessed Virgin should not be a source of division, but rather a central force for communion among those who acknowledge her Son Jesus Christ as Saviour and Lord.

Fr. Bill M. McLoughlin, OSM
Honorary General Secretary of ESBVM
BATH
21st April 2010
Feast of St. Anselm of Canterbury

Preface

Rev. Dr. Edward J. Ondrako, OFM Conv

In "Discourses to Mixed Congregations," John Henry Newman offers offer two moving accounts of his own progressive understanding of Mary in his life and in the life of the Church, "The Glories of Mary for the Sake of Her Son," and, "On the Fitness of the Glories of Mary." These discourses published in 1849 are hortatory and polemical. Born on February 21, 1801, the young John Henry knew nothing about Mary, until his faithful and dear friend Richard Hurrell Froude began to enlighten him with a balanced understanding of Mary. In 1843, his fifteenth university sermon given to the faculty of Oxford, on the Feast of the Presentation, John Henry advanced the view that Mary is the "pattern of faith." This insight helped him to move from what really mattered in his life, from a notional theory of the development of doctrine, to real assent. Newman continued as an illuminating trajectory of a person panting for truth all his life. Mary remained central to that personal quest for truth through his humble contemplation and sustained intellectual effort. Newman's writings about Mary, along with the circumstances and persons that helped him to get it right, are a most significant key to understanding his intellectual honesty.

The Ecumenical Society of the Blessed Virgin Mary lives this vision of Newman implicitly and explicitly, even with the welcomed multiplicity of views about Mary. The United States group met recently at Vienna, Virginia, on the feast of St. Joseph the Worker, the spouse of Our Lady, a not insignificant coincidence. The esteemed Mariologist, Rev. Dr. Peter Damian Fehlner, FI, summarizes succinctly: "The virginal maternity of Mary is sometimes casually referred to as that of an 'unwed mother.'" The maternity being virginal was most perfect, but at the same time within "holy wedlock" in the proper sense of the term. The properly "virginal" fatherhood of Joseph in the Holy Family and in the Church cannot be under-stressed and will certainly not be under-stressed if Blessed John Duns Scotus is taken seriously.

After some discussion of the ground breaking ESBVM International Meeting held in the United States, at Pittsburgh in August 2008, the governing body looked forward with anticipation to the publishing of "Mary for the Love and Glory of God," edited by Dr. Virginia Kimball and Dr. Maura Hearden. This volume is part of the rising tide of the resources by Christian searchers with an ecumenical motivation who are devoted to Mary. Academic research by its nature gives respectful space for reasonable minds to disagree. Hence, the papers "Mary for the Love and Glory of God" serendipitously imply a definition of theology from St. Bonaventure that is three fold: the importance of following rigorous academic principles, along with the study of the Creeds and their true development, as well as humble prayer and contemplation of the life and doctrines about Mary. That is St. Bonaventure's view of authentic Mariology. It is in this spirit, with varying degrees of conviction for understandable reasons, that the papers given at Pittsburgh elicit serious reflection and promise to move Marian understanding forward.

To this end, one of the most inspiring and memorable statements about Mary came from the Archbishop of Canterbury, Rowan Williams, who led a pilgrimage together with Walter Cardinal Kasper from the Shrine of Our Lady of Walsingham in England to Lourdes in September 2009. The Archbishop said that the ecumenical movement will not make progress without Our Lady. That is a clarion cry to take time and to study in a calm, hope-filled manner that gets beneath the historical controversies about Mary. Moreover, the example and words of the Archbishop and Cardinal are clear: to join together in prayer and pilgrimage. One practical way is to begin each meeting with one of the beautiful Marian prayers handed down from antiquity. The earliest extant is "Sub Tuum Praesidum" from the third century (which is in the Rylands Library , Manchester, England).

To recapitulate, the papers from the International meetings of the ESBVM are one helpful means to fulfill the will for unity as willed by Jesus. May these papers and humble efforts bear fruit! May they contribute to be effective and enlightened conversations that work for the unity of the Church even with so many of her members truly holy and deeply devoted to the Mother of God! Mary, whose glories are for the sake of your Son, pray for us!.

Sub Tuum Praesidium
Under Your Protection
c. 250 AD

Greek Text	English Translation
Ὑπὸ τὴν σὴν εὐσπλαγχνίαν, καταφεύγομεν, Θεοτόκε. Τὰς ἡμῶν ἱκεσίας, μὴ παρίδῃς ἐν περιστάσει, ἀλλ᾽ ἐκ κινδύνων λύτρωσαι ἡμᾶς, μόνη Ἁγνή, μόνη εὐλογημένη.	Beneath your compassion, We take refuge, O Mother of God: do not despise our petitions in time of trouble: but rescue us from dangers, only pure, only blessed one.

1.
Tribute

Robert Andrews
America's Own Byzantine
Mosaic Iconographer

Virginia M. Kimball

When Robert Andrews was a very young man he probed the heavens as a Navy flier, but then God pierced his heart and took him to the true Heavens ... becoming America's only Byzantine mosaic iconographer.

Andrews' journey as an iconographer has embraced a lifetime. Prior to this First International Congress of the Ecumenical Society of the Blessed Virgin Mary, in August 2008, Andrews had just completed the largest mosaic face of Christ in the western hemisphere, mounted 90 feet above the floor in the central dome of the Holy Trinity Greek Orthodox Church in San Francisco, California, in the United States. The face of Christ measures an astounding 23 feet long.

Modest and quiet, Andrews usually finds it difficult to talk about his work. The work of an iconographer's calling is truly spiritual in nature. Artistic skill has to be combined with an appreciation and deep knowledge of a long Christian tradition. The conversation that best suits him is carried out high on scaffolding while he is at work.

His latest project involved hands-on placement of *tesserae*, whose color and design dwelt creatively in his head, and then went to paper plans using a selection of 5,000 tile colors. In this mosaic there are approximately 1,360,000 pieces of *tesserae* used to cover the entire 3400 square foot dome. It was fascinating for ESBVM members at our 2008 Congress banquet to hear Andrews describe this magnificent and spiritual work.

In unassuming fashion, Andrews shared a few words about the work of an iconographer as the tradition has been carried down through the centuries from early Byzantium. Technically, it is not artwork. The elements of an icon are "written" -- considered to be inspired "words" that open up the mystery of God's good news on earth. Figures appear almost surrealistic, elongated, and facing forward using inverted perspective -- meant to open doors to spiritual illumination.

Mary's son in the dome of the Holy Trinity Greek Orthodox Church on Brotherhood Way in San Francisco, California, is a momentous achievement. High in the central dome, it is Christ the *Pantocrator*, the Sustainer of All. Yet, to stand on the church floor beneath this piece and look up, one can't help but be drawn to Christ's loving and embracing eyes.

Andrews let his work speak for him. Members of the ESBVM were treated to a video presentation of the process of creating and installing this unique representation of the Son of God, son of Mary. The documentary can be seen at:

http://www.vimeo.com/1119924

The video provides a comprehensive look at the long process in creating this *Pantocrator* mosaic. Questions after the video led to awe as Andrews explained the mathematical calculations required to create a realistic image -- understandable to the human eye far below. The engineering task of preparing the dome to hold the great mosaic was fascinating enough, but then the skilled mosaic master began his work. Long before in the studio of his home, Andrews prepared the angles and positions of the icon's elements.

Mosaic icons by Andrews can be found in more than twenty-five locations across the United States – from San Francisco, Irvine, and Stockton, California; to Seattle, Washington; Salt Lake City, Utah; Albuquerque, New Mexico; Phoenix, Arizona; Merrillville, Indiana; Rochester, New York; Washington, DC; Binghamton, New York; Tacoma, Washington; Dover, New Hampshire (his original hometown);

at the Greek Orthodox Memorial Park in Colma, CA and the
Serbian Orthodox Cemetery in South San Francisco, CA; and
near to his home now in Massachusetts -- Fall River, Hyannis,
Lowell, Marlboro, Pittsfield, Somerville, Springfield, Cohasset,
Haverhill, Quincy, and Boston. In Europe, Andrews has
written icons in St. Sophia Cathedral in London, UK. It was at
the Transfiguration of the Saviour Greek Orthodox Church, in
Lowell, Massachusetts, that I first met Andrews, learning that
the process also represents the life, faith, and contribution of
parish members throughout a years-long installation.

These icons are for everyone, not just the Orthodox.
St. John of Damascus, during the attack on icons during the 8th
century (long before major Christian divisions), wrote to defend
iconographic images which he termed "Divine Images." In his
first treatise in defense of religious pictures, St. John of
Damascus based his justification for iconography as it refers to
the incarnation of God:

> Therefore, I boldly draw an image of the invisible God,
> not as invisible, but as having become visible for our
> sakes by partaking of flesh and blood (cf. Heb 2:14).[1]

The Almighty took on flesh and this was St. John's defense of
religious images. For members of the ESBVM that night, the
work of Andrews brought us to contemplate that majesty of
God, the Judge of All – Son of the Virgin Mary.

> How can the invisible be depicted? How does one
> picture the inconceivable? How can one draw what is
> limitless, immeasurable, infinite? How does one paint
> the bodiless? How can you describe what is a mystery? It
> is obvious that when you contemplate God becoming
> man, then you may depict Him clothed in human form.[2]

---

[1] St. John of Damascus, *On the Divine Images, Three Apologies Against Those Who
Attack the Divine Images,* translated by David Anderson (Crestwood, New
York: St. Vladimir's Seminary Press, 1980), § 4, 16.
[2] St. John of Damascus, § 8, 18.

Mary and Doctrine

2.

Speaking of Mary and the Church[1]

John Behr

My subject today is how we speak of the Virgin Mother of God – specifically, how we speak of Mary and how our discourse about her is shaped by how we speak of the Church. We speak in many different ways of Mary – whose womb is more spacious than the heavens, for she gave birth to God – but we don't often step back to think of *how* it is that we speak like this. Rowan Williams commented that "Theology is perennially tempted to be seduced by the prospect of by-passing the question of how it learns its own language."[2]

This is not just a question of history, recalling how we learnt in the past, for the evolution of a discourse profoundly informs how that discourse itself speaks and shapes the world in which it speaks. In the case of theology, this is especially important. And perhaps in a way that has yet to be fully recognized, this is true of Mary. When we begin to look at the development of discourse about Mary, the Virgin Mother, the Mother of our Lord, we will begin to hear resonances within this that bring us into a very profound understanding of our own relationship to Christ, in the Church, and also of the transforming power of the Gospel in history, for, as we will see, in the history of theological reflection, it seems that Christians began by reflecting on the motherhood of the Church, and then came to speak of Mary in ways that reflect this.

---

[1] Much of the material for this essay comes from, and occasionally develops, Chapter Four, "The Virgin Mother" in John Behr, *The Mystery of Christ: Life in Death* (Crestwood, NY: SVS Press, 2006).
[2] Rowan Williams, *On Christian Theology* (Oxford: Blackwell, 2000), 131.

We should start by recalling that within the canonical gospels, there are two main places in which Mary appears: in the infancy narratives and at the crucifixion as it is described in the Gospel of John. In the liturgical tradition of the Orthodox Church, however, there are four main Marian feasts: her Nativity, her Entry into the Temple, the Annunciation, and her Dormition. And it is instructive to consider the scriptural readings assigned for these feasts. The Annunciation, as the only event, of the four, recorded within the canonical gospels, has its own reading for the festal liturgy; but the gospel reading prescribed for the liturgy of the other feasts is the passage describing Jesus' conversation with Mary and Martha, and then concludes with a woman from the crowd crying out: "'Blessed is the womb that bore you, and the breasts that you sucked.' But he said, 'Blessed rather are those that hear the Word of God and keep it.'" (Luke 11:27-8).[3]

Christ's words are striking because they direct our attention away from his biological mother – the womb that bore him and the breasts that he sucked – and focus our attention instead on the condition of faith – hearing the Word and keeping it. As Christ says earlier in the same Gospel, when told that his mother and brothers standing outside want to see him: "My mother and my brothers are those who hear the word of God and do it" (Luke 8:21). Those who hear the word of God, receiving the Word and embodying it, giving it flesh, are, in Christ's own words, his mother and brother.

These words of Christ are not read at the Annunciation because, quite simply, Mary here embodies this. The gospels present no one else as keeping the Word of God in a pure heart apart from Mary, the Mother of Jesus; and this is what we celebrate in the Feast of the Annunciation: that Mary hears the Word of God announced by the angel, accepts it, and conceives Christ in her womb.

---

[3] Biblical quotations in this article are taken from *The New Oxford Annotated Bible with the Apocrypha, Expanded Edition*, Revised Standard Version (New York: Oxford University Press, 1977) except where noted.

As mentioned, the other main place where Mary appears is the crucifixion as described in the Gospel According to John; and here again it is her faithfulness to the Word that is emphasized, in distinction to the Synoptic Gospels where Mary is not mentioned as present at the crucifixion: the disciples had abandoned Christ (or even, as Peter, denied him), while the women who had ministered to him stood some distance apart: Mary Magdalene, Mary the mother of James and Joseph, and the mother of the sons of Zebedee (Matt 27:56 and Mark 15:41; Luke 23:49 just mentions women from Galilee).

But in the Gospel of John we have the scene thereafter depicted in Byzantine iconography: Jesus on the cross with his mother and the beloved disciple standing at its foot (the Gospel also mentions his mother's sister, Mary, the wife of Cleopas, and Mary Magdalene – but they recede into the background on the icon, if there at all). And the words spoken by Christ from the cross relate, once again, to motherhood: "Woman, behold, your son"; and to the disciple, "Behold, your mother" (John 19:26-7). Those who stand by the cross, and are not ashamed of it, receive as their mother the one who embodies this fertile, generative faithfulness, and they themselves become sons, as Christ himself is the Son of God – they have put on this identity of Christ.

In the Annunciation and crucifixion, then, we focus on Mary as the one who is obedient to God, enabling the birth of the Son of God and opening the way for others to become sons of God. This is the starting point for how we speak of Mary.

But, before we go on, it is important to note that this is not the only way that the mother of Jesus appears in the gospels. When she appears elsewhere, which is not all that often, she is portrayed in strikingly different terms: she searches anxiously for her young son, and is astonished to find him in his Father's house debating with the teachers – and then she reproaches him!(Luke 2:41-51); when Jesus was rumored to be

27

"beside himself," "possessed by Beelzebub," his mother and his brothers[4] went "to seize him," but he said in return that "whoever does the will of God is my brother, and sister, and mother" (Mark 3: 21-35); and when she makes her request at the marriage celebration in Cana, she receives a sharp rebuke from Christ ... "what have you to do with me? My time has not yet come!" (John 2:4). It is also noteworthy that in these passages the mother of Jesus is not actually called "Mary," a point we will take up later.

When we hear these words, our tendency is to mollify them, to soften them. We start with what we think we already know of Mary (the all-pure Virgin) and then find a way of explaining these passages. St John Chrysostom, on the other hand, takes a very different approach (and, to be sure, he is unique in this). Commenting on such passages and the words of Christ about his mother and his brothers, St John Chrysostom describes her as being a demanding mother, overconfident in her authority over her son, "not yet thinking," as Chrysostom says, "anything great about him." His conclusion is that "we learn here that even to have borne Christ in the womb, and to have brought forth that marvelous birth, has no profit, if there is not virtue." But, he continues, Christ "has pointed out a spacious road: and it is granted not only to women but also to men, to be of this rank, or rather of one yet higher. For this makes one his mother much more than those birth-pangs did."[5]

What should we make of this? Rather than explaining St John Chrysostom away (he was the only one to speak of Mary this way), I would suggest that we should rather be challenged by his boldness and allow these words about the mother of Jesus to also challenge us, to allow this tension between these two images to lead us to a deeper understanding of how it is

---

[4] The word "family" in this section is understood to be his mother and his brothers. See Mark 3:31.

[5] St John Chrysostom, *Homily 44 on Matthew* (on Matt 12.46-9). In NPNF first series, vol. 10.

that we speak specifically of Mary. I would suggest that what we have is two different ways of viewing Jesus' mother, and two correspondingly different ways of speaking about her.

In one, she is seen as beginning, as it were, *in* the condition to which Eve had reduced the human race. Here she is very much Jesus' mother, acting in the way that St John Chrysostom's view characterizes it. With her in this condition, we focus on Christ alone as the one who has brought us back into paradise, for his work recreates all of creation and its history.

The second way of speaking of her, however, *builds upon this basis*, to speak now of Mary as the New Eve, the one who, by her obedience to God, conceives or gives flesh to the Word. This is already at work in the infancy narratives of Matthew and Luke, events we celebrate in the Annunciation. The scripture readings for the other Marian feasts also direct us to this condition of faith, hearing and receiving the Word of God. And the other Marian feasts also extend this contemplation to the celebration of the key events in her life: Nativity, her Entry into the Temple (or her identification with the Temple), and her Dormition.

It must be stated emphatically that, theologically and historically, the first way of speaking is primary: Christ alone is the mediator, redeemer and savior. Only slowly does the feast of the Annunciation come to be celebrated (I'll come back to this later), and then much later the other feasts of Mary. And these feasts develop later on, not by the discovery of previously unknown historical information, but rather by thinking through what is effected by Christ's saving work, how it redeems and transforms all of human history, beginning, most intimately, with his mother.

In other words, there is a theological principle at work in the development of the language of theology, one which we cannot afford to ignore. Christian theology always speaks in the light of the risen Christ – a light which illumes and transfigures all of creation and its history – understanding him by turning back to the scriptures inspired by the same Spirit, and now also seeing that the Lord Jesus has been at work in it all and through it all to lead to him. Because of this, we need to pay careful attention to how it is that we speak of Mary in the liturgical feasts celebrating her, lest we take what is said of Mary, by virtue of Christ's work of salvation, as applied to his mother throughout her life, independently of the work of Christ.

This is really what is at issue in the debates about the Immaculate Conception: whether prior to, and independent of Christ, Mary is pure, without original sin, and so apart from us; or whether the purity necessary for giving birth to Christ is dependent upon his (later) work of redemption. As we will see, the Annunciation and conception of Christ is already intimately related to the Passion of Christ and the proclamation of the Gospel; and what we celebrate about the life of Mary in the Marian Feasts of her Nativity, Entrance into the Temple and Dormition, are always already described in terms of what has happened in and through Christ, even to the point of Thomas again being late at her Dormition, as he was for the resurrection of Christ. The Marian feasts of the Church present a theological reflection on who Mary is and what she has done, reflection made in the light of Christ's work of salvation. They are confessional statements of faith, a theological reflection based upon Christ, not an attempt to bypass his work, to get at what "really happened" prior to, and independent of, that work. As Anselm put it (after discussing the Immaculate Conception, and insisting that Mary is pure because of the work of Christ – so that he is pure from himself, not because of her):

> When God does anything, once it is done it is
> impossible for it not to have been done, but it is
> always true that it has been done; and yet it is not

right to say that it is impossible for God to make what is past not to be past.[6]

In these scriptural descriptions of the Annunciation and the Nativity of Christ, and in the other liturgical celebrations of Mary, we are directed not simply to his mother, "the womb that bore him and the breasts that he sucked." We are directed rather to Mary as the one who received the Word and gave birth to Christ, and whose whole life is transfigured by this. Moreover, we are given all this as an exhortation for us also to receive the Word, standing firmly by the cross and putting on the identity of Christ.

And this is, in fact, the way in which the reception of the gospel was described from the beginning. Paul, who wrote his letters before any of the evangelists put pen to paper, already speaks in these terms. Although he speaks of Christ as being "born of a woman" (Gal 4:4) Paul does not even mention the name of Mary. Instead, he describes himself directly as the one who begets his converts "in Christ Jesus through the gospel" (1 Cor 4:15). And in even more dramatic terms, he describes himself as a mother giving birth to Christ in the Galatians: "My little children, with whom I am again in travail, until Christ be formed in you!" (Gal 4:19).

Christians are those who have been born again in Christ Jesus through the gospel; they are the ones who are having Christ formed in them. And, Paul is not only the one who is in travail with them, but he is the paradigm of the state to which they are called:

> I have been crucified with Christ: It is no longer I who live, but Christ who lives in me; and the life I now live in the flesh I live by faith in the Son of God, who loved me and gave himself for me. (Gal 2:20)

---

[6] Anselm of Canterbury, *Cur Deus homo*, 17.

Having been crucified with Christ, Christ not only now lives in Paul, but Paul no longer lives – he identifies himself with Christ. Writing to the Galatians, Paul speaks of God having "revealed his Son in me"[7] (1.16, not "to" me, as the RSV translates it), and praises them for having received him "as an angel of God, as Christ Jesus" (4.14). Born again through the gospel in Christ Jesus, or having Christ formed in them, Christians are the body of Christ. This isn't simply a loose analogy or metaphor. Paul makes the identification without qualification: "You are the body of Christ and individually members of it." He says, "all", that is, who "by the one Spirit we were all baptized into one body" (1 Cor 12:27, 13). Christians are called to be "the one body," by living in subjection to the head, Christ, and allowing his peace to rule in their hearts (Col 3:15). As members of his body, they depend for their life and being upon their head, who is Christ, "the head of the body, the Church" (Col 1.18-19, 2.9). By holding fast to the head "the whole body, [is] nourished and knit together through its joints and ligaments, grows with a growth that is from God" (Col 2:19). And Christians also depend upon one another: "we, though many, are one body in Christ, and individually members one of another" (Rom 12:5). The grace given to each is for the benefit of the one body, so that everything is to be done in love for the building up of the one body (1 Cor 12: 12-13).

The proclamation of the gospel is clearly understood by Paul the Apostle in terms of giving birth to Christians, those who respond to the Word of the Cross, the Word of God, in faith – standing by the cross as did the Beloved Disciple. Paul is in travail with them, forming Christ in them, in those, that is, who are both individually and collectively the body of Christ. The gospel brings Christians into a new relationship with God, whereby, sharing in the Spirit bestowed in the risen Christ, they also can call upon God as "Abba, Father."

---

[7] Translation of the Greek original text would be "in."

This generative power of the gospel also stands out very clearly in our liturgical use of a passage from Isaiah, one which was probably the most important scriptural text for understanding the person and work of Christ: what is called the "fourth hymn of the suffering servant" (Isaiah 52:13-53:12), which speaks of the suffering of the servant, bruised for our iniquities and pouring out his soul unto death. This passage is read, in the Orthodox tradition, only at Vespers on Holy Friday afternoon. Having read on Holy Thursday evening the Passion Gospels at the foot of the cross placed in the middle of the church, we celebrate then at Holy Friday Vespers the "Rite of Entombment": reenacting how Joseph of Arimathea took down the body of Christ from the cross and placed it in the newly-hewn tomb, where no one had ever yet been laid (cf. Luke 23:53 et par). It is at this service that the Isaiah hymn is read. But, while this hymn is usually reckoned to finish at Isaiah 53: 12, the prescribed reading includes the following verse:

> Sing, O barren one, who did not bear; break forth
> into singing and cry aloud, you who have not been
> in travail! For the children of the desolate one will
> be more than the children of her that is married,
> says the LORD (Is 54:1).

Modern scholarship would take this verse as belonging to a different oracle. However, within the tradition of the Orthodox Church, the proclamation of the Suffering Servant concludes with the joyful exclamation that the barren one will give birth – read at the tomb of Christ. For it is, after all, into Christ's death and resurrection that Christians are baptized, being born again of the water and the Spirit, putting on Christ, and living in him by the grace of the Spirit as sons of God (Rom 6ff). The effect of this passage from Isaiah must have been all the more vivid when, as used to be the custom, Easter night was the time for the baptism of those who had been catechized during the forty days of Great Lent.

33

Given what we have seen of the generative power of the gospel – begetting sons of God, those in whom Christ is formed – it is not surprising that from the earliest times onwards Christians have taken Isaiah's barren unmarried woman, or virgin, as the Church – their Mother, or Virgin Mother. This image is already found in the book of Revelation, and from many writings from the second century, most vividly in a letter, probably written by St Irenaeus of Lyons, which describes, in very graphic terms, what had happened during a violent persecution in 177AD.[8] Some Christians were not ready for the conflict in the arena, and so they initially backed down – they were, in the terms of the letter, "stillborn" or "miscarried."[9] However, these stillborn Christians were encouraged through the zeal of the others, especially the slave girl Blandina, who was hung on a stake to be devoured by the wild beasts: the other Christians looking on her saw her as the embodiment of Christ, "in their agony they saw with their outward eyes in the person of their sister the One who was crucified for them."[10] Through the powerful witness in death of this lowly slave girl, the letter continues,

> ... the dead were made alive ... And there was great joy for the Virgin Mother in receiving back alive those who she had miscarried as dead. For through [Blandina and others] the majority of those who had denied were again brought to birth and again conceived and again brought to life and learned to confess; and now living and strengthened, they went to the judgment seat.[11]

---

[8] The Letter is preserved in Eusebius, *Ecclesiastical History* 5.1-2. Ed. and trans. K. Lake, LCL (Cambridge, MA: Harvard University Press, 1980 [1926]).

[9] *Ecclesiastical History* 5.1.11.

[10] *Ecclesiastical History* 5.1.41.

[11] *Ecclesiastical History* 5.1.45-6.

34

The Christians who turned away from making their confession are simply dead – their lack of preparation has meant that they are stillborn children of the Virgin Mother, the Church; but strengthened by the witness of others, they also are able to go to their death, and so the Virgin Mother receives them back alive – finally giving birth to living children of God. The death of the martyr, the letter says later on, is their "new birth," and the death of the martyr is celebrated as their true birthday.[12]

One of the most unusual examples of using the term "Virgin" to refer to the Church comes from Clement of Alexandria – again, writing at the end of the second century. The *virgin* is not only our mother, giving us birth into the life of God, but is also the one who supplies nourishment to her infants:

> The Lord Jesus, fruit of the Virgin, did not proclaim women's breasts to be blessed, nor did he choose them to give nourishment. But when the Father, full of goodness and love for men, rained down his Word upon the earth, this same Word became the spiritual nourishment for virtuous men. O mysterious marvel!

> There is one Father of all, there is one Word of all, and the Holy Spirit is one and the same everywhere. There is also one Virgin Mother, whom I love to call the Church. Alone, this mother had no milk because she alone did not become a woman. She is virgin and mother simultaneously, a virgin undefiled and a mother full of love. She draws her children to herself and nurses them with holy milk, that is, the Word for infants. She had not milk because the milk was this child, beautiful and familiar, the body of Christ.[13]

---

[12] *Ecclesiastical History* 5.1.63.

[13] Clement of Alexandria *Paedagogus* 1.6. Ed. O. Stählin, 3rd rev. edn. U. Treu, GCS 12 (Berlin: Akademie Verlag, 1972); Eng. trans. in ANF 2.

The fruit of the Virgin here is Christ, not simply, however, as the one to whom she gives birth, but as her milk, the milk by which she nourishes those for whom she is mother, that is, the Christians. There is also the suggestion that the Church already existed, a virgin waiting to become a mother while yet preserving her virginity. It is possible that the image of milk has Eucharistic overtones, for there were Christians who used milk (sometimes with honey) in their ritual meals, often connected with baptism.[14]

That the mother preserves her virginity is stated explicitly, for the first time, by Clement of Alexandria. He affirms the perpetual virginity of Mary by a very intriguing comparison:

> It appears that even today many hold that Mary, after the birth of her Son, was found to be in the state of a woman who has given birth, while in fact she was not so. For some say that, after giving birth, she was examined by a midwife, who found her to be a virgin. Now such to us are the Scriptures of the Lord, which gave birth to the truth and remain virgin, in the hiddenness of the mysteries of truth. "She gave birth and did not give birth," Scripture says, since she conceives by herself, not by conjunction.[15]

Mary remained a virgin, just as the scriptures give birth to the truth while remaining virginal. The proclamation of the gospel according to the scriptures results in the birth of Christians to new life; yet this proclamation does not impair the purity and integrity of the scriptures. I will come back to this connection

---

[14] Cf. A. McGowan, *Ascetic Eucharists: Food and Drink in Early Christian Ritual Meals* (Oxford: Oxford University Press, 1999), 107-115.

[15] Clement of Alexandria *Stromata* 7.16, referring to the *Protoevangelium of James* 19.1-20.1, and citing *Pseudo-Ezekiel*.

between the truth conceived in the scriptures and the Virgin giving birth to her Son.

The examples I have given so far are all from the Greek world (Irenaeus was Greek and wrote in Greek), but the content belongs to both East and West. In the Latin Church of this period we can also see the same reflection on the Church as the Virgin Mother. This can be seen in pictorial form, for instance in the magnificent frescoes of the Roman catacombs – especially the portrayal of the Virgin Orans. *Orans* is a posture with arms outstretched in the position for prayer – an image which continues in Byzantine iconography – usually seen in a mandorla figure placed over the Virgin with Christ, her child.[16]

Tertullian, writing in Carthage in the early third century, often speaks of the Church as "Mother." On occasion, he also introduces into this imagery the figure of Eve. For example:

> As Adam was a figure of Christ, Adam's sleep
> shadowed out the death of Christ, who was to
> sleep a mortal slumber, that from the wound
> inflicted on his side might be figured the true
> Mother of the living, the Church.[17]

The Church, which came from the side of the crucified Christ (referring to the blood and the water. cf. John 19:34) is foreshadowed by the formation of Eve from the side of Adam when he was asleep, the sleep which foreshadowed Christ's own sleep in death. While Eve was certainly called the mother of the living (Gen 3:20), it is really the Church that is this. St

---

[16] "Mandorla" refers to an almond shape figure representing an enveloping light in a protective cloud applied usually to the glory of God. Eventually, it was used in liturgical art as a sign of the "celestial glory" of Christ and His mother, the Virgin Mary. See: Alexander P. Kazhdan, Editor in Chief, *The Oxford Dictionary of Byzantinum*, Vol. 2 (New York: Oxford University Press, 1991), 1281.

[17] Tertullian *On the Soul* 43.10. Ed. J. H. Waszink (Amsterdam: North Holland Publishing Company, 1947); Eng. trans. in ANF 3.

Cyprian of Carthage, writing a few decades later, says very simply: "You cannot have God for your Father if you no longer have the Church for your mother."[18]

We still, to this day, sing of the Church as Virgin in this way. For example, the Troparion for the Resurrection in Tone Six:

> Angelic Powers were at your grave, and those who
> guarded it became as dead, and Mary stood by the
> tomb, seeking your most pure Body.
> You despoiled Hell and emerged unscathed; you
> met the Virgin and granted life.
> O Lord, risen from the dead, glory to you![19]

Mary, here, is clearly Mary Magdalene, and just as clearly "the Virgin" is not Mary, the mother of Christ! Nor is the Virgin mentioned in this hymn as the Theotokos. Rather, the Virgin, to whom risen Christ comes, granting life, is the Church, the Virgin who now becomes a virginal mother, granting new life to her children.

Early Christians clearly reflected profoundly on the theme of the Church as Virgin Mother. During this period, the usual typology for Mary was the contrast between her, as the obedient virgin, and Eve as the disobedient virgin. But from the fourth century, Mary is brought into this reflection on the Church as Virgin Mother, and comes to be seen as a type or symbol of the Church. One very dramatic example, from St Ephrem the Syrian, must suffice:

> The Virgin Mary is a symbol of the Church, when
> she receives the first announcement of the Gospel.
> And, it is in the name of the Church that Mary
> sees the risen Jesus. Blessed be God, who filled

---

[18] Cyprian *On the Unity of the Church* 5-6. Ed. and trans. M. Bévenot, OECT (Oxford: Clarendon Press, 1971).
[19] Translation from *H ΘΕΙΑ ΛΕΙΤΟΥΡΓΙΑ – The Divine Liturgy* (Oxford: Oxford University Press, 1995).

Mary and the Church with joy. We call the Church
by the name of Mary, for she deserves a double
name.[20]

St Ephrem seems confused: he identifies the Mary that saw the
risen Jesus (i.e. Mary Magdalene, according to the gospels), with
Mary the Mother of Jesus. But the Syrian is not confused; the
identification is based on the fact that both Marys received the
gospel, first as an annunciation, and then by seeing the risen
Jesus. It is *when* she receives the proclamation of the gospel that
Mary is seen as a symbol of the Church, and not the other way
around: Mary is not the archetype of the Church, but the
symbol of the Church. The Church is older than all creation,
Isaiah's barren virgin who gives birth through Christ's work; it
is this one that Mary symbolizes, or that Mary personifies.
Theological reflection, as we have seen, begins with the work of
Christ, and what is brought into being by him – the Mother
Church – and then understands Mary in this light. So strong is
the identification between the church and her symbol, Mary
(when seen in this light), that St Ephrem can simply call the
church "Mary."

Speaking of Mary as a symbol of the church is not
meant to deny her historical reality, to make her nothing but a
type, or an allegory, an allegorical personification. Rather it is to
emphasize that we are now speaking of her in the light of the
work of Christ, a reflection which is bound up with that upon
the church. It is not allegory, but simultaneity: when we speak
of Mary, we are also speaking of the church, for how we speak
of her is based in how we speak of what has been brought into
being by the work of Christ.

With this idea of Mary being a type, image or
personification of the Church, who, as a result of Christ's
saving Passion now gives birth to numerous children, we can

---

[20] St Ephrem of Syria *On the Resurrection*, as cited in L. Gambero, *Mary and the
Fathers of the Church: The Blessed Virgin Mary In Patristic Thought*, trans. T.
Buffer (San Francisco: Ignatius Press, 1999), 115.

now begin to understand a further aspect of the Annunciation itself, the only Marian feast described in the canonical gospels, and that is the connection between the tomb of Christ and the womb of Mary. This is treated by many of the Fathers, but summed up neatly by Augustine:

> He is believed to have been conceived on 25 March, and also to have suffered on that day. Thus to the new tomb in which he was buried, where no mortal body was laid before or after, there corresponds the womb in which he was conceived, where no mortal body was sown before or after.[21]

To the tomb corresponds the womb. This connection between the tomb and the womb seems, in fact, to have been the reason for celebrating the Nativity of Christ on December 25. This feast only began to be celebrated in the East in the late fourth century,[22] and then it was bound up with solar symbolism and taken to replace pagan celebrations. But it was celebrated earlier in the West, where the date of 25 December was arrived at on the basis of the date of his Passion, which was held to have occurred on 25 March – nine months earlier.[23] So that, in the liturgical calendar, the birth of Christ occurs nine months after his passion: to the tomb corresponds the womb. Only later is the date of March 25 reckoned to the date of Christ's conception.[24]

To the tomb corresponds the womb. And so the Mary that we contemplate in the infancy narratives (but not in the other places that she appears in the canonical gospels), is already described in terms of the gospel: the infancy narratives of Matthew and Luke are already told as a proclamation of the

---

[21] Augustine *On the Trinity* 4.2.9. Trans. E. Hill (Brooklyn, NY: New City Press, 1991).
[22] T. Talley *The Origins of the Christian Year*, 2nd edition (Collegeville Liturgical Press, 1991), 135-6.
[23] Cf. Ibid. 9.
[24] Cf. Ibid. 91-9:

gospel (in the full sense). This is also a connection made explicit in the icon for the Nativity, where Christ is depicted, not in a stable (as a historicist depiction would require), but wrapped in swaddling cloths as a corpse (with a cross in his halo), laid in a manger as food (for us who eat the body of Christ), and the manger is positioned in a cave embracing in its shape the Virgin, just as the crucified Christ was placed in a newly-hewn (i.e. virgin) cave owned by the other Joseph. The same point can be made by reference to the liturgical hymnography for the Feast of the Nativity.

Icon of the Nativity by mosaic iconographer Robert Andrews, installed in Transfiguration of the Saviour Greek Orthodox Church, Lowell, Massachusetts
[Photograph courtesy of Arthur Sparagos]

As Mary is known to have given birth to the Word of God only from the perspective of the Passion and exaltation of the Cross, when seen and understood through the matrix of scripture, her conception and birth of Christ is already presented in these terms – to the tomb corresponds the womb. It is for this reason that Clement of Alexandria, as noted earlier, connects Christ's birth from the virginal womb with the virginal scriptures which give birth to the truth.

41

There is one final passage I would like to consider which brings together the Passion of Christ and the Incarnation of the Word, woven from the fabric of scripture. In his treatise *On Christ and the Antichrist*, Hippolytus brings all of this together through an extended metaphor:

> For the Word of God, being fleshless, put on the holy flesh from the holy virgin, as a bridegroom a garment, having woven it for himself in the sufferings of the cross, so that having mixed our mortal body with his own power, and having mingled the corruptible into the incorruptible, and the weak with the strong, he might save perishing man.

> The web-beam, therefore, is the passion of the Lord upon the cross, and the warp on it is the power of the Holy Spirit, and the woof is the holy flesh woven by the Spirit, and the thread is the grace which by the love of Christ binds and unites the two in one, and the rods are the Word; and the workers are the patriarchs and prophets who weave the fair, long, perfect tunic for Christ; and the Word passing through these, like the combs (or rods), completes through them that which his Father wills.[1]

The flesh of the Word, received from the Virgin and "woven in the sufferings of the cross," is woven by the patriarchs and prophets, whose actions and words proclaim the manner in which the Word became present and manifest. That is, it is in the preaching of Jesus Christ, the proclamation of the One who died on the cross, interpreted and understood in the matrix, the womb, of Scripture, that the Word receives flesh from the Virgin. The "virgin" in this case, Hippolytus later affirms

---

[1] Hippolytus *On Christ and the Antichrist* 4. Ed. H. Achelis, GCS 1.2 (Leipzig: Hinrichs Verlag, 1987); Eng. trans. in ANF 5.

following Revelation 12, is the Church, who will never cease "bearing from her heart the Word that is persecuted by the unbelieving in the world," while the male child she bears is Christ, God and man, announced by the prophets, "whom the Church continually bears as she teaches all nations."[26] The Virgin Church continually gives birth to Christ by her pure teaching, the gospel proclaimed according to scripture so that the Word is made flesh in her children.

By reflecting on the way in which Mary is presented in the scriptures, and how we celebrate her in our hymnography and iconography, we have seen how we are always brought back to the mystery of Christ himself, and invited to see everything in the light of the crucified and exalted One, the light which illumines and transforms all of our created reality and history. The Mary that we behold is the one who is already transformed in this way by the work of her Son. Her womb corresponds to the tomb, and every aspect of her life then reflects his image, just as we are called to be conformed to the image of the Son. And, simultaneously, the body is that assumed from the Virgin by the Word, and what we confess in this light cannot be separated from the body which believers now are, having been born anew in the virgin church, having Christ born in them, so that they, we, are really his body. Given all the dimensions that we have seen going into the church's reflection on Mary, we can perhaps now begin to understand the word of John of Damascus that "it is proper and true that we call the holy Mary the Theotokos, for this name expresses the entire mystery of the economy."[27]

---

[26] *Antichrist*, 61: ὃ ἀεὶ τίκουσα ἡ ἐκκλησία διδάσκει πάντα τὰ ἔθνη.
[27] St John of Damascus *On the Orthodox Faith* 56 (= 3.12). Ed. B. Kotter, PTS 12 (Berlin and New York: De Gruyter, 1973); Eng. trans. F. H. Chase, FC 37 (Washington DC: Catholic University of America Press, 1958).

3.

Ecumenical Reflections on the Immaculate Conception

Robert Fastiggi

Adapted from a presentation given at the First International Congress of the Ecumenical Society of the Blessed Virgin Mary USA, August 11-13, 2008, Newman Library and Oratory, Pittsburgh, PA.

Introduction

On December 8, 1854, Pope Pius IX issued his Bull, *Ineffabilis Deus*, defining the dogma of the Immaculate Conception. The actual definition reads as follows:

> .....To the honor of the holy and undivided Trinity, to the glory and distinction of the Virgin Mother of God, for the exaltation of the Catholic faith and the increase of the Christian religion, by the authority of our Lord, Jesus Christ, of the blessed apostles Peter and Paul and our own authority, we declare, pronounce and define (*declaramus, pronuntiamus et definimus*): the doctrine, which maintains that the most blessed Virgin Mary, at the first instant of her conception, by the singular grace and privilege of almighty God and in view of the merits of Jesus Christ, the Savior of the human race, was preserved immune from all stain of original sin,
>
> is revealed by God and, therefore, firmly and constantly to be believed by all the faithful.[1]

---

[1] Pius IX, Bull, *Ineffabilis Deus* (December 8, 1854) in Denzinger, Heinrich and Hünermann, Peter, *Enchiridion symbolorum definitionem et*

From an ecumenical perspective, this solemn definition is somewhat problematical. Mary's Immaculate Conception is often conceived of as a uniquely Roman Catholic doctrine, which cannot claim universal Christian acceptance. The Eastern Orthodox usually look upon the Immaculate Conception only as a "theological opinion" (*theologoumenon*), and they claim that it lacks sufficient scriptural and Patristic support to claim dogmatic status.[2] Although Martin Luther, in a 1527 sermon (six years after his excommunication by Rome) seemed to affirm Mary's Immaculate Conception, he was not always consistent.[3] Protestants, by and large, see the Immaculate Conception as lacking scriptural warrant, and, therefore, incapable of demanding assent from Christians.

This essay will not try to provide a complete scriptural and historical account of the development of the Catholic dogma of the Immaculate Conception.[4] Instead, it will concentrate on the Orthodox and Protestant objections to the dogma and suggest possible points of convergence.

---

declarationem de rebus fidei et morum 40th ed (Freiburg im Breisgau, 2005)[henceforth, Denz.-H], no. 2803, p. 776 (my translation).

[2] See Fr. Vladimir Zelinsky, "The Mother of God in the Orthodox Church" in Mark Miravalle, ed. *Mariology: A Guide for Priests, Deacons, Seminarians, and Consecrated Persons* (Goleta, CA: Queenship Publishing, 2007), 798: "[T]he tradition of the undivided Church did not know such a teaching [of the Immaculate Conception]."

[3] See Michael O'Carroll, C.S.Sp., *Theotokos: A Theological Encyclopedia of the Blessed Virgin Mary* (Eugene, OR: Wipf and Stock), 227-228.

[4] For a review of the development of the Catholic dogma of the Immaculate Conception, see Fr. Peter Fehlner, F.I., "The Predestination of the Virgin Mother and her Immaculate Conception" in Mark Miravalle, ed. *Mariology: A Guide for Priests, Deacons, Seminarians, and Consecrated Persons*, 213-276. See also Paul Haffner, *The Mystery of Mary* (Chicago: Liturgy Training Publications, 2004), 73-106.

Eastern Orthodoxy and the Immaculate Conception

As is well known, Eastern Orthodox Christians honor Mary as the ever-virgin Mother of God (*Théotokos*) who is "all-holy" (*panaghia*). Mary's dignity as *Théotokos* is taught explicitly by the ecumenical Councils of Ephesus (431) and Chalcedon (451),[5] Mary is likewise referred to as "ever-virgin" (*aeiparthénou*) several times at the ecumenical Council of Constantinople II (553),[6] and she is honored as "ever-virgin" in the Byzantine liturgy.[7] Moreover, Orthodox celebrate the feast of Mary's Dormition (falling-asleep) on August 15, and, like Catholics, they believe she has been taken up, body and soul, into the glory of heaven.[8] Almost all Eastern Orthodox, however, do not affirm Mary's Immaculate Conception as a dogma of the faith. There are, however, some Orthodox theologians who are open to the idea of Mary's all holiness, even if they do not uphold it as binding dogma.[9] In a similar manner, certain Orthodox theologians "have made statements which, if not definitely affirming the doctrine of the Immaculate Conception, at any rate approach close to it."[10] In spite of this, "the great majority of Orthodox theologians have rejected the doctrine."[11]

Why do most Orthodox reject the doctrine of the Immaculate Conception? As already mentioned, one reason is historical: there does not seem to be adequate Patristic support for Mary's exemption from original sin.[12] By way of response,

---

[5] See Denz.-H, 251 and 301.

[6] Ibid., 422 and 437

[7] See Donald Attwater, *Eastern Catholic Worship* (New York: The Devin-Adair Company, 1945), 32

[8] See Zelinzky, 799 and Timothy Ware (Bishop Kallistos of Diokleia), *The Orthodox Church* New Edition (London: Penguin Books, 1993), 260-261.

[9] See Virginia M. Kimball, "The Immaculate Conception in the ecumenical dialogue with orthodoxy: how the term *theosis* can inform convergence," in *Mary for Time and Eternity: Essays on Mary and Ecumenism* (Herefordshire, UK: Gracewing, 2007), 175-218.

[10] Ware, 259.

[11] Ibid.

[12] See Zelinsky, 798.

some Catholic theologians have pointed to numerous Eastern Fathers who have provided at least embryonic support for what would later develop into the Catholic dogma of the Immaculate Conception.[13] In fact, Father Peter Fehlner, F.I. believes that "the Eastern tradition of the Church, before 1500, shows even stronger support for what the Western Church now calls the Immaculate Conception than does the Latin West."[14] According to Fehlner, the principal reason for the refusal of the Orthodox to accept the Immaculate Conception is ecclesiological,[15] i.e. the Orthodox do not believe the Pope can define a dogma for the entire Church without the support of an ecumenical council. Fehlner also believes that the Orthodox have confused "non-acceptance" of the Immaculate Conception with an inaccurate claim of "traditional support for explicit denial" of the dogma.[16]

Is there Patristic support for Mary's Immaculate Conception? There is if one accepts the principle of doctrinal development. The earliest Patristic support for the Immaculate Conception, therefore, can be found in the identification of Mary as "the New Eve." St. Justin Martyr (c. 100-165) and St. Irenaeus (c. 130-202) are two of the more prominent early Fathers who contrast Mary, the associate of Christ, the Redeemer, with Eve, the associate of Adam, who brings death and sin to humanity. Although these early Church Fathers did not explicitly affirm Mary's Immaculate Conception, the Eve/Mary parallelism led later Church Fathers to affirm Mary as "all-pure" and sinless. Thus, St. Ephraem of Syria (c. 306-373) writes: "For on you, O Lord, there is no mark; neither is there any stain in your Mother."[17] With St. Andrew of Crete (c. 660-740), there is further development. He exclaims: "Your

---

[13] See Fehlner, 241-242.
[14] Ibid., 242.
[15] Ibid.
[16] Ibid.
[17] St. Ephraem the Syrian, *Carmina Nisibena* 28, 8 as cited in Luigi Gambero, *Mary and the Fathers of the Church* trans. Thomas Buffer (San Francisco: Ignatius Press, 1999), 109.

birth was immaculate, O Virgin Immaculate"[18], and he says, "let us honor [Mary's] holy conception.[19] Although St. Andrew does not explicitly affirm Mary's Immaculate Conception, he does play a role in the development of the doctrine by comparing Mary to the uncontaminated virgin soil possessed of a "pure human nature" that "receives from God the gift of the original creation and reverts to its original purity."[20] In a similar vein, St. Germanus of Constantinople (c. 635-733) speaks of Mary as "wholly without stain."[21]

Of the Patristic writers, it is St. John of Damascus (c. 690-749) who affirms, in most explicit terms, the doctrine of Mary's original holiness. In praising the holiness of Mary's conception, he writes:

> Oh blessed loins of Joachim, whence the all-
> pure seed (*spérma panámomon*) was poured out.
> Oh glorious womb of Anna, in which the most
> holy fetus grew and was formed.[22]

Francis Dvornik believes this passage provides "a direct proof that John regarded Mary as exempt from all sin from the moment of her passive conception. In other words, the Catholic dogma of the Immaculate Conception is clearly expressed in this statement."[23] Thus, we can see that one of the most eminent Eastern Fathers of the Church affirmed the Catholic dogma of the Immaculate Conception in terms of Mary's original holiness and preservation from all defilement of sin.

---

[18] Andrew of Crete, *Canon on the Nativity* in J.P. Migne, *Patrologia Graeca* [PG] 162 vols. (Paris 1857-1866) Vol. 97: 1321 C.

[19] Ibid. Vol. 97:1309 A.

[20] Andrew of Crete, *Homily 1 on the Nativity*, PG 87, 809 D- 812 A; as cited in Gambero, 394.

[21] PG 98:292-309

[22] John of Damascus, *Homily on the Nativity of the Blessed Virgin* 2; PG 96 664 A; as cited in Gambero. 402

[23] Francis Dvornik, "The Byzantine Church and the Immaculate Conception," in *The Dogma of the Immaculate Conception* ed. by E.D. O'Connor, CSC (Notre Dame, IN: University of Notre Dame Press, 1958), 97.

The Catholic reading of the Patristic record, therefore, is different from that of most contemporary Orthodox. Without claiming a unanimous Patristic consensus in favor of Mary's preservation from original sin, Catholic scholars like Fehlner believe there is significant support among the Fathers, especially from the East, for an affirmation of Mary's all-holiness, which logically implies her Immaculate Conception.[24]

In addition to the questions of tradition and ecclesiology, many Orthodox today reject the Immaculate Conception because of its link to a certain view of original sin that they, by and large, do not share. Bishop Kallistos Ware, for example, believes that, for the majority of the Orthodox, the doctrine of Mary's Immaculate Conception, "implies a false understanding of original sin" and "seems to separate Mary from the rest of the descendents of Adam, putting her in a completely different class from the righteous men and women of the Old Testament."[25] James Likoudis locates Orthodox resistance to the doctrine principally in the Orthodox belief "that the descendents of Adam do not inherit the guilt of Original Sin but only the consequences of sin: bodily death and corruption."[26] Fr. John Meyendorff, in a similar manner, maintains that there is "a consensus in Greek patristic and Byzantine traditions in identifying the inheritance of the Fall as an inheritance essentially of mortality rather than of sinfulness, sinfulness being merely a consequence of mortality."[27] According to Meyendorff, most Eastern Fathers believed that

---

[24] See Fehlner, 239, where he states that "theological speaking" the Eastern title of Mary as all-holy (*Panhagia*) "means Immaculate Conception."

[25] Ware, 259-260.

[26] Prof. James Likoudis, "An Inadequate Understanding of Original Sin as Source of Eastern Orthodox Objections to the Immaculate Conception," in *Mary at the Foot of the Cross – IV: Mater Viventium (Gen. 3:20): Acts of the Fourth International Symposium on Marian Coredemption* (New Bedford, MA: Academy of the Immaculate, 2004), 352.

[27] John Meyendorff, *Byzantine Theology* (New York: Fordham University press, 1974), 145.

"'the wrong choice made Adam brought in passion, corruption, and mortality,' but not inherited guilt."[28]

Meyendorff traces the Latin understanding of original sin as "inherited guilt" in the Vulgate translation of Rom 5:12 as: "Sin came into the world through one man and death through sin, and so death spread to all men as all sinned in him (*in quo omnes peccaverunt*)."[29] According to Meyendorff, this translation reflects an incorrect rendering of the Greek phrase, *eph ho pantes hemarton*, which should be more accurately translated as "because all have sinned." Thus, the meaning of Rom 5:12 is not that all men sinned in Adam but that death spread to all men through Adam and "*because of death*, all men have sinned."[30] This death, which resulted from Adam's sin, is what "makes sin inevitable, and in this sense 'corrupts' nature."[31]

Because Orthodox theologians, as a rule, do not accept the idea of original sin as an inherited guilt, they do not see the point of Mary's Immaculate Conception. Moreover, the consensus of the Eastern Fathers (and Western) is that Mary died, even though her body, not undergoing corruption, was assumed into heaven. Since death is the primary effect of original sin, it is not clear to the Orthodox how Mary is preserved from death and, therefore, from original sin.

If the Orthodox do not accept Mary's Immaculate Conception, why then do they call her "all holy"? The Greek Orthodox theologian, Constantine N. Tsirpanlis, provides this explanation:

---

[28] Ibid.
[29] Cf. Ibid., 144. It should be noted that the "*in quo omnes peccaverunt*" of the Vulgate and other Latin translations has been changed to *eo quod omnes peccaverunt* ("because all have sinned") in the *Nova Vulgata* published in 1979: see
http://www.vatican.va/archive/bible_vulgata/documents/nova-vulgata_nt_epist-romanos_lt.html
[30] Meyendorff, 144 (italics in original).
[31] Ibid., 145.

Mary was born under the law of original sin, which in Eastern Patristic thought means *inherited mortality*, not guilt. But sin could never become actual in her person; the sinful heritage of the fall had no mastery over her right will. The sanctity of the Mother of God is the fruit of free will and grace. That is, although the Virgin Mary, having inherited Adam's nature, was under original sin, she was able to heal this natural tendency towards sin and become "truly pure, more than anyone else, after God, " "more holy than the saints."[32]

Following this interpretation, Mary was "full of grace," not from the moment of her conception, but as a result of "her own growth in grace."[33] In Eastern Christian terms, this means that Mary became "all holy" as a result of the process of *theosis* (deification or divinization), [34] and this was the result of both "her free will and consent and ... of the grace of the Logos of God."[35]

In an interview, published in 2004, Bartholomew I, the Patriarch of Constantinople, speaks in a similar way of Mary's spiritual progress towards purity:

> [Mary's] holiness and purity were not blemished by the corruption, handed on to her by original sin as to every man, precisely because she was reborn in Christ like all the saints, sanctified above every saint.
>
> Her reinstatement in the condition prior to the Fall did not necessarily take place at the

---

[32] Constantine N. Tsirpanlis, *Introduction to Eastern Patristic Thought and Orthodox Theology* (Collegeville, MN: The Liturgical Press, 1991), 56

[33] Ibid., 57.

[34] See Kimball, 175-177.

[35] Tsirpanlis, 58.

moment of her conception. We believe that it happened afterwards, as consequence of the progress in her of the action of the uncreated divine grace through the visit of the Holy Spirit, which brought about the conception of the Lord within her, purifying her from every stain of sin ... the All-holy [Mary] participated in the hereditary corruption, like all mankind, but with her love for God and her purity – understood as an imperturbable and unhesitating dedication of her love to God alone –she succeeded through the grace of God, in sanctifying herself in Christ and making herself worthy of becoming the house of God, as God wants all human beings to become. Therefore, we in the Orthodox Church honor the all-holy Mother of God above all the saints, albeit we don't accept the dogma of her Immaculate Conception.[36]

Here we see that the Orthodox, as a whole, do not believe that Mary was all-holy (*panagia*) from the moment of her conception. Rather, they believe she became all-holy as a result of spiritual progress in God's uncreated grace, a process known as *theosis* or deification.

How can Catholics reply to these Orthodox objections to the Immaculate Conception? I believe several responses are possible. First, with respect to the translation issue of Rom 5:12, it should be noted that the Catholic understanding does not stand or fall on this verse alone. Rom 5:12-21 needs to be read as a unified passage in which Paul affirms that, "condemnation came upon all" through the transgression of Adam (Rom 5:18) and "through the disobedience of one man the many were made [or constituted (*katestáthesan*)] sinners"

[36] Gianni Valente, "The Sweet Victory of Mary" [interview with Bartholomew I,Ecumenical Patriarch of Constantinople] in *30 Days* [English edition] no. 12 [2004], 42.

(Rom 5:19). Thus, the idea of an inherited "guilt" or deprivation of holiness and justice is a legitimate reading of Paul's intent, and there are some Eastern Fathers who do speak of human beings inheriting sinfulness and guilt from Adam.[37]

A second point is that the Catholic theology of original sin involves the distinction, found in St. Thomas Aquinas and others, between the *formal* aspect of original sin (the deprivation of original holiness and justice) and the *material* effects of bodily death, ignorance, suffering and concupiscence.[38] St. Thomas writes that,

> [T]he privation of original justice, whereby the will was made subject to God, is the formal element in original sin; while every other disorder of the soul's powers, is a kind of material element in respect to original sin … Hence original sin is concupiscence, materially, but privation of original justice, formally.[39]

This distinction between the formal and the material aspects of original sin leads to a third point: the definition of the Immaculate Conception in 1854 concerns Mary's preservation from the *formal* aspect of original sin (i.e. the deprivation of sanctifying grace) and not necessarily the *material* aspects of bodily death, suffering, ignorance and concupiscence (though it is generally held that these material effects cannot be linked to any defect of justice or grace in Mary). In other words Mary was preserved from the absence of holiness and sanctifying grace in the human nature passed on through human generation since the fall of Adam. This deprivation of holiness and justice is "guilt" only in the sense that it is an inherited

---

[37] Cf. J.N. D Kelly, *Early Christian Doctrines* (New York: Harper & Row, 1960), 351

[38] Cf. *Catechism of the Catholic Church*, 404-405; St. Thomas Aquinas, *Summa theologica*, I-II, q. 82, a. 3).

[39] St.Thomas Aquinas, *Summa theologica*, I-II, q. 82, a. 3). Christian Classics edition ed. Vol. II, 958.

condition deprived of holiness and justice. The *Catechism of the Catholic Church* makes clear that original sin is sin only "in an analogical sense" (no. 404).

The Catholic doctrine of the Immaculate Conception, therefore, can be recast as an affirmation that Mary was "full of grace" from the first instant of her conception in her mother's womb. She was preserved from the formal aspect of original sin, the deprivation of holiness and justice. She did not need to be "purified" from sin, either original or personal. Mary was "all holy" (*panagia*) from her conception because, as the "New Eve," she was the new "mother of the living," representing the new creation of those redeemed by her Son.

Was Mary preserved from the material aspects of original sin, namely bodily death, ignorance, suffering and concupiscence? With regard to bodily death, Pius XII left the matter open in his definition of the Assumption in 1950, stating only that Mary's assumption into heaven occurred "when the course of her earthly life was completed" (*expleto terretis vitae cursu*).[40] The Catholic Magisterium, however, has rejected the idea that Mary died as a result of original sin.[41] Catholics who believe Mary did die maintain she did so in order to be in solidarity with her Son. John Paul II, for example, noted that Mary's freedom from original sin,

> ... does not lead to the conclusion that she also received physical immortality. The Mother is not superior to the Son who underwent death, giving it a new meaning and changing it into a means of salvation ... To share in Christ's resurrection, Mary had first to share in his death.[42]

---

[40] Denzinger-Hünermann, 3903.
[41] Ibid., 1973..
[42] John Paul II, General Audience, June 25, 1997: cited in Likoudis, 365.

With regard to ignorance, the standard Catholic position is that Mary did not have any ignorance brought about by sin. As a creature, though, Mary did not possess omniscience, though Catholic tradition affirms special forms of acquired, infused and beatific knowledge in Mary.[43] With respect to suffering, it is clear that Mary certainly did suffer (cf. Lk 2:35), even though a long-standing Catholic tradition is that Mary, in light of Gen 3:16, gave birth to Jesus without experiencing "any pain of sense."[44]

Did Mary have concupiscence, i.e. the inclination to sin? Catholics, like most Orthodox, believe that Mary, as a special privilege of grace, was "free from every personal sin during her whole life."[45] With respect to concupiscence, St. Thomas Aquinas believed that Mary had the tinder for sin (*fomes peccati*) in its essence, but it remained bound or fettered (*ligatus*) "by reason of the abundant grace bestowed on her in her sanctification."[46] St. Thomas' position, however, assumes that Mary was purified from original sin. Most Catholics, however, following the definition of the Immaculate Conception, believe that Mary "was, from the beginning, entirely free from concupiscence."[47]

Catholics, therefore, can respond to the Orthodox by noting that Mary's Immaculate Conception in no way separates her from the rest of humanity. Like all other human beings, Mary's holiness is derived from the uncreated grace of God that enabled her to "share in the divine nature" (2 Pet 1:4). In Mary's case, however, this *theosis* began at the moment of her conception.

---

[43] See O'Carroll, 212-214.

[44] *Catechism of the Council of Trent* trans. J.A. McHugh, O.P. and C.J. Callan, O.P. (Rockford, IL: Tan Publishers, 1982), 46.

[45] Ludwig Ott, *Fundamentals of Catholic Dogma* trans. James Canon Bastible (St. Louis: Herder, 1958), 203; cf. the teaching on this of the Council of Trent in Denzinger-Hünermann, 1573 and the teaching of the Orthodox on this in Ware, 259.

[46] *Summa theologica*, III, q. 27, a. 3.

[47] Ott, 203.

Why, though, was it necessary for Mary to be "all-holy" from the time of her conception? Why could her holiness not be a result of her progress in grace and subsequent purification? The answer, I believe, is that Mary would not be truly "all-holy" if she needed to be purified from sin. And if she had no personal sins, as most Orthodox claim,[48] from what type of sin did she need to be purified? The only other possibility is original sin, which, as we have seen, Orthodox theologians prefer not to describe as an inherited guilt. But if Mary, by the power of the Holy Spirit, was purified "from every stain,"[49] as Patriarch Bartholomew I has said, from what exactly was she purified if not some type of inherited stain or sin? From a Catholic perspective, it makes more sense to say that Mary's preservation from actual sin was only possible because of her preservation from original sin.

The Catholic position, therefore, can be harmonized with the Orthodox description of Mary as "all-holy." By affirming Mary's all-holiness from the time of her conception, the Catholic Church has claimed as her own the teaching of St. John of Damascus, who, by speaking of the all-holy seed of Mary's father, Joachim, recognized in his own way that Mary was conceived in St. Anne's womb free from all stain of sin and defect of grace.[50] Preserved from any defect of grace from the first moment of her conception, Mary is truly the *panagia*, the all-holy Mother of God.

Protestants and the Immaculate Conception

As noted above, Protestants usually deny the Immaculate Conception either because they think it is unscriptural or because it separates Mary from those in need of redemption by Jesus, the universal Savior. In this regard, the words of Paul in

---

[48] Cf. Ware, 259: "and all Orthodox are agreed in believing that Our Lady was free from *actual* sin" (italics in original).

[49] Valente, 42.

[50] Cf. John of Damascus, *Homily on the Nativity of the Blessed Virgin* 2; PG 96 664 A; as cited in Gambero, 402.

Rom 3:23 seem decisive: "All have sinned and fall short of the glory of God." Moreover, Mary rejoices in God her Savior (Lk 1:47). If she were conceived without original sin, she would not need a Savior.

A Catholic response to these challenges can be found in Pius IX's definition of the Immaculate Conception. Mary was preserved from original sin "by the singular grace and privilege of almighty God and in view of the merits of Jesus Christ, the Savior of the human race."[51] In other words, Jesus is Mary's Savior, but he saves her not by purifying her from original sin but by preserving her from it. As for the "all" of Rom 3:23, it can be noted: first, Jesus is clearly not included in the "all" so the passage does admit of at least one exception; and, second, the use of "all" is general not specific; otherwise, one could argue that Rom 5:18 supports the idea of universal salvation since, through Jesus, "acquittal and life" came to "all human beings" (*eis pantas anthropous*).

Catholics will also note that Mary's plenitude of grace from the moment of her conception finds support in the greeting of the angel in Luke 1:28. Mary is spoken of as "full of grace" (*kecharitoméne*) which in Greek means one who has been and continues to be "favored" or "graced" by God (alternate translations could be "completely graced" or "thoroughly graced"). As Fr. Settimio M. Manelli, F.I. observes:

> [*kecharitoméne*] is a perfect passive participle, translated as *full of grace*, or as *fore-loved, privileged, gratified*. As perfect passive participle, the Greek word means, "to be enriched by grace in a stable, lasting way." In fact, the Greek perfect denotes an action completed in the past whose effects endure. Hence, the angel greets Mary by announcing that she has been enriched by grace in the past and that the effects of this gift remain. Without doubt this is a singular form of

---

[51] Denz.-H, 2803.

address. No one else in the Bible was ever greeted thus. Only Mary has been so addressed, and this in the moment when she was about to accomplish the "fullness of time," to realize the prophecies of old, and when the Word of God stood ready to take of her our human nature."[52]

Mary is "full of grace" because Jesus, in assuming his human nature, becomes like us in all things but without sin (cf. Heb. 4:15). Thus, it was fitting for Him to take his human nature from one who is "full of grace" and free from sin (original as well as personal). As Pope Leo I writes:

> [Christ] assumed the form of a servant without the defilement of sin, enriching the human without diminishing the divine ... He is generated, however, by a new birth: because an inviolate virginity, not knowing concupiscence has supplied the matter of the flesh. (*quia inviolata virginitas concupiscentiam nescivit, carnis materiam ministravit*), From the mother of the Lord, nature, not guilt, was assumed (*Assumpta est de matre Domini natura, non culpa*).[53]

In addition to Luke 1:28, Gen 3:15 provides support for Mary's Immaculate Conception. The "woman" of Gen. 3:15 is connected with the "woman" of John 2:4, 19:26 and Rev. 12:1 and 6. Mary is the "new woman" and the "new Eve" who gives birth to the "new Adam" who brings forth the "new humanity" redeemed by grace.

---

[52] Fr. Settimo M. Manelli, F.I., "The Virgin Mary in the New Testament," in *Mariology: A Guide for Priests, Deacons, Seminarians, and Consecrated Persons* ed. by Mark Miravalle (Goleta, CA: Queenship Publishing, 2007), 75.

[53] Pope Leo I, Tome to Flavian, Denzinger-Hünermann, 293-294 (the translations from Denzinger are my own).

Besides the scriptural support, there are, I believe, two possible points of convergence between the Catholic dogma of Mary's Immaculate Conception and traditional Protestant theology. First, Mary's Immaculate Conception is an illustration of the principle of *sola gratia* (by grace alone), which is favored by Protestants. Mary's preservation from original sin was due to the singular privilege and grace of almighty God, and it was totally unmerited. Secondly, Mary's Immaculate Conception is a sign of divine election and predestination and, therefore, can be harmonized with these notions, which are important for Protestant theology. Mary was chosen by God to be the mother of the Incarnate Word "from the beginning and before all ages."[54] Because God chose to redeem sinful humanity by the Word made flesh (cf. Jn 1:29), the Mother of the Incarnate Word is at the center of salvation history. As St. Paul writes: "When the fullness of time came, God sent his son, born of a woman" (Gal 4:4).

Mary's predestination as the Mother of the Word Incarnate does not take away from the full freedom of her yes to God's invitation. Grace does not take away free will but perfects it. Mary, therefore, was predestined by God's grace alone (*sola gratia*) to say yes to God freely. In this sense, she is the model of all Christians who rely upon divine grace for holiness and salvation.

Conclusion

In this essay, I have tried to show possible points of convergence between the Catholic dogma of Mary's Immaculate Conception and traditional Orthodox and Protestant perspectives. I do not pretend to have provided enough material to convince either Orthodox or Protestants on the truth of the Immaculate Conception. My more modest hope is that Orthodox and Protestant Christians will see that the Catholic dogma of the Immaculate Conception should not challenge anything they hold as sacred and true.

---

[54] Pius IX, *Ineffabilis Deus* [the definition of the Immaculate Conception], A.D. 1854]; Denzinger-Hünermann, 2800.

For Catholics, it is a sign of hope that members of the Anglican Communion recognize that the papal definitions of Immaculate Conception and Assumption "can be said to be consonant with the teaching of the Scriptures and the ancient common traditions."[55] Perhaps Orthodox and Protestant Christians can come to the same assessment. When Mary proclaimed: "God who is mighty has done great things for me" (cf. Lk 1:49), she affirmed God as the source of all the holiness that is in her. Catholics recognize Mary's dependence on God's grace and election in the dogma of the Immaculate Conception. By God's own choice, Mary was filled with deifying grace from the moment of her conception so she might be fittingly honored as the all-holy Mother of the Incarnate Word.

The ultimate reason for Mary's Immaculate Conception is her dignity as the Mother of the Incarnate Word. When some argue that Mary's preservation from original sin separates her from the rest of humanity, a Catholic can respond by noting that God has already separated her from all other humans by choosing her as birth-giver of the Incarnate Word. Mary, after all, is, "blessed among women" (Lk 1:42), because the "fruit of her womb" is the Word of God. And all of this is due to "the singular grace and privilege of almighty God"[56] who, in his sovereignty, has done great things for Mary and "holy is his name" (Lk 1:49).

---

[55] *Mary: Grace and Hope in Christ* [common statement of the Anglican-Roman Catholic International Commission of 2004], no. 60 available from http://www.ecumenism.net/archive/arcic/mary_en.htm.
[56] Denz.-H, 2803.

4.

Entrance of the Theotokos into the Temple: Daughter of Zion Dwells in Heaven's Presence

Virginia M. Kimball

The temple most pure of the Savior,
the bridal chamber most precious, the Virgin,
the sacred treasury of the glory of God
enters today into the Temple of the Lord,
bringing with her the grace of the Divine Spirit.
Therefore, the angels of God sing to her:
"This is the heavenly tabernacle!"[1]

The ancient Eastern tradition of Christianity, in its iconography and liturgy, offers a gateway of illumination on mystical aspects of the entry of the Virgin Mary into the Temple, revealing the Theotokos as Daughter of Zion, a young woman taking residence in the Heavenly Temple so that the Son of God may take residence in her and in humanity. Elements of the icon of the Feast of the Entrance are built on scriptural concepts and symbols, evidently related to the environment of Jewish mystical concepts existing from the first and second centuries, and corroborated by studies of manuscripts and fragments from the Dead Sea region. The account of the Entry is found in the apocryphal *Protoevangelium of James* (*PJ*), with a few added details in the Pseudo-Gospel of Matthew, a Latin text, called *The Book about the Origin of the Blessed Mary and the Childhood of the Savior* (*PM.*) The Pseudo-Gospel of Matthew (*PM*) is apparently a later writing that

---

[1] George the Hymnist, *Kondakion for the Presentation of Mary in the Temple* in *Mary Mother of God, Her Life in Icons and Scripture*, edited by Giovanna Parravicini and translated by Peter Heinegg (Ligouri, Missouri: Ligouri/Triumph, 2004), 51.

incorporated the earlier tradition of *PJ*. Both the *PM* and the *PJ* provide an account of Mary's entrance into the Temple, which offer strange and mysterious elements, but all of which represent a typology of holiness, replicated and told over countless ages in Eastern Orthodox liturgy and iconography. The account of the Virgin's entry into "the Temple" is brief:

> And after [Anna] having weaned her [the child Mary] in her third year, Joachim, and Anna, his wife, went together to the temple of the Lord to offer sacrifices to God, and placed the infant, Mary by name, in the community of virgins, in which the virgins remained day and night praising God. And when she was put down before the doors of the temple, she went up the fifteen steps so swiftly, that she did not look back at all; nor did she, as children are wont to do, seek for her parents. Whereupon her parents, each of them anxiously seeking for the child, were both alike astonished, until they found her in the temple, and the priests of the temple themselves wondered.[2]

Eastern iconography and liturgy are unabashed in affirming the story: three year old Mary is taken to the Temple by Anna and Joachim. According to *PM*, three year old Mary is simply "placed [there] in the community of virgins." Yet, more is found in *PJ*: there, the small child leads a procession of virgins carrying lights.

> And the child was three years old, and Joachim said: Invite the daughters of the Hebrews that are undefiled, and let them take each a lamp, and let them stand with the lamps burning, that the child may not turn back, and her heart be captivated

---

[2] *The Gnostic Society Library*, "The Gospel of Pseudo-Matthew," Chapter 4, http://www.gnosis.org/library/psudomat.htm [Accessed February 10, 2009].

from the temple of the Lord. And they did so until they went up into the temple of the Lord.[3]

High Priest Zechariah meets little Mary at the entrance to the Temple of Jerusalem, she ascends 15 steps and enters the Temple, where she grows and is cared for by angels who feed her the "bread of Heaven." *PJ* describes this: ". . . she received food from the hand of an angel."[4] We will explore later what this food truly is. The 7th century George the Hymnist spoke of this event in his homily for the feast: "Her parents received the Chaste One as a sign of faith, promising to offer her to the Lord with joy and love. She is the super-celestial tabernacle."[5] Not only is she entering "the Temple," but she is the tabernacle [who will come to hold the Divine Child].

Eastern Orthodox writer Frederica Mathewes-Green in her study of the *Gospel of Mary* (which is what she calls the *PJ*) rather boldly asks a problematic question:

> It's hard to believe that the priests would have accepted a three-year-old girl and allowed her to reside in the temple. This is the example of Samuel, however, who was presented to the priest Eli as soon as he was weaned, maybe even younger than three. When Hannah presents her son to the priest Eli, she explains that she had made this vow before the child was conceived. This is certainly an odd idea, to hand a priest a baby and saddle him with its upbringing. Was this

---

[3] New Advent Fathers, "The Protoevangelium of James," translated by Alexander Walker in *Ante-Nicene Fathers*, Vol. 8, edited by Alexander Roberts, James Donaldson, and A. Cleveland Coxe (Buffalo, NY: Christian Literature Publishing Co., 1886, revised and edited for *New Advent* by Kevin Knight), http://www.newadvent.org/fathers/0847.htm , sec. 7 [Accessed February 10, 2009].
[4] New Advent Fathers, *PJ*, sec. 8.
[5] Parravicini, 51.

a well-known practice, or did Hannah come up with the idea on her own?[6]

It's not a new question. St. Tarasios of 7th century Constantinople in his homily on the feast asked: "What was the virgin doing as she spent her life within the confines of the Holy of Holies? ... What name, then, shall we give to Mary?"[7] Tarasios considered a number of mystical signs to represent the meaning of the event: Heaven, Sun, Moon, Cloud, Candelabrum, Throne, Paradise, Mountain, Earth, Altar and Sea. Mathewes-Green answers her question by comparing young Mary to the prophetess Anna described in Luke's gospel "who greeted Mary and Joseph when they came to offer doves for Jesus' birth."[8] In this, Mathewes-Green subtly infers there could have been some way that Mary "entered" the Temple to live there because of the biblical testimony that at least one woman was closely associated with the temple and living near it, or at least "never leaving it." Indeed, it is strange to think of a young female toddler "living in the Holy of Holies" where no woman was allowed to go and only one priest at a time dared enter the holy space. The problem is that there is no evidence historically of any female residence *in* the temple, orphanages, or existence of girls "living in the temple" in the first century. We only have that one scriptural reference to Anna, a kind of monastic who lived and prayed close to the temple.

---

[6] Frederika Mathewes-Green, *The Lost Gospel of Mary, The Mother of Jesus in Three Ancient Texts* (Brewster, MA: Paraclete Press, 2007), 42.
[7] Tarasius of Constantinople, *Homily on the Presentation of Mary in the Temple* in *Mary Mother of God, Her Life in Icons and Scripture*, edited by Giovanna Parravicini and translated by Peter Heinegg (Ligouri, Missouri: Ligouri/Triumph, 2004), 58. Note: Parravicini uses the Latin form of the name.
[8] Mathewes-Green, 42. [Reference to Luke 2: 36-38]

There are two words[9] used in the Greek of the New Testament to indicate the word "temple": one indicates the Holy of Holies and the other the temple compound. *PJ* uses the word *naós* which according to biblical use meant the Holy of Holies. However, very quickly there is a change in the meaning of *naós* in the New Testament because of Christ's new concept of the temple as the body of the faithful (i.e. the vine and the branches), and in post apostolic time when *naós* came to mean the temple within. The etymology of the word changed quickly then, as evidenced in the work of Gerhard Kittel and Gerhard Friedrich in a work translated by Geoffrey W. Bromiley, which demonstrates that the new meanings of *naós* are introduced in the New Testament by Paul, Mark, Luke in the Book of Acts, and in Revelation:

> A special development that gives *naós* precedence in the NT is its use for the spiritual temple. The

---

[9] In Herod's temple, the one standing at the time of this event, the Court of the Gentiles of the Jerusalem Temple surrounded the inner compounds which contained the Women's Gallery and the Women's Court, and which were entered by the Beautiful Gate. These areas were separated from entry into the area containing the altar of burnt offering, which in turn was separated from the inner sanctum containing the porch and then the Holy of Holies. In New Testament references, "two words are used in the Greek: ναός meaning the sacred building alone, and ιερόν the whole sacred area, including various auxiliary courts, side chambers, and porticoes. Both words are translated 'temple,' without distinction, but the reader needs to keep the difference in mind, especially since only priests could enter the ναός (George Arthur Buttrick, ed., *The Interpreter's Dictionary of the Bible, An Illustrated Encyclopedia* (Nashville, TN: Abingdon Press, 1962, 551, column 1.) [Schematic drawing of the Temple on 556.)" It is interesting to note that in most Greek mss of *PJ*, chapter 7, verse 1, Joachim suggests they take child Mary to the temple (ναω° - a form of *naos*). This looks like it is the Holy of Holies that Mary enters. However, these two words began to be interchanged. *Naós* was then used to indicate the place of God in the heart as the Heavenly temple, not the temple in Jerusalem. "The term *naós* is an important one in the post apostolic period. Barnabus 4:11 demands that believers become a perfect temple for God. The heart is a holy temple in 6:15. This is the true temple, not the historical temple (16ff). Yet we are also being led to God's heavenly dwelling as a temple" according to Bromiley, *Theological Dictionary of the New Testament*, Abridged in One Volume, 625.

reasons for this development are the LXX interest in the term, the fact that it goes well with the idea of upbuilding, and the rich potential of the word. ... At the trial Jesus is accused of saying that he would destroy the temple (cf. Mk. 14:58; Mt. 26:61; Acts 6:14; also Jn. 19,21). Mark states that the witness is false. He also contrasts the temple made with hands and the wonderful new temple of the eschatological community, whereas Matthew and John stress the person and power of Jesus. ... [In Revelation] the temple is the abode of God's majesty and the source of his commands. The temple may also be the community, as in 3:12. In the new Jerusalem there is no temple, for God himself is the temple (21:22). The point is that God is now present in person.[10]

What does it all mean, then?

For our fellow Christians in ecumenical discussion, who are solely biblically-based and are unfamiliar with Eastern tradition, the Entry of the Virgin into the Temple may seem to be merely a fairy tale and immaterial to faith. In the first century, a little girl only three years old going to live in the inner sanctum of the temple in Jerusalem seems hardly plausible. However, looking at the symbolic elements in the account and finding their biblical meaning -- as often provided by Patristic homilies and hymns, and looking at the possibility of Jewish mystical thought of the first century, the ancient tradition of Christianity begins to provide for all of us deep illuminations of the mystery of this young woman's preparation in becoming the mother of God's Son.

Realizing the undeniable bond between early liturgical and iconographic sources with the *PJ* and the *PM*, we can begin to probe the symbolic meaning of details and typology used. As

---

[10] Bromiley, 626.

the account unfolds in the *PJ*, we identify symbols that do play a central role in the account, namely the "temple," "lamps and light," the "altar" or Holy of Holies in the Temple (beyond the third step), and "angels."

> When Mary turned three Joachim said, "Call the undefiled daughters of the Hebrews, and let each one take a **lamp**, and let it be burning, so that the child will not turn back and her heart be captured from the **temple** of the Lord." And they did this, and went up to the temple of the Lord. There the priest welcomed Mary and kissed her, and blessed her saying, "The Lord has magnified your name to all generations of the earth. By you, unto the last of days, the Lord God will reveal redemption to the children of Israel."
>
> There he sat her down on the **third step of the altar**, and the Lord God poured out grace upon her. And she danced with her feet, and all the house of Israel loved her.
>
> Her parents went down marveling and praising God that the child did not turn back. Mary lived like a nurtured dove in the temple, and received food from the hand of **an angel**.[11]

In this simple account of *PJ*, certain symbols thrust our attention to the spiritual aspects of the narrative, which in turn obviously predominate eastern liturgical hymns and prayers for the feast on the Entrance of the Theotokos into the Temple in the *Menaion* of the Orthodox Church. Here are a few examples:

> **Temple** – representing the actual presence of God.
> *Let the gate of the temple* **wherein God dwells** *be opened; for Joachim brings within today in glory the*

---

[11] Mathewes-Green, 43 and 45. [re: *PJ* chapter 7: 1, 2, and 3; chapter 8: 1.]

Temple and Throne of the King of all, and he consecrates
as an offering to God her whom the Lord has chosen to be
his Mother.[12]

Lamp and lamps - represents light as holiness, honor to the presence of God.

Into the holy places the Holy of Holies is fittingly brought
to dwell, as a sacrifice to God. The virgin adorned by
*virtues go before her carrying **torches**, and offer her to*
God as a most sacred Vessel.[13]

Third Step – indicates an entry into the presence of God.

The Theotokos, when she was three years old after the
flesh, was led to the Lord; and Zacharias, the priest of
God, received her in the temple with rejoicing and
established her there.[14]

Angel – abounding in the presence of prayer.

The hosts of angels and the multitude of all mankind
dance today before thy face, O all-pure Lady, and
carrying lamps they go before thee, proclaiming the
greatness in the house of God.[15]

Throughout the liturgical texts for the feast there is a sense of great joy. Archimandrite Kallistos Ware describes the feast: "Permeating all the hymnography of the day and giving to the feast a distinctive flavor, there is an ever-present note of rejoicing. For Orthodoxy, the Mother of God is *par excellence* a sign and expression of joy."[16] In liturgical texts, we see the

---

[12] 21 November, "The Entry of the Most Holy Theotokos into the Temple" in *The Festal Menaion*, by Mother Mary and Archimandrite Kallistos Ware (South Canaan, Pennsylvania: St. Tikhon's Seminary Press, 1998), Small Vespers, Tone One, 164.

[13] November 21, *Festal Menaion*.

[14] November 21, *Festal Menaion*, Mattins, Second Canon, Tone One, 176.

[15] November 21, *Festal Menaion*, Mattins, Canticle Three, First Canon, 177.

[16] Rev. Kallistos of Diokleia, [Kallistos Ware] "The Feast of Mary's Silence: The Entry into the Temple (21 Nov)" in *Mary in Doctrine and Devotion, Papers of the Liverpool Congress, 1989, of the Ecumenical Society of the Blessed Virgin Mary*, edited by Alberic Stacpoole OSB (Collegeville, Minnesota: The Liturgical Press, 1990), 37.

virgins leading joyfully with lights and then Mary dancing up the steps of the altar. Joy is shown to be at the heart of the experience of God, as demonstrated in Luke's special term used in the angel's greeting to her: *Chaire*, usually translated "Hail" but which is best translated as "Rejoice!" (Luke 1:28)

> *The most holy virgin, Temple that is to hold God, is dedicated with the temple of the Lord; and young girls, bearing lamps, now go before her. Her noble parents, Joachim and Ann, leap for joy and dance, for they have borne her that is to bear the Creator; and she, the All-Pure, with rejoicing goes round the divine habitations and is fed by the hands of an angel. She it is that shall become Mother of Christ, who grants the world mercy.*[17]

Bishop Kallistos Ware points out the holy silence of the Virgin in the event implies her great holiness. In the 14th century, St. Gregory Palamas sensed this value of holy silence in the *PJ* account as it is reflected in his homily for the feast. He embraced the Entry as "a symbol of mystical ascent of the soul to God," seeing Mary "as a contemplative, as the supreme *hesychast*, the one who more than any other has attained true *hesychia*, stillness or silence of heart."[18] For Kallistos Ware, the Virgin we find in the Entry is the "Mary of Palamas, Mary the hesychast in the temple, [who] turns out in the end to be not so very different from the Mary of St. Luke's Gospel who listens to God in humble and attentive silence."[19] These aspects of "joy" and "silence" identified by Kallistos Ware are intrinsically similar to the elements of Jewish mysticism in the early centuries.

In biblical exegesis of Luke, we identify similar temple mysticism. Cyprian Robert Hutcheon has identified the Temple as a "word-sign" element in the Gospel of Luke. This "sacramental approach" to God's *economia*, as it is revealed in

---

[17] November 21, *Festal Menaion*, Great Vespers, Tone Five, 171.

[18] Kallistos Ware in *Mary in Doctrine and Devotion*, 38.

[19] Kallistos Ware in *Mary in Doctrine and Devotion*, 39.

Luke's gospel, he claims, is integral to Luke's theological method. The "temple" is a method the evangelist uses to organize his gospel, if one understands that the "temple" is an equation to "Jerusalem." The Gospel of Luke begins and ends in the Temple, as does the ministry of Jesus. Using this "word-sign" as establishing an order, Hutcheon divides Luke's Gospel into three parts: Luke 1-2, the infancy and childhood narratives that begin and end in the Jerusalem Temple; Luke 3:1 – 19:27, the Galilean ministry and Christ's journey to Jerusalem; and Luke 19:28 – 24:52, surrounding Christ's ministry in the Temple and his death, resurrection and ascension in Jerusalem. He points out that "temple" forms a "literary *inclusio* for the Book of Acts as well."[20]   Therefore, exegetically, Hutcheon demonstrates a model for a mystical framework that is a Lucan "Temple theology." He finds "a sort of 'cosmic liturgy': a series of 'descents' and 'ascents' between a 'heavenly realm' and an 'earthly realm' involving 'the Kobod' (*shekinah, doxa 'glory'*) and 'the Spirit' (*ruach, pneuma, dynamis*)."[21] This "Temple" word/sign order in Luke's gospel resembles closely the sign of "temple" in early Jewish mysticism. In this sense, it suggests that the apocryphal documents may easily represent a culture of the same early mysticism. We should note that there are three main sections in the ancient temple of Luke's day that surrounded the Holy of Holies: the Court of the Women, the Court of the Men of Israel, and the Court of the Priests.

The temple in the time of Mary and her parents, Joachim and Anna, had been expanded and enlarged by Herod. The New Testament makes frequent allusions to this temple, including Solomon's Porch, the Beautiful Gate, its altar, the sanctuary and veil, the Holy Place, and the Holy of Holies. The Herodian temple sat atop a hill, "originally sloped in all directions from the summit, with varying grades ... [and to the south were] a magnificent system of substructural arches commonly called ... 'Solomon's Stables' to support the level

---

[20] Cyprian Robert Hutcheon, "'God is with Us': The Temple in Luke-Acts," *St. Vladimir's Theological Quarterly*, 44 no.1, 2000, 3-4.
[21] Hutcheon, 32.

platform. The whole area was paved with stone."[22] Logistically, then, the temple's physical elevation accessed after a climb up the slope and through arches could be understood to be little Mary's "ascent" to the Court of Women which was part of the temple. The very inner temple, the sanctuary, must have been magnificent. The Holy of Holies was distinguished by separation behind curtains. As we see in the iconographic tradition, there is a draped cloth or curtain which often is placed above the Virgin – indicating both that she is not in the holy of Holies and that at the Incarnation she, herself, became the locus of the Holy, the Holy of Holies, and is the Holy of Holies:

> The inner temple, or sanctuary stood on a raised platform in the Court of Priests, approached by a flight of twelve steps. It was probably of the same shape and size as that constructed by Solomon. Facing the east, it towered aloft, and made a most impressive appearance as the crown of the whole great sacred inclosure. The sanctuary contained a magnificent entrance hall, and the two rooms designate "the Holy Place," separated from each other by a heavy tapestry curtain or curtains. The entrance to the sanctuary was a porch one hundred and fifty feet high, one hundred and fifty feet broad, and thirty feet deep. It had no doors, but a gateway one hundred and five feet high and thirty feet broad. Great double doors led into the next chamber of the sanctuary, and probably a massive, elegant curtain hung before them. This chamber, known as the Holy Place (Heb 9:2, 8), was thirty by sixty feet in size. It contained the altar of incense in the middle, with the table of showbread to the north, and the seven-branched

[22] Clyde Weber Votaw, "The Temple in Jerusalem in Jesus' Day" in *The Biblical World*, Volume 23, No. 3 (March 1904), 174.
www.jstor.org.lib.assumption.edu (Accessed at Assumption College, Salisbury Street, Worcester, MA, August 1, 2008)

golden candlestick to the south. Only officiating
priests might enter this room. The Holy of
Holies, entered only through the curtain or
curtains described, was thirty feet square,
perfectly dark, and contained absolutely nothing.
This was the most sacred place, the earthly
locality of God.[23]

Icon of the Entry of the Theotokos into the Temple

The Orthodox maintain a close relationship between
liturgy and iconography as a language of tradition, as in the icon
of the Entry of the Theotokos into the Temple. An inspiring
source for iconography has traditionally rested on the scripture
and the apocryphal texts - believed to contain sacred tradition
at their center .

In the course of time apocryphal texts have been
variously treated. At times they were condemned
by the Church (especially in the West), at others
they fostered secular piety or inspired works of art.
Byzantine art includes scenes derived from the
Apocrypha. It suffices to mention here by way of
example wall-paintings in Cappadocian churches,
the mosaics in the narthex of the Chora monastery
on Mt. Athos and of the Peribleptos monastery at
Mystras, etc. All are inspired by the *Protoevangelium
of James* and include scenes from the childhood of
the Virgin, an important iconographic cycle from
the life of the Virgin is preserved in illuminated

---

[23] Votaw, 178-179. [FN 7 on page 178: The New Testament speaks of
"the veil," as of a single curtain (Matt. 15:38; Heb 6:19; 9:3); but the Mishna
(*Yema, V, 1*) speaks of two curtains, eighteen inches apart, the outer one
loose on the south side, the inner one loose on the north side – an
arrangement which permitted the high priest to enter the Holy of the
Holies without exposing that chamber to the view of others. This indicates
the growing awareness of the most sacred holiness of the Holy of Holies.]

manuscripts of the homilies of the monk James of Kokkinobaphos. [24]

Ouspensky and Lossky and the *Dictionary of Byzantium* provide an analysis of the icon that is associated with the Feast of the Entry. They explain that this feast was not an ancient festival and was probably developed no earlier than the 7th century, testified to by direct reference by Andrew of Crete in the 8th century. It is documented that the feast was officially introduced into Constantinople in the 8th century by Patriarch Tarasios, and adopted in the West under Pope Gregory XI in 1374,[25] being brought to the West via Hungary. Both iconography and liturgical texts trace the early development of this feast:

> Though believed to originate in Jerusalem in the dedication of the Nea (New St. Mary) church under Justinian I (21 Nov. 543), the feast is not found in the Jerusalem lectionaries through the 8th C. It appears in Constantinople in the *Typikon of the Great Church* and in the Menologion of Basil II. In this period, the emperor regularly celebrated the feast in the Church of the Chalkoprateia; in the 14th C. he went to Peribleptos monastery instead. Manual I Komnenos included the Presentation in a list of holidays. The West received the feast from Byzantium, apparently via Hungary ca. 1200. [26]

In the iconographic tradition, the icons of a feast day usually include similar elements and arrangement as they are copied

---

[24] Maria Vassilaki, *Mother of God, Representations of the Virgin in Byzantine Art* (Athens, Greece: Benaki Museum AND Milan: Skira Editore, 2000), 68.

[25] Leonid Ouspensky and Vladimir Lossky, *The Meaning of Icons* (Crestwood, NY: St. Vladimir's Seminary Press, 1989), 153.

[26] Alexander P. Kazhdan and Alice-Mary Talbot, editors, *The Oxford Dictionary of Byzantium*, Volume 3 (New York: Oxford University Press, 1991), 1715.

and repeated through the ages, a written testimony to revelation in image form, a "scripture" expressing the tradition of faith. The Feast of the Entry of the Virgin into the Temple features the following elements:

- A procession of virgins carrying candles
- The presence of Joachim and Anna
- The priest, Zacharias, standing in front of the Holy of Holies
- Virgin Mary in the Holy of Holies, fed bread by an angel/s [often "lifted to the top of the icon in a corner suggesting an ascent like the chariot of Ezekiel]
- Temple architecture, draped with the red veil
- Virgin Mary as a young woman, only quite small in size

If, indeed, it is understood that these elements derive from ancient 1st century mystical concepts, it is clear that these symbolic elements were not concocted in the 7th to 8th century when the feast day was established and when iconography related to the feast was established. Instead, they appear to express a mystical tradition that had its inception in first century Christianity in relationship to mystical Judaism.

Looking for Meaning

Despite the fact that this feast celebrates an event that, at first, appears non-Jewish and non-practical, perhaps even Gnostic in its descriptions, there remains the possibility that hidden in the apocryphal texts there abides a mystical theology, an illumination of God's plan, and all that pertains to the young woman who was to bear the Son of God. Since the major sources of this feast are the *PJ* and *PM,* we can ask if this feast, one of the twelve great feasts in the Byzantine rite, relies on Gnostic Christian thought. For example, do the *PJ* and *PM* hint at any Judaic culture? Contemporary scholarship on early

Jewish mysticism demonstrates that it is incorrect to label them purely as "Gnostic."

Gnostic or Judaic?

Although the *PJ* was condemned by Pope Gelasius in the *Decretum Gelasianum* in the 5th century and proclaimed "apocryphal," elements of the account crept into the Western tradition "with the production of the *Gospel of Pseudo-Matthew*," containing nearly all of the elements of *PJ* and more narrative drawn from the *Infancy Gospel of Thomas*.[27] According to a meditation on the Marian Library's *Mary Page*, "This story is a legend with no foundation in history."[28] Is this true? Pope Paul VI in his 1974 encyclical *Marialis Cultus*, wrote "despite its apocryphal content, it presents lofty and exemplary values and carries on the venerable traditions having their origins in the Eastern churches."[29] It should be noted that the definition of "apocrypha" itself is broad in meaning as described by Karl Rahner and Herbert Vorgrimler, "hidden; books not used in the liturgy or in theology because of their fantastic tenor, unknown origin, and heretical authorship."[30] Although declared and considered "apocryphal," which in many minds means "Gnostic" (the philosophical origin of second century heresies), evidently elements of the *PJ* account were known by Justin. Would Justin draw from sources he thought "Gnostic"? Tim Horner considers this in his work, "Jewish Aspects of the *Protoevangelium of James*."

---

[27] Tim Horner, "Jewish Aspects of the *Protoevangelium of James*," *Journal of Early Christian Studies 12.3* (Baltimore: Johns Hopkins University Press and the North American Patristics Studies, 2004), 315. This condemnation was evidently fueled by Jerome's condemnation of the idea that Joseph was a widower and had children prior to his betrothal to Virgin Mary.

[28] Rev. Matthew Mauriello, "A Meditation on the Feast of the Presentation of Mary," *Mary Page*, http://campus.udayton.edu/mary/meditations/Nov21.html (Accessed 08/03-2008.)

[29] Pope Paul VI, *Marialis Cultus*, 1974, §8.

[30] Karl Rahner and Herbert Vorgrimler, *Dictionary of Theology*, Second Edition (New York, Crossroad Publishing Company, 1990), 22.

The oldest copy of *Prot. Jas.* that we possess can be dated to the early fourth century C.E. (*Papyrus Bodmer V*), but there is evidence that suggests Justin Martyr knew of *Prot. Jas.* This means that Prot. Jas. probably comes from one of the most mysterious centuries in Jewish history.[31]

What does it mean to consider a text as "Gnostic"? Marvin Meyer in his work on the Nag Hammadi Library points out that the term "Gnostic" has been considered by Michael William and Karen King of Harvard as a flawed term. "The term 'Gnosticism' is so flawed, King concludes, that it may need to be rejected outright."[32] Michael William "proposes ... that we reconsider ancient gnosis and dismantle 'a dubious category,' the category he has in mind is 'gnosticism' itself. ... Williams recommends that we replace the old, vague category of 'Gnosticism' with 'biblical demiurgical traditions.'"[33] In this sense, *PJ* couldn't possibly be called "Gnostic." Williams is suggesting that there was a more specific tradition than the general category of "Gnostic" in the early centuries which looked at scripture through the Platonic eyes and conceiving of an apparent demiurge, a lesser god who was connected with creation, albeit in a negative aspect.

Tim Horner contends that *PJ* is an assertion of Christian belief on the virginity of Mary "soaked in a Jewish narrative."[34] Horner's work is a "reexamination of Prot. Jas.'s Jewish imagery and its implications for our understanding of Jewish/Christian relations."[35] He sees a Jewish matrix in the writing – exhibiting details that correspond to traditions which are included in the Mishnah, claiming that parallels between *PJ* and the Mishnah help to deconstruct the assumption that *PJ*

31 Horner, 315.
32 Marvin Meyer, *The Gnostic Discoveries, The Impact of the Nag Hammadi Library* (San Francisco: HarperSanFrancisco, 2005), 40.
33 Meyer, 38-39.
34 Horner, 335.
35 Horner, 314.

may have more in common with contemporary Judaism, or at least one part of it, than is often assumed. He looks into various Jewish aspects of "childlessness"; the shining priest's headband confirming to Joachim that God would bring birth to Anna; a Jewish attitude on betrothal and marriage using long held laws and traditions to point out the unusual situation with Mary that determined her virginity; and the significant meaning of Mary's age -- entering the temple at three years old and having to leave the temple at 12 years old.

In the *PJ*, Joachim tries to offer a gift at the temple but it is refused since he is childless. The biblical view would place childlessness on the woman but the later Mishnah, however, places responsibility for childlessness on the man *and* the woman. Horner feels this shows a connection to the tradition of the Mishnah.[36] In the *PJ*, Joachim asks forgiveness and recognizes God's blessing in the shining headpiece of the priest, considering it an oracle and revelation. According to Horner, this links directly to the idea of oracle and revelatory power "in a few Qumran fragments that refer to Moses' tongues of fire (1Q29, 4Q376, 4Q408). All of these texts describe the oracular, light/fire giving properties of the high priest's breastplate in relation to the mysterious Umin and Thummin."[37] The Umin and Thummin were twelve jewels representing the twelve tribes of Israel found on the breastplate of the priest in early temple worship. They represented an oracular type of source for the priest to determine God's will. It was understood to be a mystical way of God speaking to the heart of the people.[38]

In the Jewish laws on betrothal and marriage there were three distinct stages, which are reflected in the Mishnah. These stages are (1) birth to three years, (2) three years to 12 years, and (3) 12 years to the birth of a child. Mary's life in the *PJ* is

---

[36] Horner, 319.
[37] Horner, 320.
[38] This means of mystically hearing the voice of God was later replaced in the oracles of the prophets.

divided into these same three stages, with the variation that some documents of the *PJ* relate the birth of Jesus when Mary was 16. These stages fit tightly with purity concerns. "But when we read this through the lens of the Mishnah, it takes on a significant meaning. *Prot. Jas.*'s exacting language focuses attention on Mary's purity and her betrothal."[39] For example, the detail of Mary's entry into the temple just before her third birthday stresses her protection in purity. According to Mishnah law, at age 12 the young woman must be betrothed and usually before that age. Horner notes:

> The fact that she is given over to the temple at three harkens to betrothal language, but who is her betrothed? And if she is betrothed to the temple – a provocative and strange notion – how, when, and by whom will this "betrothal" be consummated? I believe these are exactly the questions that *Prot. Jas.* wants the reader to ask because they lead the reader to a distinctly radical, Christian conclusion.[40]

Utilizing Jewish law, the *PJ* explains the remarkable mystery held by Christians concerning Mary, the Virgin. The main point of the *PJ* may have been missed by those who object on the basis that a young girl living in the temple is an anachronism. Horner claims: "So while the idea of temple virgins may seem exotic in academic discussions of Judaism, this does not mean that second-century readers, even those of Jewish origins, would have found this wholly inappropriate."[41] In other words, the tale is set up to explain in Jewish terms how extraordinary the situation truly was.

Yet another anachronistic detail that has prompted some to say that *PJ* is not a Jewish writing is the test of bitter water required by the temple priest when Mary is found

---

[39] Horner, 322.
[40] Horner, 323.
[41] Horner, 324.

pregnant. This test is mentioned only once in the Bible in Numbers 5:11-31. In that case, it was administered only to the woman. However, in the Mishnah there is a consideration to give the test to both the man and the woman, with the central concern being "a matter of revealing guilt."[42] The Jewish reader of the second century might understand this account in mystical, deeper terms and descriptions as a testimony that Mary and Joseph were proven steadfast in God's will. The test itself was archaic but perhaps was used with a metaphorical and symbolic meaning, attempting to be understandable to the Jewish/Christian mind.

Lastly, Horner points to a study that linked the use of the term *Ioudaioi* [referring to "the Jews," a term describing themselves] used in the *PJ*, as a term that was actually "'insider language' [that] reflects a Jewish, if not specifically Palestinian, provenance. ... The earliest MS of *Prot. Jas.* (*Bodmer Papyrus V*, early third century CE) consistently follows insider usage."[43] Key words such as these provide us an illumination on what the meaning will be as it is used in liturgy and iconography of the Feast of the Presentation later on.

1st century Jewish mysticism

Once we look at the early text of the *PJ* with new vision, realizing that it may have been written for Jewish Christian eyes in the second century, the more revealing the aspects of the account become. Harrison turned to the idea of Christian myth in understanding the Feast of the Entry of the Theotokos in the Temple: "This is done through rituals that re-enact the myths of origin. In this context, a 'myth' is not a falsehood but a story of profound insight that explains the meaning of life and delineates an archetypal pattern to be re-

---

[42] Horner, 328.
[43] Horner, 330.

lived again and again."[44] By examining the temple symbolism, the mystery of Mary's obedient response to God's call is told.

> Our Lady's presence in the temple vividly
> portrays the depth and intensity of her spiritual
> formation and preparation. ... The rich temple
> imagery of the feast, with its vast and variegated
> historic and religious associations, discloses a little
> of the mystery of her inner life. Her heart, the
> inmost core of her being, becomes the holy of
> holies, where God is enthroned and surrounded
> by angels.[45]

Harrison sees the connection between the temple details and Eastern hymnology, iconography and even church structure. For example, the liturgical prayers for the feast include Psalm 44/45, a royal wedding psalm "where the queen-to-be is escorted into the throne room to meet her king."[46] Ancient symbolism of the temple as an entry into the presence of God and God's realm appears associated with the symbolic elements in the Entry of the Theotokos into the temple:

> To enter the temple is to enter again into
> paradise, a garden adorned with palm trees and
> cherubim, fire and light. The court of Israel
> where sacrifices are offered daily is identified with
> the material cosmos, the earthly realm, while the
> holy of holies is identified with heaven, the abode
> of God and the angels. God's work of creation
> was believed to have started from the place where
> the temple stands, where heaven and earth, angels
> and humans, are united. ... All this is fulfilled in

---

[44] Nonna Verna Harrison, "The Entry of the Mother of God into the Temple," *St. Vladimir's Theological Quarterly* 50:1-2, 2006, 152.
[45] Harrison, 156. Here she refers to Margaret Barker's *The Gate of Heaven: The History and Symbolism of the Temple in Jerusalem*, Sheffield Phoenix Press Ltd., 2008.
[46] Harrison, 157.

the Mother of God, in her body and soul. She is
the new heaven where God incarnate is
enthroned, or rather is more spacious than the
heavens which cannot contain him.[47]

This detail "articulates a theology in the form of a story that
expresses the meaning of events that we can be sure
occurred."[48] In the Eastern hymn of the day, we hear Anna
saying to her little daughter: "Go into the place which none
may enter: learn its mysteries and prepare thyself to become the
pleasing and beautiful dwelling place of Jesus."[49] With the
continuing study of ancient, early Jewish mysticism, there is
sure to be even more to be discovered that sheds light on the
Feast of the Entry. It is clear these studies will take the details
even beyond Harrison's description of "myth." These studies
will propel us into realizing that the mystical depths of silence
and presence with God cannot be described, but they were and
can be experienced.

In a serious study of Jewish mysticism, Rachel Elior
states that mysticism has not been well received in our
contemporary world.

The corpus of mystical writings in the traditional
Jewish world developed over the course of
thousands of years. ... The creators of mystical
thought and those who gave expression to
mystical experiences tried to decode the mystery
of divine existence by penetrating to the depths of
consciousness, language, memory, myth, and
symbolism. They strove to rescue reality from its

---

[47] Harrison, 158.
[48] Harrison, 154.
[49] Harrison, 155 citing from Mother Mary and Archimandrite Kallistos
Ware, *The Festal Menaion*, 1969, 171.

concrete, univocal meaning by delving deep into the psyche.[50]

In many ways, Jewish mysticism is the same mode of expression as found in early Christian liturgy, ancient iconographic typological (symbolic) images, and seen in the apocryphal writings themselves. Elior sees the voice of the mystic as one who has experienced an indescribable vision and often communicates this in terms of an encounter with the Heavenly realm:

> Mystics are those who mediate in their dreams
> and visions, in their thoughts and consciousness,
> in their soul and spirit, in their poetry and ritual,
> between the fire blazing at Sinai and the fire
> blazing around the beholders of the merkavah,
> between the fire of the angels and the heavenly
> fire that envelops Ezekiel's chariot.[51]

Study of the Dead Sea scrolls opens the possibility of seeing how first century Jewish mysticism might illuminate the account of the Entry of the Theotokos into the Temple. It has become evident that there is an identity at Qumran that is probably Essene, but not in the narrow sense once thought. Jean-Baptiste Humbert states that the Qumran manuscripts speak of "saints" and the "pious." Those called "Essene" can now be identified as "a conservative political-religious movement, diversified and scattered in a number of communities all over Palestine and probably beyond."[52] This indicates that an Essene-like spirituality may have prevailed at the time of Christ throughout the region, albeit in various sects and communities of Jewish Christians during the first century

---

[50] Rachel Elior, *Jewish Mysticism, The Infinite Expression of Freedom* (Oxford, UK: The Littman Library of Jewish Civilization, 2007), 1.

[51] Elior, 81.

[52] Jean-Baptiste Humbert, EBAF, translated by Claude Grenache, A.A., "An Essene Identity at Qumran," *Near Eastern Archaeology*, Volume 63, No. 3, September 2000, 174.

and afterward. These faithful Jews were not only disappointed with the failing influence of the Temple but appear to have developed spiritual alternatives to experience the sacred presence of God.

Florentino Garcia Martinez has determined in his work on the Temple Scroll that there was a period of formation prior to the community at Qumran. He has determined that the *Temple Scroll* is "a compilation of various sources thoroughly edited and revised by an author/redactor who added new material of his own to them."[53] This finding leads us to see that the spiritual, cultural environment in which we find Anna and Joachim and little Mary was parallel to Jewish eschatological expression, and through which the experiences of this holy family could be told. Martinez organized[54] the material into four main themes: 1) the Temple – rules on the sanctuary and the altar, and the Temple's courtyards and various buildings; 2) a description of festivals; 3) purity rules for both the Temple and the holy city along with other purity rules; and 4) a rewriting of Deuteronomy 12 to 23. Martinez doesn't see the Temple Scroll as eschatological but more pertaining to its contemporary time.

> The detailed description of the temple and all its buildings, of the sacrificial system, the purity laws and the laws of the polity, according to the will of God as it should be understood, painfully shows the inadequacy of the situation of the time of its author and creates a powerful instrument for reform. By presenting this program as directly revealed at Sinai, the author underscores the urgency of implementing it. The present reality (and the present temple) does not correspond to the will of God.[55]

---

[53] Florentino Garcia Martinez, "The Temple Scrolls," *Near Eastern Archaeology*, Volume 63, No. 3, September 2000, 172.

[55] Martinez, 173.

The Temple Scroll, dated as early as the 5th century BCE or as late at the 1st century CE, may help in conceiving how 2nd century Jewish Christians may have seen the elements and importance of the Temple as key to Mary's preparation to be the mother bearing God's son. In fact, Martinez concludes his report in claiming the high importance of this very meaning in the scroll:

> [The *Temple Scroll*] belongs, therefore, to the [Essene-like community at Qumran] formative period. This implies that the composition of the *Temple Scroll* is more or less contemporaneous with 4QMMT (*Some of the Works of the Torah*) which shows us that a well-defined group existed within these priestly circles and can be placed within the same priestly circles in which 4QMMT originated – the same priestly circles from which the Qumran community was later to emerge. This solution explains the similarities and differences by allowing us to take into account the inevitable evolution, the modifications imposed due to the break from the Jerusalem temple, and ideological and halakhic developments that arose in the new situation. ... Whatever the case, the anonymous person who redacted the *Temple Scroll* around the middle of the second century BCE, using earlier written sources, succeeded in creating one of the most interesting documents for understanding the Judaism of his period.[56]

This is not to say that the *Temple Scroll* is directly connected to the *PJ* tradition but only to say that there was a milieu in Judea in the first century that prompted mystical concepts, creating a culture in which the Entry of Mary into the Temple could be interpreted and communicated. As the situation at the Jerusalem temple worsened after the time of Christ and sects

---

[56] Martinez, 174.

like those at Qumran had to realize a new locus of God in the community of believers, such as the concept of the Mystical Body explained by Christ, the mystical temple came to be comprehended as the "place" of encounter with God. A tangible document like the *Temple Scroll* helps us to understand new mystical realizations describing the power and glory of God who never abandons the marginalized. Angels who minister to God are present among the community of the faithful and the righteous. Let us see this in a brief example from the *Hodayot*, psalms found at Qumran (which are not in the Bible.)

> Blessed art Thou, O Lord,
> for Thou hast never abandoned the orphan
> neither despised the poor.
> [Unbounded is] Thy power,
> and Thy glory hath no measure.
>
> Angels of wondrous strength
> minister unto Thee,
> and [they walk] at the side of the meek
> and of them that are fearful or right-doing,
> and of all the lost and lorn
> that stand in need of mercy,
> lifting them out of the slough [Jer 32:19]
> when that their feet are mired. [Ex 34:6][57]

Temple and the angels

This brings us now to a fascinating collection of essays collected in *Paradise Now, Essays on Early Jewish and Christian Mysticism,* edited by April D. DeConick. Although these comprehensive and scholarly essays provide a wealth of possibilities for insight into first century mysticism, we can only touch on some. To begin, DeConick tackles the meaning of

---

[57] Theodor H. Gaster, *The Dead Sea Scriptures in English Translation* (Garden City, New York: Anchor Books / Doubleday & Company, Inc., 1964), 155.

"mysticism" in first century context. The word "mysticism" is not one used in ancient vocabulary in describing the experience of God, but rather "apocalypse" or "revelation."

> It [mysticism] corresponds to no single term in the ancient literature. In fact, when the early Jews and Christians describe their mystical experiences in a single word, they do so most often by employing the term *apokalypsis,* an "apocalypse" or "revelation." In the Jewish and Christian period-literature, these religious experiences are described emically as waking visions, dreams, trances, and auditions that can involve spirit possession and ascent journeys. Usually these experiences are garnered after certain preparations are made or rituals performed, although they can also be the result of rapture. The culmination of the experience is transformative in the sense that the Jewish and Christian mystics thought they could be invested with heavenly knowledge, join the choir of angels in worship before the throne, or be glorified in body.[58]

DeConick states that the earliest Christian mysticism would be considered essentially "Jewish," and "beginning to take on its own individuality only by the mid-to-late second century, for instance in the Alexandrian school run by Clement and then Origen."[59] The tradition in early Jewish and Christian mystical tradition emerges in what is called "period literature": apocalyptic literature; writings of Philo of Alexandria; in Qumran literature; and "possibly in the teachings of the Palestinian school of Yohanan ben Zakkai."[60] DeConick believes, along with others, that "these early currents of

---

[58] April D. DeConick, editor, *Paradise Now, Essays on Early Jewish and Christian Mysticism* (Atlanta: Society of Biblical Literature, 2006), 2.
[59] DeConick, 2-3.
[60] DeConick, 3.

mysticism form the basis for *merkabah* and *hekhalot* speculation. Subsequently, these mystical traditions were absorbed into the Pharisaic and Tannaitic trajectory, some forms of Christianity, gnostic schools, and later kabbalistic materials."[61] "Merkabah" refers to the biblical and later mystical traditions as the realm of angels, relating to Heaven's domain described in Ezekiel. "Hekkhalot," too, refers to mystical experience in the region of angels.

In another essay in the DeConick collection, Rachel Elior treats the "Emergence of the Mystical Traditions of the *Merkabah*." She begins her essay with a fascinating quotation from a Qumran scroll which is pertinent to our topic, describing the presence of angels in the midst of one who experiences the presence of God: "The cherubim fall before him and bless. They give blessing as they raise themselves. The sound of divine stillness [is heard]… and there is a tumult of jubilation as they lift their wings. A sound of divine stillness."[62] Here is the element of "silence" which Palamas later identified. Elior referred to the 1941 work of Gershom Scholem, a scholar of Jewish mysticism. Scholem did not have the advantage of knowing the material found in the Dead Sea caves and, therefore, could not have imagined how the history had started far earlier. Elior says "In the sixty-five years that have passed since the publication of [Scholem's] *Major Trends in Jewish Mysticism*, we have learned that the first chapter in the history of Jewish mysticism in the postbiblical period started a number of centuries earlier, in the period during which the extensive priestly library known as the Dead Sea scrolls was written."[63] This is an indication that it is possible that the Galilean community and the Jewish Christians would have begun a tradition about the mother of Christ clearly within this culture of Jewish mysticism. Elior distinguishes that mystical

---

[61] DeConick, 4.
[62] Rachel Elior, "The Emergence of the Mystical Tradition of the *Merkabah*" in *Paradise Now, Essays on Early Jewish and Christian Mysticism*, edited by April D. DeConick, 43.
[63] Elior, *Paradise Now*, 84.

traditions, particularly about the *merkabah*, referring to the divine chariot of the cherubim shown to seers and prophets as well as its ritual representation in the tabernacle and in the temple, were written between several centuries before Christ and until the first half of the first millennium C.E., with variations. Both Jewish and Jewish Christian mysticism demonstrated parallel concepts:

> 1. An exceptional interest in celestial sanctuaries and holy angels related to priestly understanding of "holy time, holy place, and holy ritual."

> 2. A heavenly domain that is revealed to mystics who ascend to the heavenly sanctuaries.

> 3. An interest in "mystical descriptions of the *holy space* in heaven (seven *merkabot*; seven *hekhalot*; *pardes* – paradise; garden of righteousness) and in the sacred ritual performed by the angelic watches in the celestial realm in eternal cycles.

> 4. They see *holy angels* as guardians of *holy time* in sevenfold divisions within the *seven heavenly sanctuaries.*[64]

The account of Mary's Entry into the Temple and the detail that she was fed by angels appears to lie coherently in this mystical perception. The mystical tradition of the *merkabah* relates scripturally to Enoch and, according to Elior, [were] ... [like] the heavenly chariot, the "heavenly chariots" of cosmic time divisions and seven chariots of sacred ritual, and a sevenfold angelic liturgy – all written before the Common Era.[65]

Another aspect of early Jewish mysticism was the concept of the "temple within." Christopher R.A. Morray-Jones

---

[64] Elior, *Paradise Now*, 85.
[65] Elior, *Paradise Now*, 102.

explains that the *"merkabah mystical"* traditions were preserved in *hekhalot* writings.

> In these sources, the ascent into heaven is envisaged as a journey through the courts of a cosmic temple to the innermost sanctuary where God form of a vast manlike figure of fire or light, called the "Power" (δύναμιζηρωβγ) or "Glory" (δοζᾶδωββ), seated upon the throne of glory (δωββη αοβ), also called the "chariot" (ηββρμ). This imagery is deeply rooted in the Hebrew biblical tradition. The term *merkabah* is derived from 1 Chr 28:18, where it refers to "the chariot of the cherubim" that carried the ark of the covenant in the holy of holies. In Isa 6, a central text of the later mystical tradition, the prophet encounters the enthroned deity in the holy of holies of the temple.[66]

When looking at the icon of the Entry of the Theotokos into the Temple, it is hard not to think of this mystical imagery when we see Mary seated high above and being fed by angels. Morray-Jones comments that this is mystical language, meaning that the prophets may not have literally ascended but experienced a deep and profound vision on earth, perhaps in the earthly temple. During the exile, it was impossible to have access to the temple and its Holy of Holies where the earlier prophets may have experienced their visions. In 1 Enoch: 14, there appears a cosmology of three heavens, which later increases to a cosmology of seven heavens. "Here again the highest heaven, the dwelling place of the 'the Great Glory' (η δόζα η μεγάλη), is called "the holy of holies."[67]

---

[66] Christopher R.A. Morray-Jones, "The Temple Within" in *Paradise Now, Essays on Early Jewish and Christian Mysticism*, edited by April D. DeConick, 145-146.
[67] Morray-Jones, 148-149.

In Qumran literature, there is a concept of a "temple within," a sense of God's presence within the worshipping community of initiated faithful – surrounded by angels. In contrast, rabbinic writings see a three-way relationship between cosmos, temple, and body but don't refer to a "correspondence between temple and community."[68] It is obvious that the mystical ideas of temple and community are incorporated in Christian faith, with Christ as "great High Priest who has passed through the heavens, Jesus the Son of God."[69] Therefore, with the development of the "mystical descent" to the *merkabah* within, there may be an illumination in comprehending what the young woman Mary experienced mystically in preparing to become the mother who bore Christ.

Another element, which may be reflected in Mary's dining with the angels, is developed by Andrea Lieber in the DeConick collection. There is a "relationship in ancient Jewish literature between sacrificial meals and eschatological banquets, both of which are meals that mediate the human and divine realms."[70] This is an area, she notes, that has not been explored in scholarly literature. "Similarly, the motif of a heavenly banquet, described in rabbinic midrash and in Hellenistic sources, is also represented as a meal consumed in God's presence, shared among the righteous of Israel."[71] The sharing of a meal in God's presence is a mystical way of "seeing" oneness with God.

Reading this mythic tradition alongside the early Christian sources, we can see the way in which heavenly meal imagery functions to articulate

---

[68] Morray-Jones, 178.

[69] *Orthodox Study Bible, New Testament and Psalms* (Nashville, Tennessee: Thomas Nelson Publishers, 1993), Hebrews 4:14. This biblical verse given in Morray-Jones.

[70] Andrea Lieber, "Jewish and Christian Heavenly Meal Traditions" in *Paradise Now, Essays on Early Jewish and Christian Mysticism*, edited by April D. DeConick, 313.

[71] Lieber, 313.

powerful statements about the divine-human relationship. Philo uses cultic meal imagery to affirm the legitimacy of a pious life apart from the Jerusalem temple; in New Testament sources meal symbolism is used to assert a collapsing of the boundaries that formerly structured humanity's relationship to the divine ... .[72]

The detail of the young Mary ascending into the Temple and being fed by the angels is an illumination of the beginning of an actual coming together of God and humanity, celebrated in mystical language as she is fed by the angels.

Gates of temple – ascending on steps

In the *PJ* account, there is direct reference to the Temple in Jerusalem, including the area known as the "Court of Women." In an Orthodox work on the life of the Theotokos, we find the following details:

Now there were fifteen steps at the temple that led from the Court of the Women to that of the men. The significance of the number fifteen, to the Jews, was that it corresponded to the fifteen Psalms of Degrees [Ps 119-133 LXX]. The temple had been built on a mountain, thus the altar of burnt offering could not be reached except by steps. On one of these steps, they placed the little maiden Mary. Then the whole company ascended into the temple of the Lord: the maidens bearing lamps and singing psalms. And Mary, without anyone leading her or lifting her, ascended the steps one after the other.[73]

---

[72] Lieber, 339.
[73] Holy Apostles Convent, *The Life of the Virgin Mary, the Theotokos* (Buena Vista, Colorado: Holy Apostles Convent and Dormition Skete, 1989), 26. This aspect is taken from Rev. Alexander Roberts and James Donaldson, editors, *Apocrypha of the New Testament: The Gospels of the Nativity of Mary* in

The "Psalms of Degrees" are associated with "ascent" and relate to the "the Songs of Ascent." This appears to depend on the account given in the *Pseudo Gospel of Matthew*, chapter 4:

> And when she was put down before the doors of the temple, she went up the fifteen steps so swiftly, that she did not look back at all; nor did she, as children are wont to do, seek for her parents. Whereupon her parents, each of them anxiously seeking for the child, were both alike astonished, until they found her in the temple, and the priests of the temple themselves wondered.[74]

The Jerusalem temple, built on a hill, meant that one must "go up" to its courtyards to then approach the area of sacrifice and be near the Holy of Holies where only the priest would enter. It is thought that pilgrims, making the journey to the Temple for great feast days, would sing and pray together. Connected to this is the category of the Psalms in the Psalter (Hebrew: שיר תולעמה Shir Hama'aloth) called "the Songs of Ascent," "Fifteen Songs of Degrees," or "Song of Ascents," Psalms 120 to 134 (119-133 LXX). The 15 steps were associated with the actual ascent to the temple for pilgrim festivals as mentioned in Deuteronomy 16:16.[75] These psalms are short and identify keywords in repetitions making them suitable for group singing. The short phrase attached to all these psalms, "A song of ascents," is the Hebrew word *ma'alah* and is "typically translated

---

The Ante-Nicene Fathers, The Writings of the Fathers down to A.D. 325, Volume VIII, 385.

[74] *Ante Nicene Fathers, translated by* Philip Schaff *et al.* http://en.wikisource.org/wiki/Ante-Nicene_Fathers/Volume_VIII/Apocrypha_of_the_New_Testament/The_Gospel_of_Pseudo-Matthew [Accessed February 12, 2009]

[75] "Three times a year all your males shall appear before the Lord your God in the place the Lord chooses; at the Feast of the Unleavened bread, at the Feast of Weeks, and at the feast of Tabernacles; and they shall not appear before the Lord your God empty-handed," *The Orthodox Study Bible* (St. Athanasius Academy of Orthodox Theology, 2008), Deuteronomy 16:16.

'ascent,' may refer to a step (see, e.g. Ezekiel 40.26). Early rabbinic tradition thus connects these fifteen psalms to the fifteen steps of the Temple according to Ezek. 40.26, 31, where the Levites sang (*m. Mid. 2.5; b.Sukkah 51b*)."[76] Again, we see a mystical origin for the detail given in the apocryphal literature of the Entry of the Theotokos into the Temple.

Burning lamps

The meaning of the procession of virgins carrying lamps to accompany little Mary to the temple does not seem so remote to us. We are familiar with the many biblical metaphors of light. However, after exploring the early mystical tradition, we can see that this is a "ritual" and carrying lights gives us illumination of the significance:

> The connection between lamps and the central sanctuary is very strong. Perhaps all but two of the literal references to lamps (2 Kings 8:19; 1 Chron 28:15) are to lamps in the central sanctuary. The golden lampstand in the tabernacle, with its vertical shaft, its three branches on each side and its cups "shaped like almond flowers with buds and blossoms" (Ex 25:31-40). It is very likely that this lamp symbolized the tree of life in the garden of Eden, which is otherwise evoked in features of the tabernacle and in the inner courts of Solomon's temple. ... The lamp in the shrine at Shiloh is called "the lamp of God" in 1 Samuel 3:3; this suggests that its light symbolized God's presence. The lamp for the tabernacle was to be trimmed

[76] Adele Berlin and Marc Zvi Brettler, editors, *The Jewish Study Bible* (Oxford: Oxford University Press, 2004), footnote on 1424.

night and morning to give constant light (Ex 30:7-8.)[77]

Once we can begin to think in terms of "myth" as Harrison indicates, and we approach the mystery of this event of the Entry realizing the symbolism of the temple is closely connected to ritual, aspects of the tradition's story speak with more clarity.

Qumran

In his work on the theology of Qumran, Helmer Ringgren explains that the manuscripts at Qumran develop a spiritual sense of "temple" which replaces the actual physical temple of Herod.

> Community was like an antechamber of heaven. Indeed, the suggestion that the Qumran Community was occasionally portrayed as, or better functioned as, the Temple, which is developed by G. Klinzing, seems confirmed by the copy of the Rule of the Community which seems to depict the Community as *Miqdash*, "Temple" ... .[78]

If the early Christian community was an Essene-like community, then these early Christians could easily describe a similar concept as a mystical tradition: that within the community of initiated faithful there was a temple-like presence of God. Ringgren describes this concept: "the earthly services mirrored the singing of the heavenly ones; in fact the Angelic Liturgy describes the angels' worship of God in the heavenly Temple, but the Qumranites on earth participated in this

---

[77] Leland Ryken, James C. Wilhoit, and Tremper Longman III, editors, *Dictionary of Biblical Imagery* (Downers Grove, Illinois: InterVarsity Press, 1998), 486.

[78] Helmr Ringgren, *The Faith of Qumran, Theology of the Dead Sea Scrolls* (New York: Crossroad Publishing Company, 1995), xx.

worship (Schwemer)." [79] In Jewish mysticism of the early centuries, there is an emphasis on God's transcendence and the need for intermediaries such as angels. Ringgren provides the fascinating detail that "in a couple of passages ($_1$QSb, The Blessings, iv. 25 and QH vi.13) there is also mention of angels of the presence, i.e., angels of a special higher rank who stand before the face (presence) of God; this term is also known from the rest of Judaism. The so-called Angelic Liturgy names a large number of angels and classes of angels as participants in adoration and worship." [80] As Orthodox will know, even today, it is believed that angels flourish around the altar during the Divine Liturgy.

Conclusion:
Daughter of Zion dwells in Heaven's Presence

"Zion" is biblically the city of Jerusalem, and in an eschatological sense -- the new Jerusalem. However, imbedded in this word symbol are layers of mystical illuminations:

- The Temple as Yahweh's dwelling place
- The covenant people of God as God's dwelling place
- Kingship leading to the idea of a Messiah
- The world center for God's law
- The renewed heavens and earth where peace and prosperity will reign. [81]

Theotokos, the woman who bore Christ, is a personification of all these. "Perhaps the most striking metaphor used to describe Zion is the metaphor of a woman. She is the 'daughter of Zion, that is, the Lady Zion." [82] By associating the Temple with the Theotokos -- the very Presence of Holy God within its inner

---

[79] Ringgren.
[80] Ringgren, 83.
[81] Ryken, Wilhoit and Longman, 980.
[82] Ryken, Wilhoit and Longman, 981.

sanctuary, and her association with angels having climbed the 15 steps of ascent, we are illumined by her purity – her presence in the Presence of the Transcendent God, her preparation at the hands of angels, her care in the gifts of God, her steadfast faith, and her all-holiness. Having explored the foundations in early Jewish mysticism, we do not have to see the little Mary of three years of age literally entering the Holy of Holies. She is entering the initiated community in which God abides. She will become the Holy of Holies with the Transcendent God in her womb. As St. Germanos, Patriarch of Constantinople in the 8th century, wrote in his homily:

> Hail, new Zion and divine Jerusalem, holy "city of God the Great King, in whose towers God is made known," (Psalm 48:3) making kings bow down in veneration of your glory and disposing the whole world to celebrate in exultation the solemnity of your presentation; you are truly the seven-branched candelabra, (Daniel 2:34) golden and resplendent, lit by the timeless flame that is fed by the oil of purity and that guarantees the dawning of light upon those who are blinded by the gloomy darkness of sins.[83]

---

[83] Germanus of Constantinople, Homily I, *The Entrance of the Most Holy Mother of God* in *Mary Mother of God, Her Life in Icons and Scripture*, edited by Giovanna Parravicini and translated by Peter Heinegg (Ligouri, Missouri: Ligouri/Triumph, 2004), 24.

Mary and Islam

5.

Mary and Islam: A Sign for All the World, A Model of Salvation

Mary Catherine Nolan, O.P.

Background of Muslim Understanding of Mary

Some 200 years after the Council of Ephesus in 431 C.E. declared Mary to be Theotokos[1] and 180 years after the Council of Chalcedon, 451 C.E., defined the doctrine of the hypostatic union of the divine and human natures in the One Person of Jesus Christ, there remained on the Arabian peninsula ancient Christian Churches which disputed some of the teachings of these Councils. Monophysites held that Jesus had one nature, divine. Nestorians held that human and divine natures were conjoined in Jesus and they rejected the title "*Theotokos*" (*God-bearer*) for Mary, the Mother of God, considering *Christotokos* (Christ-bearer) as the appropriate title for Mary who was held to be the Mother of Jesus' human nature only.[2] The controversy over the identity of Jesus and thus Mary's status continued to cause conflict in the Churches. Later, it was observed by the Prophet Muhammad and his followers that Christians disagreed among themselves about their faith.

About the year 622 C.E., the Prophet Muhammad had led his followers from the city of Mecca to the city of Yathrib, about 180 miles north of Mecca. This city is now known as Medina, the City of the Prophet. The Muslim calendar began at this time. The year of the migration, *Hijra*, is year one of the

---

[1] Luigi Gambero, *Mary and the Fathers of the Church: The Blessed Virgin Mary in Patristic Thought*, Trans. Tom Buffer (San Francisco: Ignatius Press, 1999), 235-237.

[2] Gambero, 235.

Muslim era. It was at this time and in this place that Muhammad received the revelation concerning Mary the Mother of Jesus. In Arabic she is called Maryam. This revelation is contained in the third and nineteenth *Suras* or chapters of the Holy Qur'an.

The occasion of this revelation is described in the following story: A delegation of richly garbed Christians, consisting of sixty horsemen, came from Najran, an ancient town in southern Arabia the Messenger of God. It was noted that they belonged to the *King's religion.* Among them were fourteen of their notables, three of whom held special authority among their people. One was a leader and guardian of the affairs of the people, another was their chief, and the third was their bishop and the head of their religious school. The bishop was held in high honor because he had studied all the sacred books and had acquired great wisdom and learning. Even the Byzantine kings honored him. The delegation came to the Messenger of God in his mosque at the time of mid-afternoon prayers. The companions of the Messenger of God were awed by their elegance. An invitation was extended to the visiting delegation to join in the prayers and they accepted, facing East as was the custom. After prayers the Christian leaders spoke with the Messenger of God and he said to them, "Accept *Islam.*" They replied, "We have been *muslims* long before you" (*muslim* refers to one who submits to God.)[3]

What followed was a disputation concerning the person of Jesus. Muhammad argued against the Christian belief in the divinity of Jesus. Part of the argument is that God is pure spirit and does not have a son. Moreover, Jesus was born of a human mother, subject to human bodily needs, and he died. The Christians then asked, "If Jesus is not the Son of God then who is his Father?" Muhammad stated, "It is Our Lord who formed Jesus in the womb as he willed. The mother of Jesus bore him

[3] Mahmoud M. Ayoub, *The Qur'an and Its Interpreters, Vol. II: The House of 'Imam* (Albany: State University of New York Press, 1992), 1-2.

in the same manner as women bear their children, and delivered him as they do, and he was then nurtured as would be any child."[4]

According to commentators the men of Najran who spoke to the Prophet were adherents of the *King's religion* which probably meant that they were Melkites and held to the Christological definition of Chalcedon. However, at this time, Najran had a large and wealthy Christian population; Nestorian and Monophysite Christians were also in Arabia at this time. The visitors were not swayed by Muhammad's argument and Muhammad called them unbelievers.

There are various traditions concerning this legend but most Islamic commentators agree that it was on this occasion that God, *Allah*, sent down the eighty-two verses of the third Sura, *The 'Imrans*. This chapter contains the revelation concerning the birth of Mary, her consecration and life in the temple. Also, the annunciation and birth of Jesus are depicted in the text. Christians who read the Qur'an will note some similarities with the accounts in the Gospel of Luke and a non-canonical text, the *Protoevangelium of James*. There are also significant differences. Concerning the cause of the revelation of this Sura, the modern commentator, Sayyid Qutb writes: "…it is clear from the subjects that these verses treat that they confront the errors of the Christians, especially those relating to Jesus, peace be upon him. They also revolve around the creed of unadulterated divine oneness which Islam brought."[5]

Before looking at the accounts it is well to note that Catholic view their sacred texts much differently than Muslims

---

[4] Ayoub, 2-3.
[5] Ayoub, 3-4. Islamic commentators to which Ayoub refers in the story of Najran are A. Wahidi, A. Tabari, S. Qutb and F. Razi. Regarding the reports of the disputation between the Prophet and the Najran delegation, Ayoub quotes Islamic scholar F. Razi: "You should know that this report proves that the use of disputation for the purpose of confirming the faith and removing errors was the way of the prophets, peace be upon them."

view their sacred text. For Muslims the real Qur'an is in heaven. The word, *Qur'an*, means *recitation*. The book which we know as the *Qur'an* is authentically the word of Allah sent down to Allah's Messenger, Muhammad. Muhammad received and recited the revelation which was then written by scribes. The language of the text is Arabic as it was spoken in the sixth century and is beautiful in its poetry. Only the original Arabic *Qur'an* is considered the authentic one. Devout Muslims commit the entire *Qur'an* in its original language to memory.

For Catholics, Jesus, the Christ, is the Son of God, and the presence of Jesus is experienced in a special way in the Eucharist. For Muslims the presence of Allah is experienced in the *Qur'an*. The *Qur'an* is held in reverence in much the same way that Catholics reverence the Eucharist. According to Dr. Scott Alexander, Jesus is the *Christian* equivalent of the *Qur'an*. Christians are, according to Dr. Scott Alexander, *people of the Person*.[6]

In 1965, the Second Vatican Council document *Nostra Aetate* proclaimed that "the Church has a high regard for Muslims." The two communities of Catholics and Muslims were asked to seek *mutual understanding*. Also, they were asked to work together in the fields of social justice, moral values, peace and liberty.[7] Pope Paul VI had created the Secretariat for Non-Christians in 1964 with the intention of helping Christians come to a deeper knowledge of other religions so that through dialogue mutual respect and cooperation would be built.

The purpose of Catholic-Muslim dialogue, today, is not to seek to convince or convert but to understand and respect each other. With this in mind I proceed to look at the understanding of Mary in the Muslim faith tradition. There is a

---

[6] Interview with Islamic scholar, Dr. Scott Alexander, professor at Catholic Theological Union.
[7] *Nostrae Aetate* is the Declaration on the Relation of the Church with Non-Christian Religions of the Second Vatican Council. The title is taken from the first line in Latin of the declaration.

large body of literature outside of the *Qur'an* which contributes to the formation of the Muslim faith. The *Hadith* literature contains sayings and deeds of the Prophet and his followers. There are also *tales* with an exegetical bent which elaborate the stories of the *Qur'an*. These are stories about the lives of the prophets and messengers of God such as Adam, Abraham, Noah, Moses and Jesus.

How Mary is Presented in the Qur'an

There are thirty-four references to Mary, the Mother of Jesus in the *Qur'an*. She is the only woman mentioned by name in the text. The high esteem of the Prophet Muhammad for Mary is shown in the Hadith where the Prophet states that the best of all the women of humankind are: Mary, daughter of *'Imran*; Asiyah, the wife of Pharaoh; Khadijah, wife of Muhammad; Fatima, daughter of Muhammad and the wife of Ali. Of these women, many commentators consider Mary the most excellent due to God's election.[8]

According to Muslims, the miracles that God worked in and for Mary are a sign of God's power. Mary, as she is presented in the *Qur'an*, is a *model for salvation*. She symbolizes purity, piety and beauty. Together with Jesus she is a *Sign* (Arabic: *âya*) for all peoples, for the whole world.

The Birth of Mary

The election of Mary and her birth is related in the third Sura of the *Qur'an* titled, *The 'Imrans*. The title gives the name of Mary's father, *'Imran*, and also indicates her ancestry. It is the name of the great grandson of Jacob who was the father of Moses, Aaron and Miriam (Exodus 6:18). The name of Mary's mother is not given. She is simply referred to as the *wife of 'Imran*. The *House of 'Imran* is the family of prominent prophets and messengers. The story of Mary follows mention of the

---

[8] Ayoub, 97.

prophets Adam, Noah, Abraham and his descendents. The *Qur'an* states: "Allah chose Adam and Noah, Abraham, and the Imrans above all beings," (Sura 2:77.) Thus Mary is situated among the elect.

The Christian gospels place Mary, the mother of Jesus, in the royal line of David. The *Qur'an* places Mary in the line of the great prophets: Mary is a chosen one, blessed and nurtured by Allah.

The third Sura states:

> 35. Remember, when the wife of 'Imran [Mary's mother] prayed: "O Lord, I offer what I carry in my womb in dedication to your service, accept it, for You hear all and know every thing."

> 36. And when she had given birth to the child, she said: "O Lord, I have delivered but a girl." – But God knew better what she had delivered: A boy could not be as that girl was. "I have named her Mary," (she said), "and I give her into Your keeping. Preserve her and her children from Satan the ostracized."

> 37. Her Lord accepted her graciously, and she grew up with excellence, and was given into the care of Zachariah. Whenever Zachariah came to see her in the chamber, he found her provided with food, and he asked: "Where has this come from, O Mary?" And she said: "From God who gives food in abundance to whomsoever He will."[9]

In Islamic tradition all humans are touched by Satan at birth. This is why the newborn cries. Some

---

[9] *Al-Qur'ān, A Contemporary Translation* by Ahmed Ali (Princeton, New Jersey: Princeton University Press, 1984) Sura 3: 35-37.

commentators interpret these verses to mean that because of the dedication of Mary to Allah, she was preserved from this touch as, also, was her son, Jesus.[10]

The Annunciation

Following the account in the *Qur'an* on the prayer of Zacharias for a child and the birth of the prophet John the Baptist is the account of the visit of the Angel Gabriel to Mary. I note here that in the *Qur'an*, Mary is a chosen one. She questions the angel but she is not asked to give her consent. There is no *fiat* as there is in the Gospel of Luke. Mary's perfection assures her total submission to God.

> 42. The angels said: "O Mary, indeed God has favoured you and made you immaculate and chosen you from all the women of the world. 43. So adore your Lord, O Mary, and pay homage and bow with those who bow in prayer."

> 45. When the angels said: "O Mary, God gives you news of a thing from Him, for rejoicing, (news of one) whose name will be Messiah, Jesus, son of Mary, illustrious in this world and the next, and one among the honoured, 46. Who will speak to the people in the cradle and when in the prime of life, and will be among the upright and doers of good."

> 47. She said, "How can I have a son, O Lord, when no man has touched me?" He said: "That

---

[10] George Tavard, *The Thousand Faces of Mary* (Collegeville: The Liturgical Press, 1996) 36. In Christian theology this belief may be seen as a version of original sin. Islamic theology has no doctrine of original sin.

is how God creates what He wills. When He decrees a thing, He says 'Be', and it is."[11]

There is a second, more detailed, account of the Annunciation in Sura 19. The title of this Sura is *Mary* (*Maryam*). The story, again, is preceded by the account of the birth of John the Baptist. Unlike the account in the Gospel of Luke, the *Qur'an* is not specific about the time or place of the Annunciation and the birth of Jesus.

> 16. Commemorate Mary in the Book. When she withdrew from her family to a place in the East.

> 17. And took cover from them, We sent a spirit of Ours to her who appeared before her in the concrete form of a man.

> 18. "I seek refuge in the Merciful from you, if you fear Him," she said.

> 19. He replied: "I am only a messenger from your Lord (sent) to bestow a good son on you."

> 20. "How can I have a son," she said, "when no man has touched me, nor am I sinful?"

> 21. He said: "Thus will it be. Your Lord said: 'It is easy for Me,' and that: 'We shall make him a sign for men and a blessing from Us.' This is a thing already decreed."[12]

The Birth of Jesus

In the account of the birth of Jesus and Mary's presentation of him to her people, we again are told that the

---

[11] *Al-Qur'an, A Contemporary Translation,* Sura 3: 42-43, 45-47.
[12] *Al-Qur'an, A Contemporary Translation,* Sura 19: 16-21.

Christians are arguing among themselves. Two hundred years after the Council of Chalcedon, the Christological question of the identity of Jesus had not been settled among the Churches of Arabia. Historically, the non-Chalcedonian Churches, that would include the Nestorian Christian Churches and the Monophysite Christian Churches, deemed that they were being oppressed by the Byzantine Churches and began to dialogue with the Muslims. The account in the *Qur'an* makes clear that Jesus is a holy child but he is born as any human child.

> 22. When she conceived him she went away to a distant place. 23. The birth pangs led her to the trunk of a date-palm tree. "Would that I had died before this," she said, "and become a thing forgotten, unremembered."

> 24. Then (a voice) called to her from below: "Grieve not; your Lord has made a rivulet gush forth right below you. 25. Shake the trunk of the date-palm tree, and it will drop ripe dates for you. 26. Eat and drink, and be a peace. If you see any man, tell him: 'I have verily vowed a fast to Ar-Rahman and cannot speak to any one this day.'"

> 27. Then she brought the child to her people. They exclaimed: "O Mary, you have done a most astonishing thing! 28. O sister of Aaron, your father was not a wicked person, nor your mother sinful!"

> 29. But she pointed towards him. "How can we talk to one," they said, "who is only an infant in the cradle?

> 30. "I am a servant of God," he answered. "He has given me a Book and made me a prophet,
> 31. And blessed me wherever I may be and enjoined on me worship and zakat [to give alms] for as long as I live,

32. And be dutiful to my mother. He has not made me haughty or rebellious. There was peace on me the day I was born, and will be the day I die, and on the day I will be raised from the dead."

34. This was Jesus, son of Mary: a true account they contend about. 35. It does not behove God to have a son. Too immaculate is He! When He decrees a thing He has only to say: "Be", and it is.[13]

In the Sufi tradition, Mary's withdrawal to the East is understood as an invitation to prayer and silent contemplation. That Mary is instructed to shake the palm tree is an invitation to action rather than waiting for Allah to do something. [14]

The Sufi mystic and poet, Ibn al-Arabi extols Mary as attaining perfect presence with Allah. The angel blew Jesus into her. The angel was transmitting Allah's Word to Mary just as an apostle transmits his word to the community. The Sufi poet, Jalal al Din Rumi, reports that another Sufi mystic, Abu Yazid al-Bistani, feeling himself to be one with Allah, envisioned an identification with Mary.

... His form is vanished, he is a mere mirror:
Nothing is seen in him but the reflection of another ...
If you see Jesus there, you are his mother Mariyam.
He is neither this nor that – he is void of form ...[15]

---

[13] *Al-Qur'an, A Contemporary Translation,* Sura 19:22-35.
[14] Tavard, 41-42. Mary is the perfect model for the Sufi in that she embodies the ideal of passive waiting for God in prayer and of active personal effort.
[15] Tavard, 42. That one can identify with Mary to the point of being Mary is echoed by the medieval Dominican mystic, Meister Eckhart, when he states, "We must all be mothers of God."

Mary as a Sign for the World according to Islam

In 2004, Archbishop Michael Fitzgerald, then president of the Pontifical Council for Interreligious Dialogue, addressed the Ecumenical Society of the Blessed Virgin Mary, in Bath, England, on the texts of the Qur'an that present Mary together with Jesus as a sign for the whole of humanity. He began by quoting Sura 21: 91:

> And (remember) her who guarded her chastity. We breathed into her of Our Spirit, and We made her and her son a sign for all peoples.[16]

Mary and her son together form a single *sign* or *miracle* for all time, for all places, and for all people. Jesus is a sign and manifestation of God's mercy. By his wonderful birth and wonderful life he is to turn an ungodly world back to God. Jesus being born without a father was to bring to the people's mind the Omnipotence of God.

> The insistence on God's omnipotence is striking. It will be seen that this excludes all human participation. Mary does not have to consent to what is being announced to her. There could be no Muslim text equivalent to the homily of St. Bernard where he imagines the heavens and the earth suspended, waiting for Mary to pronounce her *fiat*. God has merely to say to something, "Be," and it is (cf. Q 3:47). It is easy for him. It is a thing decreed.[17]

---

[16] Michael Fitzgerald, "Mary as a sign for the world according to Islam" in *Mary for Time and Eternity, Essays on Mary and Ecumenism,* edited by William McLoughlin and Jill Pinnock (Herefordshire, UK: Gracewing, 2007), 298. Archbishop Fitzgerald quotes from *The Holy Qur'an, Text, Translation and Commentary,* translated by Yusuf Ali, 1968.

[17] Fitzgerald, *Mary for Time and Eternity,* 301.

Archbishop Fitzgerald notes that there are divisions among Christians themselves concerning Jesus: "There is a real need for ecumenical endeavour so that Christians can give united witness to Jesus, son of Mary and Son of God, truly a Sign for the whole of humankind."[18]

Some Teachings from Islamic Scholars and Imams on Mary's Role in Islam

From many conversations with American Muslims concerning the position of Mary the Mother of Jesus in Islam, three themes have emerged: the theme of Mary as model of purity, prayer and beauty; as a sign of salvation; and as the personification of the eschatological community of believers.

Professor Shahrzad Hushmand, in a reflection on Mary, states that she is the only creature who was immaculate even before she took human form. Mary was preserved from sin but not from suffering. Her greatest suffering was when she was about to offer Jesus to the world, because she knew that she was offering him to a world that does not understand and that will try to extend its sinfulness to two beings who are immaculate. Referring to (Q 19: 23) "…Would that I had died before this…and become a thing forgotten, unremembered," Hushmand asks "why this enormous suffering?" She explains Mary's terrible cry.

> "El Rahman" the name par excellence, of God
> in the Qur'an expresses the Mercy, the infinite
> love of God, a love which does not expect
> anything in return, which offers itself to anyone,
> sinner or saint, grateful or ungrateful, believer
> or unbeliever. To reach that level of love is the
> final goal of a human being's spiritual journey: a
> very difficult journey which leads to becoming a

---

[18] Fitzgerald, *Mary for Time and Eternity,* 303-304.

true image of God, a representative of his (khalifat Allah) on earth.

...She, (Mary), is offering Jesus, the love of God (raHmatan minna) to a world that will even persecute him and will want to kill him. And Mary knows this. But it is precisely in that act of donation that love becomes a source of life. Then after this offering, as the Qur'an reminds us, from her own feet will surge a spring of living water and the tree that was already dried up and dead, thanks to her will regain life and, as if by a miracle, it will become green again and give fresh and ripe fruits (Q 19: 23-25).

This is why the Qur'an proposes Mary as the perfect model to follow, for believers, men and women, of all places and times.[19]

In a beautiful discourse on Mary, Dr. Walid Khayr, Imam of a mosque in Vernon Hills, Illinois, calls Mary a model for salvation. He notes that the presentation of Mary in the *Qur'an* follows a line of prophets. Of the prophetic experience, he says:

First prophetic experience is potentially a universal human experience. The selection for this blessed experience is done by God regardless of race, ethnicity or biological lineage. Secondly, Mother Mary chosen for a very high position close to God along the side of all these men is further liberating such experience from gender discrimination.[20]

---

[19] Dr. Shahrzad Hushmand, *Mary in Islam.* Paper presented at a Marian Congress in Castlegandolfo, Italy in 2003. Dr Hushmand, a Muslim theologian, has a close association with the Catholic ecclesial movement, the Focolari.
[20] Dr. Walid Khayr, text of a homily given at Vernon Hills Mosque, January, 2004.

He presents Mary as the model and prototype for attaining
higher altitudes and stations near to God. She is a model of
purity, piety and beauty. As a model of prayer, "Mary was
capable of transcending this sensual world into the intelligible
world; connecting with the world of angels, the world of
absolute reality, and receiving the divine word of God without a
mediator."[21]

Mary is a model for our age of materialism because
people can see in her the possibility for transformation and
attaining a high level of spirituality. "When she gave birth to
Jesus, she gave a new birth to humanity and to her people a
new direction towards salvation. … If creation of Adam
represented the beginning of humanity, Jesus represented the
rebirth of humanity."[22]

Mary as Symbol of the Eschatological Community

In the Fall of 2006, I attended a series of lectures
sponsored by the Medieval Institute at the University of New
Mexico. Several of the lectures centered on the building of the
great cathedrals of Europe, e.g. Notre Dame de Paris. That
many of the great medieval cathedrals were named after Our
Lady is not surprising. Mary was understood as an icon of the
Church. It was mentioned that entering through the door of the
cathedral was akin to entering the womb of Mary who
personifies the faithful, worshipping community.

W. Deen Mohammed, a Muslim leader in America,
speaks of Mary as the personification of the faithful Muslim
community. Mary birthed a new humanity in giving birth to
Jesus. At the end time, Mary will give birth to the final universal
community of the faithful. "Can't you see that Mary is the
woman that Allah has raised above all the women of the world?
The *Ummah* (community) of Muhammed is the woman that

---

[21] Dr. Walid Khayr.
[22] Dr. Walid Khayr.

114

Allah has raised above all the women (communities) of the world and that's it exactly."[23]

Mary as Intercessor

There are various opinions in Islam regarding Mary as intercessor. Some insist that Muslims do not pray to Mary because in Islam there is no mediation between God and the person praying. However, a young Turkish woman, Betul Avci, who is a Sufi, told me that one can seek intercession from those who are beloved of God. In certain circumstances, sections of the *Qur'an* are recited as prayer. For example, a woman who is asking God for safety in childbirth might recite the part of Sura 19 which describes the birth of Jesus. If she is praying for a beautiful child, she might recite the Sura which tells of Joseph the son of Jacob because he was supposed to be very good-looking. Many families name their daughters Maryam in the hope that these children will be blessed.[24]

In an account of an apparition of Mary above St. Mark's Coptic Church in Zeitoun, Cairo, Egypt in April, 1968, it is recorded that while Christians prayed the rosary, Muslim workmen at a garage across from the church recited a verse from the *Qur'an* praising Mary.

Mary as Prophet

In Islam, the role of prophet confers the highest status upon a person. Jesus, son of Mary, is revered by Muslims as the greatest prophet until Muhammed, the Seal of the Prophets.

---

[23] W. Deen Mohammed on how Muslims are to see Mary, the mother of Jesus Christ.

[24] Betul Avci, a doctoral student in theology at University of Chicago and member of a Sufi Order, shared her understanding of Mary as a sign of God's power to work miracles and as a sign of God's loving care for us. I interviewed her in March, 2005, in Chicago. She has since completed her studies, graduated, and returned to her home in Istanbul, Turkey. I am grateful for the explanation she gave me of what it means to be a Sufi.

Mary is understood to be born of the *House of 'Imran* which is the family of the prophets, Moses and Jesus. Many commentators, while highly revering Mary, do not give her the status of prophet. Yet, there is a minority opinion that Mary is a prophet.[25]

Images of Mary

There is a story from the Hadith that when Muhammad had all the idols and images removed from the Ka'aba at Mecca, he instructed his followers to leave an image of Mary. This is the only image that Muslims are permitted to have. Mary symbolizes beauty.

In ancient Christian icons of Mary and her child, we often see Mary pointing to Jesus. In the account of the birth of Jesus in the *Qur'an,* we read that after the birth of Jesus Mary does not speak or defend herself to her relatives. She points to the child and Jesus speaks in defense of his mother.

In 2006, at a Catholic-Muslim symposium at Catholic Theological Union, Mr. Ian Linden from Britain shared a story from his time in Teheran, Iran. He mentioned that there are large pictures of Mary in the city. When there was a demonstration in front of the Danish Embassy in protest against the cartoons negatively caricaturing the Prophet Muhammad, Linden observed an angry scene. An artist, who had lost the use of both arms in the Iran-Iraq war, had managed, while holding the paint brush in his teeth, to create a beautiful painting of Mary. He put the image in front of the embassy with the caption: *This is our faith. What is yours?*

Woman of Peace

---

[25] This position is argued by the 11th century Andalusian jurist and poet, Ibn Hazam.

Today in many shrines dedicated to the Virgin Mary, prayers are raised for world peace. Mary is the woman of peace. Her presence in both Christianity and Islam is the presence of one whose entire being was in union with God, who lived in total obedience to God's will. A small house in Ephesus, thought to be the home to which the Apostle John took Jesus' Mother, is a place where Christians and Muslims kneel together in prayer. The house has been restored and is now a shrine. Christians and Muslims brought together in prayer by their reverence for Mary the Mother of Jesus can live together in peace.

Conclusion

In Islam, Mary the Mother of Jesus is highly revered. She is considered the perfect woman in her piety and faithfulness to God. Thus, she is a model for all people. Because she conceived Jesus as a virgin, she is a sign of the omnipotence of God. She represents beauty. She is mother of a new creation.

In Egypt, Mary is considered the *Golden Bridge* between Coptic Christianity and Islam. Catholics and Muslims revere Mary. May she be the bridge to peace and reconciliation for all who are at enmity with one another. Mother Mary, lead us in the ways of peace in our troubled world.

Mary and Protestant Thought

6.

Our Lady of Spiritual Solidarity: Reflections on the Marian Dimension of Catholic-Methodist Dialogue[1]

Maura Hearden

The French ecumenical Dombes Group observed, "the Virgin Mary…is perhaps the point at which all the underlying confessional differences, especially in soteriology, anthropology, ecclesiology, and hermeneutics, become most clear."[2] Hers is the story of the way in which God has chosen to save mankind. It concretizes the afore-mentioned doctrines resulting in a uniquely powerful immediacy of understanding. For this reason, post-Reformation Christianity has often regarded the Mother of our Lord as a symbol of that which divides us, and a potentially inflammatory topic for those engaged in ecumenical dialogue. Such a state of affairs can be nothing less than tragic for all who desire a common Christian household, a household that must surely include the woman from whom the Son drew his humanity.

Fortunately, nearly a century of intra-Christian dialogue has chipped away at the walls that divide us and laid the groundwork for some significant progress in the area of mariology. The most obvious signs of progress can be found in laudable dialogue efforts focusing specifically on "Marian" topics, each resulting in varying degrees of agreement.[3]

---

[1] A modified version of this essay, titled "Our Lady of Sacramental Communion: Marian Possibilities Emerging from Catholic-Methodist Dialogue," appeared in *Pro Ecclesia* vol. XIX, no. 1 (Jan. 2010): 69-92.

[2] Alain Blancy, Maurice Jourjon, and the Dombes Group, *Mary in the Plan of God and in the Communion of Saints*, trans., Matthew J. O'Connell (New York: Paulist Press, 2002), 51.

However, I would suggest that the most intriguing possibilities to date are emerging from ecclesiological discussions that have not included Marian topics as such but are inextricable from them for the reasons mentioned above. Specifically, recent Catholic-Methodist dialogues focusing on the Church as a "sacramental communion" have opened the door wide to some startling convergences in the area of Marian doctrine and the devotions that flow from it.

It must be said at the outset that I am a Catholic and am motivated by Catholic doctrinal concerns. I am also a believer in the ecumenical cause and am convinced that Catholics and Methodists might take great strides in the direction of unity—improving our understanding of and strengthening our solidarity within the Body of Christ—by examining these issues within the context of each tradition's theological heritage. The following reflections are offered in the hope of initiating a more in-depth analysis by those who are formally involved in ecumenical endeavors.

"Sacramental Communion" and Spiritual Solidarity: Preliminary Remarks

The image of the Church as a "sacramental communion" has been a subject of discussion among Catholic and Methodist ecumenists since the 1982 Nairobi Report, *Towards a Statement on the Church.*[4] This particular way of

---

[3] I am referring here to such landmark dialogues as H. George Aderson, J. Francis Stafford, Joseph A. Burgess, eds., *The One Mediator, the Saints and Mary: Lutherans and Catholics in Dialogue VIII* (Minneapolis MN: Augsburg, 1992); the Dombes Group cited above; and the Anglican-Roman Catholic International Committee, *Mary, Grace and Hope in Christ* (2005) available on-line at http://ecumenism.net/archive/2005/07/the_full_text_o.htm

[4] The theme has been developed over time within the international dialogue statements listed below and the U.S. statement by the United Methodist Church and the National Conference of Catholic Bishops titled *Through Divine Love: The Church in Each Place and All Places.* The complete texts of the international dialogues are available from Report of the Joint Commission

speaking of the Church has gained fairly universal acceptance among Catholics since its incorporation into the documents of the Second Vatican Council and has been examined by Catholic and Methodist ecumenists in light of the Council's understanding of the term. I will therefore provide a brief explanation of important Catholic concepts embedded within this description of the Church before proceeding with an overview of its use within the dialogues.

Acceptance of the term "sacramental communion" as it is applied to the Church in post-Vatican II Catholicism, is contingent upon understanding and acceptance of at least two key theological concepts: creaturely *participation in* and *mediation of* divine grace. These concepts are fundamental to Catholic sacramentology, which is based on the notion that God works *through* creation as opposed to circumventing it. Thus, a sacrament is composed of a sensible sign, which contains and conveys invisible grace.

Traditionally, the word, "sacrament," has been confined to discussions about specific sacraments (baptism, confirmation, Eucharist, penance, marriage, holy orders, and anointing of the sick) as means instituted by Christ through which believers who possess the necessary spiritual disposition may receive sanctifying grace.[5] Since the close of the Second Vatican Council, a broader application of the term has been applied. Jesus Christ, the source of saving grace, the one who makes the invisible presence of God visible, is said to be the "primordial" sacrament. The Church is the visible sign and instrument of Christ, imbued with the Holy Spirit, and commissioned with the task of continuing Christ's saving work

---

Between the Roman Catholic Church and World Methodist Council, (Lake Junaluska, NC: World Methodist Council). For the U.S. statement, see http://www.usccb.org/seia/finalUMC-RC5-13masterintro.pdf

[5] A concise definition of the seven sacraments can be found in Robert C. Broderick, *The Catholic Encyclopedia* (Nashville, TN: Thomas Nelson Publishers, 1976).

to the glory of the Father. For this reason, it is considered the sacrament of Christ, sometimes called the "fundamental" sacrament.[6] The *Catechism of the Catholic Church* describes the currently accepted use of these terms in this way:

> Christ himself is the mystery of salvation....The saving work of his holy and sanctifying humanity is the sacrament of salvation, which is revealed and active in the Church's sacraments....The seven sacraments are the signs and instruments by which the Holy Spirit spreads the grace of Christ the head throughout the Church which is his Body. The Church, then, both contains and communicates the invisible grace she signifies. It is in this analogical sense, that the Church is called a 'sacrament' (*Catechism of the Catholic Church*, n. 774).

Finally, it must be said that the concepts of creaturely participation in and mediation of grace are intimately related to the notion that human beings exist, to some degree, in communion with God *and* with one another, particularly those who are united within the mystical body of Christ. These bonds of unity allow for the distribution of grace *through* human beings in general and, in a special way, through the members of Christ's body—a body within which the eschatological church and its earthly aspect are united. The notions of creaturely participation, mediation, and communion within Christ's body form the bedrock of Catholic doctrines and devotions concerning the communion of saints in general and the mother of Christ in particular. However, this connection has yet to be

---

[6] A more detailed analysis of the history and meaning of "sacrament" is provided by Herbert Vorgrimler, *Sacramental Theology* (Collegeville, MN: Liturgical Press, 1992). The terms "primordial" and "fundamental" are not necessarily universally applied by Catholic theologians. However, the relationship between the Incarnation and His Church that is indicated by the terminology is universally accepted.

explored in any of the international or U.S. Catholic-Methodist dialogues.[7]

"Sacramental Communion" and Spiritual Solidarity: The Dialogues

Towards a Statement on the Church, commonly known as the Nairobi Report, introduced the concept of sacramental communion, saying that:

> Christ works through his Church, and it is for this reason that Vatican II speaks of the Church as a kind of sacrament, both as an outward manifestation of God's grace among us and as signifying in some way the grace and call to salvation addressed by God to the whole human race (cf. Vatican II, *Lumen Gentium* I, 1).[8] This is a perspective that many Methodists also find helpful (*Towards a Statement on the Church*, n., 9).

Note the reserve on the part of the Methodist participants evident in that last sentence.[9] Catholic observers were not

---

[7] It should be noted that, thanks in great part to the efforts of members of the ESBVM, there has been a British Catholic-Methodist statement published on the subject of Mary. See British Methodist/Roman Catholic Committee, *Mary, Mother of the Lord, Sign of Grace, Faith and Holiness: Towards a Shared Understanding* (Peterborough; London: Methodist Publishing House; Catholic Truth Society, 1995).

[8] *Lumen Gentium* is the Second Vatican Council's Dogmatic Constitution on the Church. Hereafter, LG. All citations in this paper are from the Vatican translations available on-line:
http://www.vatican.va/archive/hist_councils/ii_vatican_council/documents/vat-ii.html.
LG may be found at:
http://www.vatican.va/archive/hist_councils/ii_vatican_council/documents/vat-ii_const_19641121_lumen-gentium_en.html

[9] David Chapman observes that "not all Methodists feel comfortable with this idea" in his comprehensive analysis of Catholic-Methodist

entirely pleased with the treatment of this subject in the *Nairobi Report* either. Jean Marie Tillard, O.P., made the following observation:

> Surprisingly…one is dissatisfied by the rather ambiguous description the text gives of this sacramentality while referring explicitly to *Lumen Gentium*. Effectively, reference is only made to sacrament as a manifestation of God's grace and as signifying the grace and call to salvation (no. 9). The dimension of effective help, of service and of co-operation is, if not forgotten, certainly put very much in the shade….The Report does not follow through with the vision it has adopted.[10]

To be fair, the *Nairobi Report* touches upon these themes by saying that "Christ works through his Church" (n., 9), and the notion of mankind's co-operation with God's grace had been introduced more than a decade earlier in the 1971 *Denver Report*.[11] The ideas were not, however, developed in this particular statement.

The Church as a sacramental communion remained an important topic for discussion in the international and U.S. Catholic-Methodist dialogues for the next twenty years.[12]

---

dialogue, *In Search of the Catholic Spirit: Methodists and Roman Catholics in dialogue* (Peterborough UK: Epworth, 2004), 145.

[10] J. M. R. Tillard, O.P., "Commentary on 'Towards a Statement on the Church'," *One in Christ.* Vol. 22, n. 3 (1986): 261.

[11] The Denver Report states, "Both traditions hold man's cooperation with God in the mystery of salvation as necessary." See n. 55. The document is available online at http://www.prounione.urbe.it/dia-int/m-rc/doc/e_m-rc_denver3.html .

[12] The specific documents dealing with the question of the Church as a sacramental communion are as follows:

- Fourth international series. *Towards a Statement on the Church*, 1982-1986 (Nairobi). Also, the *Nairobi Report*.

Gradually, ideas about Christ as the "primary sacrament," the believer's effective help as God's co-worker, the Church as a channel of divine grace and the related topic, the present reality of the eschatological Church, became more fully developed and explicitly affirmed. Finally, in the 2006 *Seoul Report*, we read that in the Church,

> The invisible and the visible come together, and the former is made known through the latter. This holding together of the invisible and the visible is essential to our understanding of the Church as Catholics and Methodists (n., 48).[13]

The document of the *Seoul Report* goes on to affirm the Church as a place in which the God who is revealed is truly present, quoting Pope Paul VI's opening address to the second session of Vatican II: " 'The Church is a mystery. It is a reality imbued

---

- Fifth international series. *The Apostolic Tradition*, 1986-1991 (Singapore). Also, the *Singapore Report*.

- Sixth international series. *The Word of Life: A Statement on Revelation and Faith*, 1992-1996 (Rio de Janeiro). Also, the *Rio Report*.

- Seventh international series. *Speaking the Truth in Love: Teaching Authority Among Catholics and Methodists*, 1997-2001 (Brighton). Also, the *Brighton Report*.

- United States national dialogue report. *Through Divine Love: The Church in Each Place and All Places*, 2005.

- Eighth international series. *The Grace Given You in Christ: Catholics and Methodists Reflect Further on the Church*, 2006 (Seoul). Also the *Seoul Report*.

[13] Christian traditions disagree as to the nature and extent of the connection between the invisible and visible aspects of the Church and there is a related argument as to the necessity of institutional unity. I would like to clarify my point of view on this matter as the narrow focus of this paper does not include discussion about the institutional aspect of unity and I would not want its absence to be misconstrued. I hold a traditional Catholic point of view, which maintains that the visible, institutional, aspect of the Church emerges from its mystical aspect and that institutional unity is necessary if we are to be truly one as Christ intended.

with the hidden presence of God'" (n., 49). Furthermore, "The nature and mission of the Church are inseparable" (n., 73). As a reality imbued with the presence of God, the Church is called to "actively... participate in his saving work" (n., 75). Believers become God's "co-workers" (n., 76) and "agents" (n., 76), and the Church is a "channel of God's grace to the world" (n., 76). Thus, the dimensions of effective help, service, and co-operation are affirmed.

The eschatological dimension of the Church is also affirmed:

> Within the Church, the Spirit is the bond of communion and connection across both space and time. The eternal Spirit is God's great eschatological gift (cf. Joel 2:28-29), giving us even now a foretaste of the heavenly banquet and an anticipation of eventual full communion with the Holy Trinity (*Seoul Report,* n., 58).

In keeping with this statement, number 82 of the *Seoul Report* quotes the Charles Wesley hymn "Come, let us join our friends above," which speaks of Christians on earth praising God in unison with those who have passed into the heavenly realm. In this hymn, past and present Christians are identified as "one family" and "one church" dwelling in Christ, although "now divided by the stream...of death." In this way, the authors of the document acknowledge a connection between discussions of the Church as a "sacramental communion" and discussions about the communion of saints. The following pages will provide reasons for and outline potential benefits of further exploration of this connection first from a Catholic perspective and then from a Methodist perspective.

Our Lady of Spiritual Solidarity: A Catholic Perspective

Because the published Catholic-Methodist dialogue reports lend great authoritative weight to *Lumen Gentium* the following section will focus on connections between the concept of "sacramental communion" and doctrines on Mary

and the saints found within this document. [14] *Lumen Gentium*
begins with discussion about the Holy Trinity as the
supernatural life, power, and reason for the Church's being. It
then proceeds with expositions of the human and hierarchical
aspects of the Church, which are sinful and imperfect, but are
nonetheless grounded in, emerge from and reflect the life of
the Trinity. *Lumen Gentium's* seventh and eighth chapters, "The
Eschatological Nature of the Pilgrim Church and Its union with
the Church in Heaven" and "The Blessed Virgin Mary, Mother
of God in the Mystery of Christ and the Church," bring the
Council's ecclesiological statement to its climax, clarifying the
Church's nature and breadth and revealing the essential
character of the saints within it as members of Christ's Mystical
Body. In addition, the final chapter, which is the chapter on
Mary, is particularly relevant to the traditional, Catholic
understanding of eschatology. Thus, *Lumen Gentium* provides
the reader with a

> ... mysteric opening and an eschatological
> consummation, between an exposé of the mystery

---

[14] The reports' conciliar references are outnumbered only by references to
Scripture. There are, in fact, nearly 100 such conciliar references within the
international dialogues, the vast majority of which are from portions of
Lumen Gentium. The special attention given the Council's dogmatic
constitution on the Church is understandable, given the fact that the last five
of the eight international dialogues have focused specifically on the nature of
and means for achieving ecclesial communion. Indeed, the 2005 U.S.
Catholic-Methodist report, *Through Divine Love*, which understands itself to
be in continuity with the international statements, explains reliance on the
conciliar documents by recalling the fact that the reports are exploring
communion ecclesiology and that "Roman Catholics link communion
ecclesiology with the Second Vatican Council..." (n., 41).
An excellent summary of the communion ecclesiology emerging from
Vatican II is provided by J.M.R. Tillard, "The Church as Communion," *One
in Christ* 17, no. 1(1981): 117-31. In it Tillard discusses concepts basic to the
council documents such as the existence of both a vertical communion with
God and a horizontal communion among fellow believers. He also notes
the central role of the Eucharist in building and maintaining ecclesial
communion as well as the relationship between mystical communion and
Church hierarchy. The latter grows out of and serves the former.

of Christ and his Bride at the beginning, and an evocation of the *parousia* and its anticipation in the Virgin Mary at the end.[15]

All of this talk of the unity between the supernatural and the natural and the expanse of time within the life of the Church as well as doctrines about the saints—and Mary in particular—are intimately associated with Catholic descriptions of the Church as a sacramental communion. As previously stated, much of this understanding hinges on the acceptance of the theological concepts of creaturely participation in and mediation of God's grace. The closely woven, interdependent nature of all these discussion points is revealed in the document's three most important references to the Church as a sacrament.

The first reference to the Church as a sacrament is found in the first chapter of *Lumen Gentium*, titled "The Mystery of the Church." The title itself is laden with meaning when one considers that the word "mystery" was chosen by the Council Fathers as the eastern Christian equivalent to "sacrament": "the divine decree by which the Father realizes his salvific will in Christ, at the same time that he reveals it through the mesh of a temporal reality...."[16] The Church is imbued with Christ's presence and is the visible means by which Christ draws humanity to himself. Thus, the first section of chapter one includes the following statement:

> Since the Church is in Christ like a sacrament or as a sign and instrument both of a very closely knit union with God and of the unity of the whole

[15] George H. Tavard, *The Pilgrim Church* (New York: Herder and Herder, 1967), 116.

[16] Gerard Philips, "The Church: Mystery and Sacrament," in *Vatican II: An Interfaith Appraisal*. International Theological Conference, ed. John H. Miller, CSC (Notre Dame: Notre Dame Press, March 20-26, 1966), 189.

human race, it desires now to unfold more fully to the faithful of the Church and to the whole world its own inner nature and universal mission (LG, 1).

The second of the three most important references to the Church as a sacrament within *Lumen Gentium* occurs in its second chapter, "On The People of God":[17]

> God gathered together as one all those who in faith look upon Jesus as the author of salvation and the source of unity and peace, and established them as the Church that for each and all it may be the visible sacrament of this saving unity (LG, 9).

The "unity" here mentioned is "saving" because it is the result of incorporation into the Body of Christ, our means for partaking in divine life. Thus, the Church's sacramental "inner nature" is both the end of and means for achieving her "universal mission."

The second paragraph of *Lumen Gentium's* seventh chapter contains the third reference:

> Christ, having been lifted up from the earth has drawn all to Himself. Rising from the dead He sent His life-giving Spirit upon His disciples and through Him has established His Body which is the Church as the universal sacrament of salvation (LG, 48).

In each of the three statements above, the idea of the Church as "sacrament" is closely associated with unity among human persons as well as the unity of each person with God. The vertical (God/human) and horizontal (human/human) dimensions of this unity are treated simultaneously as two

---

[17] The third important reference is that which has been quoted from chapter seven.

dimensions of the Church's sacramental character because each is essential to the Mystical Body. The members of the Body are bonded together by Christ's Spirit who dwells within believers and simultaneously draws believers into Christ. Christ's Spirit is in His Church and the Church is in Christ's Spirit (LG, 1. cf. Jn 17:21)—a state which unifies each member with the others as well as each member with God (LG, 1, 9, and 48). Msgr. Gerard Phillips who, along with Fr. Carlos Balic, drafted chapter eight of *Lumen Gentium*, offers this commentary on the constitution's first chapter, revealing some of the thought behind its composition:

> [T]he Church is aware of being the sacrament of the encounter with God....It [the Council] defines it [the Church as sacrament] as the sign and the *instrument* by which God raises men to intimacy with him and thus realizes, in the bosom of his eternal Being, the total unification of the human race.

> Sign and instrument do not constitute two separate entities; it is through the symbol itself that divine action works....If the creature always exists in relation to his Creator...the outpouring of the divine we are speaking of here "signifies" an inconceivable degree of intimacy, by this very fact placing the unity of the human race on an infinitely superior level.[18]

Because the bond uniting the members of the Mystical Body is the Holy Spirit, the communion experienced by believers is much more than a moral unity of autonomous individuals coming together as an expression of a common cause or obedience to a common will. Although each member of the

---

[18] Philips, 188.

Body retains his or her distinction as a unique being, he or she is part of a truly corporal reality. [19]

As the Holy Spirit permeates the believer, he or she is drawn into Christ becoming a mystical component of the *one* Body of the risen Savior (LG, 7). Recalling that there are not many Bodies, but one Body in a single Spirit (cf. 1 Cor. 12:12-27), the Council Fathers state that some of its members

---

[19] Marie-Joseph le Guillou, "Church," in *Encyclopedia of Theology: The Concise Sacramentum Mundi*, ed. Karl Rahner (New York: Crossroad, 1975), 213 provides a traditional Scriptural explanation:

> In St. Paul the idea of the Body of Christ can be understood only through the notions of *mystery, fullness* and *sacrament*....the notion of the 'Body of Christ' means the actual being of the Lord, the personal body of the dead and risen Christ, the beginning of a new creation.
> Thus when St. Paul applies the expression of Body of Christ to the Church, he means the one body which gathers together within it, in the Spirit, the whole assembly of believers by means of the sacraments....it is God himself who calls the faithful together in Christ, and it is he who unites them in one body through the Holy Spirit....the unity binding them together, whilst dwelling within them, does not derive from them, being of the divine order. It is based essentially on the unity of the Body of the Lord who died and rose again.
> The Church is thus the Body of Christ, because once brought into existence through the fellowship of the faith professed in baptism...it is perfected through communion in the same eucharistic bread which puts Christians in contact with the risen body of the Saviour, drawing those who believe in him into his own body. Ecclesial unity then is something spiritual and real and quite unique (involving even the bodies of the faithful)....

Joseph Ratzinger, provides a poetic explanation of the Church's corporal reality: "The Church is the body, the flesh of Christ in the spiritual tension of love wherein the spousal mystery of Adam and Eve is consummated...." See Joseph Cardinal Ratzinger and Hans Urs von Balthasar, *Mary—The Church at the Source*, trans. Adrian Walker (San Francisco, CA: Ignatius Press, 2005), 26.

... are exiles on earth, some having died are purified, and others are in glory beholding 'clearly God Himself triune and one, as He is'; but all in various ways and degrees are in communion in the same charity of God and neighbor and all sing the same hymn of glory to our God. For all who are in Christ, having His Spirit, form one Church and cleave together in Him. Therefore the union of the wayfarers with the brethren who have gone to sleep in the peace of Christ is not in the least weakened or interrupted...(LG, n. 49)

In short, the Church is a "sacrament" in the broad sense of the term because Christ dwells within it, making it his effective sign and instrument for the purpose of drawing human members into Christ: incorporating them into His Body. Therefore, Catholic teaching on the Mystical Body of Christ has been called "the great doctrine of the Church's internal, invisible, *sacramental*, and supernatural unity"[20]—a unity which includes vertical and horizontal dimensions simultaneously.

As mentioned, both dimensions of unity are essential to the Catholic understanding of the Church as a sacramental communion because both are necessary to the character of the sign and both are involved in the efficaciousness of that sign. Union with God means salvation. Union with each other within Christ means that Christ's Body is and acts as one. The sign is one. The real presence of Christ is one. Each loving action performed by each member of the Body is a subordinate part of the one saving action of Christ. The entire Body is involved in the salvation of the human race, including those who "have gone to sleep in the peace of Christ" (LG, 49):

---

[20] Bonaventure Kloppenburg O.F.M., *The Ecclesiology of Vatican II*, trans. Matthew J. O'Connell (Chicago, IL: Franciscan Herald Press, 1974), 37.

[A]ccording to the perpetual faith of the Church, [the bond between the saints on Earth and the saints in Heaven] is strengthened by communication of spiritual goods....[Those who] have been received into their heavenly home and are present to the Lord, through Him and with Him and in Him...do not cease to intercede with the Father for us, showing forth the merits which they won on earth through the one Mediator between God and man, serving God in all things and filling up in their flesh those things which are lacking in the sufferings of Christ for His Body which is the Church. Thus by their brotherly interest our weakness is greatly strengthened (LG, 49).

So the discussion moves from the nature of sacramental communion to discussions of creaturely participation and mediation. We participate in God's salvific plan by aligning our free will with His and receiving His grace, the ability to do so itself being a gift of grace. We participate by opening ourselves to the Holy Spirit who is the bond of communion among the members of Christ's Mystical Body. Because we live in communion with other Christians, this exercise of free will redounds to other members of the Body. Thus, our participation in God's work is also a mediation of His grace. In the words of Wilhelm Breuning, the Holy Spirit, who is the communion between Christ and the Father, is "the immanent intercommunication between Father and the Son...[and] the intercommunication of the Church with its Lord. As such the Spirit is also the intercommunication between all members of Christ who are living in grace."[21]

Christ the One Mediator, operates through those who are acting through, with and in Him. This understanding of the Mystical Body leads the Council Fathers to the following

---

[21] Wilhelm Breuning, "Communion of Saints" in *Encyclopedia of Theology: The Concise Sacramentum Mundi*, ed. Karl Rahner (New York: Crossroad, 1975), 275.

conclusions: 1) Members of the Body are understood as mediators in subordination to and dependent upon Christ's mediation (LG, 49).[22] 2) The Holy Spirit as the bond of unity/intercommunication between members of the Body allows for the invocation of saints for purposes of intercession (LG, 50).[23] 3) Because of the intimate bond between the saints in heaven and Christ, "companionship with the saints joins us to Christ, from Whom as from its Fountain and Head issues every grace and the very life of the people of God" (LG, 50).[24] Therefore, veneration of the saints, which is distinguished from

---

[22] Chapter eight begins with a statement clarifying the Church's doctrine of participation in Christ's mediation. Although in the context of a discussion on the Blessed Virgin, the principle of mediation described applies to the entire Mystical Body:

> There is but one Mediator as we know from the words of the apostle, 'for there is one God and one mediator of God and men, the man Christ Jesus, who gave himself a redemption for all'. The maternal duty of Mary toward men in no wise obscures or diminishes this unique mediation of Christ, but rather shows His power. For all the salvific influence of the Blessed Virgin on men originates, not from some inner necessity, but from the divine pleasure. It flows forth from the superabundance of the merits of Christ, rests on His mediation, depends entirely on it and draws all its power from it. In no way does it impede, but rather does it foster the immediate union of the faithful with Christ (LG, 60).

[23] The Council fathers were anxious to distinguish orthodox Christian invocation of the saints from spiritualism. They therefore added note 228 to chapter seven, explaining that the distinguishing characteristics of spiritualist invocation were 1) the use of "human means" which result in a 2) "perceptible exchange." The presence of these characteristics would amount to conjuring the dead and is strictly prohibited. See Kloppenburg, 331-32.

[24] The Latin, *coniungit*, here translated as "joins us to" is used especially in the context of joining persons together in marriage or in reference to a blood relationship. Because it is used to describe our bond with Christ *through* our relationship with the saints in Heaven, the corporal nature of this bond is reinforced. For the Latin text, see *Acta Apostolicae Sedes*, vol. 57 (1965): 56.

the worship due to God alone, is deemed "supremely fitting" or "*Summopere ergo decet…*" (LG, 50).

The nature and impact of the sacramental bond described thus far is only intelligible within an eschatological context and, as indicated by chapter seven's full title, this is the reason for the chapter's inclusion in the constitution. Pope John XXIII requested (and Pope Paul VI confirmed the request) the composition of the chapter in order to underscore and explicate the Church's "eschatological dynamism," an "essential feature…without which she cannot be properly described."[25] As a result of this chapter,

> … veneration of the saints [was brought] out of isolation in which its significance could not be properly grasped, showing it to be a concrete embodiment of the Church's eschatological nature; and conversely, this discussion of the veneration of saints ensures that the conciliar doctrine on the Church must explicitly treat of her vital eschatological aspect.[26]

The "eschatological aspect" mentioned above is not an exclusively "end times" reference in the sense of a looking ahead to future events. Rather it confirms the fact that "the Church does not fully possess her sacramental form in this world."[27] The bond between the heavenly and earthly realms (which is the Holy Spirit) is not subject to the laws of time. Therefore, in a certain sense, the eschaton is eternally present.

---

[25] Otto Semmelroth, "The Eschatological Nature of the Pilgrim Church and her Union with the Heavenly Church," trans. Richard Strachan of KG Herder in *Commentary on the Documents of Vatican II*, vol. 1, trans. Lalit Adolphus, Kevin Smyth and Richard Strachan (New York: Herder and Herder, 1962), 280.

[26] Ibid.,

[27] Ibid., 281.

This idea is made explicit in the first section of *Lumen Gentium's* chapter seven:

> Already the final age of the world has come upon us and the renovation of the world is irrevocably decreed and is already anticipated in some kind of real way; for the Church already on this earth is signed with a sanctity which is real although imperfect (LG, 48).

Past, present and future. Heaven, earth, and purgatory. All these realities are present in the resurrected Christ and the Holy Spirit and in such a manner that there is no contradiction in speaking of the eschaton as a future event that is, in some sense, upon us right now.[28] In consequence of this understanding, "It would be absurd, for the Catholic mind, to think that all relations with those who have died in the Lord came to an end with their death."[29] We are, in fact, encouraged to form relationships with heavenly members of the Mystical Body in the firm conviction that the Body is never separate from the Head and that *all* its members are involved in the building up of the Church (LG, 49-50). In his commentary on chapter seven of the constitution, Otto Semmelroth reiterates the Catholic understanding of the bond of love uniting the saints in heaven and the pilgrim people on earth and adds, in keeping with *Lumen Gentium* 50, that this unity "consists above all in the solicitous intercession of the heavenly Church for the

---

[28] George Tavard explains the Church's eschatological orientation by saying that, for Catholics, one's relationship to Christ is not simply linear, referring to our relationship with the past Jesus of history and its future fulfillment. Rather, it is like a fan spread out in a semi-circle between two horizons, with the Incarnation and the Second Coming at each extreme horizon or point of the fan and Christ standing at all points along the way. There is an unbroken communion in time and space for all who live in Christ's Body. See Tavard, 120-21.

[29] Ibid., 122.

pilgrim Church on earth and the prayer of petition with which the earthly Church invokes the heavenly."[30]

To reiterate, the notion that "human nature plays its part in the work of salvation" relies on a certain doctrinal framework that begins with the following assertion: God has chosen to communicate himself *through* creation, involving the entire universe in the mediation of his grace.[31] Human beings, who were created in God's image, mediate his grace in a special way when we use our free will to cooperate with rather than reject or corrupt it:

> Here the sacramental principle emerges: the representation of God does not mean the substitution for one who is absent (or, still more, a replacement), but indicates the real, and not only the imaginary or the intellectual, making present of the one who in and of himself cannot be visible in our human dimension.[32]

Creaturely participation in and mediation of God's grace is contingent upon that creature's openness or transparency to the Holy Spirit. In other words, it is contingent upon the depth of our communion with the divine. In the long history of those who follow the God of the Old and New Covenants, there has never been so great an example of this openness to—this communion with—the divine as that found

---

[30] Semmelroth, 282.

[31] For a summary of Catholic scholarship regarding scriptural and historical support on this topic, see chapter one of Vorgrimler. For a summary of the development of Catholic scholarship relating the sacramental structure of God's relationship with humanity to the issue of salvation including the now universally accepted notion of Christ as the primordial sacrament and the notion of the Church as the fundamental sacrament, see chapter three of Vorgrimler.

[32] Ibid., 13.

in the woman who was overshadowed by the Spirit and gave birth to the Incarnate Lord.

The principle of subordinate, human mediation (which is at the heart of the Catholic understanding of sacramental communion) set forth in chapter seven is magnified in the *Theotókos* (the God-bearer) because of her uniquely intimate relationship with the Trinity. For this reason, *Lumen Gentium's* chapter eight is in many respects a more focused extension of chapter seven.[33]

The *Theotókos* is the type of the Church as participant in and mediator of Christ's grace—not in the sense of one who stands between the believer and Christ, but as one through whom Christ has chosen to manifest his power: "In no way does...[Mary's maternal mediation] impede, but rather does it foster the immediate union of the faithful with Christ" (LG, 60). It is understood as a manifestation of the magnificent power of a God (LG, 60-62) who "could have saved us without Christ [or] Mary, or with Christ alone..." but *chose* to save us via Mary's acceptance of the Incarnation.[34]

The Mother of Christ, by virtue of her election to this unique role, mediates God's grace in a unique way. Leo Jozef

---

[33] Chapters seven and eight were discussed and voted upon at the same time. Jorge Medina Estevez believes that chapter seven would have more aptly comprised the second portion of chapter two on the "People of God," but that this was not possible because the latter text had already reached its definitive form. See Jorge Medina Estevez, "The Constitution on the Church: *Lumen Gentium*," in *Vatican II: An Interfaith Appraisal.* International Theological Conference, ed. John H. Miller, CSC (Notre Dame: Notre Dame Press, March 20-26, 1966), 117-18. However, the chapter on Mary was deliberately placed last as the one "that accentuates the eschatological and pneumatological aspect of the mystery of the Church. Mary thus appears within the Church and as having a supereminent place in it." See Charles Moeller, "History of *Lumen Genitum's* Structure and Ideas" in *Vatican II: An Interfaith Appraisal.* International Theological Conference, ed. John H. Miller, CSC (Notre Dame: Notre Dame Press, March 20-26, 1966), 143.

[34] Balic, 21.

Suenens provides an example of Catholic thought regarding the nature of Marian mediation.[35] Mary as the *Theotókos* received the word in her heart and in her body in a way which is unparalleled in human history and which effected an unparalleled communion with the Lord.[36] It is no longer she who lives, but Christ who lives in her (cf. Gal. 2:20) and, as the preeminent member of the Body of Christ, she lives within him. Her mediation is not something that lies outside of or in addition to Christ, but resides within Christ. Suenens also notes that, as stated earlier, because the person who is Mary's Son is not separate from the Head of the Mystical Body, the *Theotókos* becomes the mother of the Mystical Body's members in the order of grace.[37]

The following statement written by Hans Urs von Balthasar is another example of a Catholic understanding of Marian mediation that is based on the doctrine of participation in the life of Christ applicable to all the saints, but reaching its zenith in Mary, who exceeds all Christians in terms of virtue:

---

[35] The following is a summary of L. J. Suenens, *Mary the Mother of God*, Twentieth Century Encyclopedia of Catholicism, vol. 44, section 4, The Means of Redemption, trans. a nun of Stanbrook Abbey (New York: Hawthorn Books, 1959), 96-102.

[36] Although the notion of Mary's mediation grows out of the Eve-Mary parallel developed by St. Irenaeus, it began to truly mature theologically after Mary was declared *Theotókos* at the Council of Ephesus and Cyril related her role as mediator to her office as the Mother of God. See Michael O'Carroll, C.S., Sp., *Theotokos: A Theological Encyclopedia of the Blessed Virgin Mary* (Eugene, OR: Wipf and Stock Publishers, 2000), 239. Suenens 53-56 reminds us of some of the implications of this motherhood, namely that, because Christ is born the Redeemer, rather than merely acquiring the role of redeemer, his mission is essential to his being. Similarly, by the grace of God, being the mother of the Redeemer is essential to the one from whom Christ drew his humanity and her participation in his mission is her sole vocation from the moment of his conception.

[37] For a summary of papal teaching and conventional Catholic understanding of this point, see Suenens, 56-57.

[The communion] of saints cannot be compared with an ordinary gathering of men in which individual stands next to individual, even if they are all marching in the same direction or are animated by the same concern. Rather, the selflessness of Christian love founds a kind of communism of spiritual goods, and the more perfectly a Christian develops this selfless love in himself, the more all others can live on his goods as if they were their own. Not only are individuals transparent to one another, they also radiate what is theirs into the others—although we can speak only in a loose sense of 'theirs', because perfect selflessness and transparency are nothing other than the life of God and Christ in creatures. Mary, as the purest of all creatures, irradiates what is her own least of all. Everyone within the communion of saints has something Marian about him.[38]

Traditional Catholic mariology is replete with similar statements underscoring the Blessed Virgin's special significance *within*—not apart from—the mystical Body of Christ.

Marian doctrines are of great importance to ecumenists on the levels of both doctrine and devotion. Because the story of Mary is the story of the way in which God chose to enter human history and save the human race, mariological reflection on extra-Marian issues, such as the notion of the Church as a sacramental communion, tends to clarify and illuminate them. There is, however, another, arguably greater, Marian significance for ecumenists. If the doctrine about the Mystical Body of Christ that I have presented thus far is the truth, then, more than a hope and promise of what the Church is destined to become, the eschatological aspect of the Church is instrumental in the process of its becoming. Developing

---

[38] In Ratzinger and Von Balthasar, *Mary—The Church at the Source*, 122.

relationships with and requesting the intercession of the saints (and Mary in particular) is of vital importance to the success of the ecumenical endeavor.

Methodists have not, traditionally, engaged in mariology or Marian devotion. There have, of course, been some grand exceptions to this rule, namely Neville Ward, Donald Charles Lacy, and others belonging to the Ecumenical Society of the Blessed Virgin Mary (ESBVM). These scholars and churchmen have had reason to believe that Methodists might engage in both without endangering the integrity of their own Methodist religious heritage. I heartily agree and would now like to offer some thoughts concerning aspects of John Wesley's theology that provide openings for expanded Marian studies and devotions.

Our Lady of Spiritual Solidarity: Possibilities in John Wesley's Theology

John Wesley rejected many aspects of Catholic mariology and corresponding devotions, particularly the practice of invocation and the doctrine of creaturely merit. He regarded them as idolatrous. At the core of Wesley's objection was the notion that Catholic doctrines about saintly mediation, invocation, merit, and devotions implied that the saints—and Mary in particular—were sources of grace in their *own right*, apart from Christ. He believed that Catholic doctrines placed saints as obstacles existing between believers and Christ and that their intercession was sought as something which added substantially to the intercession of the One Mediator between God and Man. So, for example, item number 14 in Wesley's pamphlet, *The Advantage of the Members of the Church of England, over Those of the Church of Rome* states that the trust Catholic believers might have

> ... in Christ alone, the one Mediator between God and man, is hindered so much the more, the more the people are referred to the merits and

intercession of the blessed Virgin, and other saints....[39]

Wesley was mistaken. To be fair, his was an easy mistake to make. The widespread abuse of Catholic doctrines during this era has been well documented. On the other hand, an "abuse" is, by definition, a perversion of a doctrine and not the doctrine itself. The official Catholic position is also well documented in historical communications such as this tract by Roman Catholic priest, Robert Manning (d. 1731):

> To prevent all mistakes relating to this matter [Marian devotion], we must lay it down as an undoubted maxim of faith, that whatever excellences we attribute to the *blessed Virgin*, or whatever terms we make use of to express the esteem and respect we have for her, we must regard her no otherwise than as a *pure creature*; and, by consequence infinitely below God, depending on him, and indebted to him for all the gifts of nature and grace possessed....
>
> [I]t has always been the undoubted faith of the Church, *first*, that *Jesus Christ* is the only *mediator* of *redemption*; *secondly*, that he alone has *immediate access* to God without the mediation of any other; and that, by consequence, the prayers of *Saints* and *Angels* in heaven as well as of the faithful on earth,

---

[39] Contained in volume 10 of *The Works of the the Rev. John Wesley, A.M*, sometime fellow of Lincoln College, Oxford, vol. 10, third edition with the last corrections of the author (London: John Mason, 1830), pp. 133-40. For additional polemics, see John Wesley's answers to, *A Roman Catechism faithfully drawn out of the allowed writings of the Church of Rome. With a reply thereto* in *The Works of the Rev. John Wesley, A.M.* The aforementioned is Wesley's reproduction and response to treatise which was originally published in 1686 and titled *A Catechism truly representing the Doctrines and Practices of the Church of Rome, with an answer thereunto – by a Protestant of the Church of England.* The original tract was not an accurate representation of Catholic doctrine.

are all offered up thro' the mediation of *Jesus Christ....*[40] (Emphasis is Manning's.)

In other words, Mary's authority (and that of the saints) is derived from and subordinate to Christ's. Creaturely intercession, whether the creature resides on earth or in heaven, is practiced only in and through Christ's unique mediation. Manning's thought, in fact, anticipates the thoughts expressed in *Lumen Gentium*, which affirm Christ as the One Mediator and source of life who distributes His grace through the subordinate mediation of the members of His Mystical Body.

Unfortunately, as has been noted by several historians, Wesley lived in a day and age in which circumstances made accurate characterizations of differing belief systems extremely difficult.[41] During this time, doctrinal polemics were often launched against positions that did not exist. Methodist historian, David Butler characterized the situation in this way:

> Wesley had little face-to-face dialogue with Catholics and the impression of Catholic-Methodist dialogue in the eighteenth century is of the antagonists shouting their respective ware across a street full of the noise and bustle of carts, horses and people. Because they are on opposite sides of the street, they are barely heard by each other, and what is heard is only a snatch of the whole. Perhaps it would be fair to say that they

---

[40] Robert Manning, *Of Devotion to the Blessed Virgin Mary. Extracted from the third volume of the Moral entertainments on the most important practical truths of the Christian religion. By the Reverend Mr. Manning* (London: Printed and sold by J. Marmaduke, Bookseller in Great Wild-Street/Lincoln's-Inn-Fields, 1787), 6, 10-11.

[41] For descriptions of religious intolerance contributing to this difficult atmosphere, see Chapman, 12; Henry Rack *Reasonable Enthusiast: John Wesley and the Rise of Methodism* (Philadelphia, PA: Trinity Press International, 2002), 22, 27-29, 39.

145

are so convinced that they know what the other believes and know it to be wrong, that it is hardly worth listening.[42]

To make matters even more difficult, Wesley's religious and cultural environment tended to breed anti-Catholic sentiments. In the words of historian, Henry Rack, Wesley was influenced by "the inherited fears and mythology of English Protestants about false Popish doctrine, deceit, cruelty and political subversion."[43] For all these reasons, it is not surprising to find that, brilliant and well-intended as Wesley was, when he argued against the Catholic doctrines that we are currently considering, his characterizations of these doctrines were incorrect.

On the other hand, Wesley's remarkably broad range of scholarly pursuits resulted in the incorporation and blending of classically Catholic as well as Protestant theological concepts and is therefore open to many areas of doctrinal convergence with the Church of Rome. Notably, he incorporated "the theme of [humanity's] *participation*"[44] in divine grace, a concept that is arguably most evident in what has come to be known as the Doctrine of Christian Perfection. Furthermore, as an Anglican priest, Methodism's patriarch turned to the Church of England for a formal definition of the term "sacrament" stating that it was "an outward sign of an inward *grace*, and a *means* whereby we receive the same,"[45] (Emphasis is Wesley's) thus confirming the notion of the material mediation of divine grace. Wesley's use of these two concepts, participation and

---

[42] David Butler, *Methodists and Papists, John Wesley and the Catholic Church in the Eighteenth Century*, (London: Darton, Longman, Todd, 1995), 22.

[43] Rack, 309.

[44] See "On Reading Wesley's Sermons," an essay in the front of vol. 1 of the bicentennial edition of Wesley's works: Frank Baker, Albert Outler, eds., *The Works of John Wesley: Sermons 1-33*, vol. 1 (Abingdon Press: Nashville, TN, 1984), 99.

[45] Wesley quotes from the Book of Common Prayer Catechism within his sermon, *The Means of Grace*.

mediation—the concepts upon which Catholics have built doctrines on the communion of saints and the Church as a sacramental communion—will be the focus for the remainder of this essay. It is impossible to do justice to these two subjects given present restrictions of time and space, so I offer these somewhat condensed reflections in the hope that they will inspire additional inquiry.

Wesley's soteriology maintained the classically Protestant distinction between justification ("salvation from the guilt of sin and restoration to God's favor") and sanctification ("salvation from the power and root of sin and restoration to God's image").[46] He therefore believed that salvation was "both instantaneous and gradual, beginning the moment we are justified and growing until we are perfected in love, attaining the fullness of Christ."[47] The latter of these two aspects of salvation includes striking similarities to Catholic notions about creaturely participation in grace.

The essence of Wesley's doctrine on sanctification was expressed in the above-mentioned Doctrine of Christian Perfection: "To the Reformers perfection was perfection in faith, but to Wesley it was an inherent ethical perfection in love and obedience."[48] This perfection was ultimately grounded in freely given grace, but, as Wesley pointed out, "Man can either cooperate with it or oppose it. As soon as God's work has begun in the souls of men they may become 'workers together with Him'."[49] Randy Maddox has summarized the idea saying, "Wesley was convinced that, while we *can* not attain holiness

---

[46] Colin Williams, *John Wesley's Theology Today* (New York & Nashville, TN: Abingdon Press, 1946), 40.

[47] Ibid.

[48] Harold Lindström, *Wesley and Sanctification: A Study in the Doctrine of Salvation* (London: Epworth Press, 1950), 136.

[49] Ibid., 46, c.f. *Predestination Calmly Considered*, 1752. Also see, Randy Maddox, *Responsible Grace: John Wesley's Practical Theology* (Nashville, TN: Kingswood Books, 1994), chapters 6 and 7.

(and wholeness) apart from God's grace, God *will* not effect holiness apart from our responsive participation."[50]

To participate in God's grace meant to participate in the divine life, for Wesley "identified grace as the personal Presence of the Holy Spirit in our lives...."[51] To be a co-worker with God involved deepening our spiritual communion with the divine and, while Wesley would not limit God's actions to particular circumstances, he believed that the ordinary way in which God made his grace available was through created means.

In his sermon, *The Means of Grace*, Wesley stated,

By 'means of grace' I understand outward signs, words, or actions ordained of God, and appointed for this end—to be the *ordinary* channels whereby he might convey to men preventing, justifying, or sanctifying grace.[52]

When commenting on Wesley's sacramentology, Ole Borgen observed that "The 'sign' and the 'signified' are not identical, but distinct, and yet not separated. There is a 'carrying over' from the one to the other, in Baptism as well as in the Lord's Supper."[53] Furthermore, Borgen asserts that, for Wesley, a sacrament "as a means and instrument...actually *conveys* what it *shows*."[54]

---

[50] Maddox, 148.

[51] Ibid., 156.

[52] Wesley, *The Means of Grace*, in *The Works of John Wesley*, vol. 1, *Sermons I 1-33*, bicentennial ed., 381.

[53] Ole Borgen, *John Wesley on the Sacraments* (Nashville, TN: Abingdon Press, 1972), 57.

[54] Ibid., 94. These observations about the material mediation of grace are NOT meant to imply that Wesley's sacramentology was identical to Catholic sacramentology. For example, Wesley rejected the Catholic notion of

Wesley's acceptance of creaturely mediation expanded beyond his application of the principle to formal sacraments. As Maddox observes,

> Wesley was convinced of the effective communication of God's grace through the sacraments of baptism and eucharist, and through means like liturgy and formal prayers that had come to be emphasized in Anglicanism. Yet, like the Reformers (and Eastern Christianity), he refused to confine grace to such official channels. Indeed, one of the central features of the Methodist revival was Wesley's expectation that his people would avail themselves of *both* the traditional means of grace present in Anglican worship and such distinctive means as class meetings, love feasts, and covenant renewal services.[55]

Wesley identifies the chief means of grace as individual and corporate prayer, Scripture study and meditation, and the Lord's Supper.[56] The Lord's Supper was the greatest of these,

---

transubstantiation. Nonetheless, for Wesley, the material sign mediated grace.

[55] Maddox, 194.

[56] Lindström, 129. Note Wesley's omission of baptism in his list of the chief means of grace. Borgen, 121 provides the following explanation:
> In no place does he [Wesley] mention Baptism among the other means of grace. Nevertheless, there is no doubt that Wesley considers it a powerful means of grace. Why he omits Baptism from the usual lists of ordinances can only be conjectured. The initiatory characteristics of this sacrament, its functioning as a beginning rather than as being constantly available for continuous use, as well as being a singular event not to be repeated, are obvious reasons for not including Baptism in lists of ordinances which Wesley exhorts his people to use constantly. When he calls upon his listeners to attend upon the ordained means, he speaks to adults, most of

"the grand channel whereby the grace of His Spirit was conveyed to the souls of all the children of God."[57] All of these aspects of creation—including human prayer—mediate God's grace, which is the personal presence of the Holy Spirit. In keeping with these thoughts, the 2004 United Methodist general conference statement on the Lord's Supper includes the following:

> Sacraments are effective means of God's presence mediated through the created world. God becoming incarnate in Jesus Christ is the supreme instance of this kind of divine action.[58]

So, by virtue of our participation in these "means of grace," we receive and participate in the divine life. We deepen our communion, our bond, with God. We also deepen our bond with one another.

In Wesley's sermon, *Of the Church*, he broadly defines "Church" as "a congregation or body of people united together in the service of God."[59] But Wesley's thoughts about the nature of the bond which exists within the Mystical Body of Christ, does not stop with the assertion of a moral unity. Rather, it extends to a vital unity effected by Christ's Spirit:

---

whom are already baptized. And, not being a parish priest, Wesley has relatively few opportunities to baptize, although his *Journal* records several events where he administers the sacrament.

[57] John Wesley, *Upon our Lord's Sermon on the Mount—VI*, in *The Works of John Wesley*, vol. 1, *Sermons I 1-33*, bicentennial ed., 585.

[58] Number 7 of *This Holy Mystery A United Methodist Understanding of Holy Communion*. Available online at http://gatewayumc.org/pdf/hcfinal2.pdf

[59] Wesley, *Of the Church* in Albert Outler, ed., *John Wesley*, A Library of Protestant Thought (New York: Oxford University Press, 1964), 308. Hereafter, Outler, *John Wesley*.

[By baptism, Christians] are mystically 'united to Christ' and made *one* with him. For 'by one Spirit we are all baptized into one body'—namely, 'the Church, the body of Christ.' From which spiritual, vital union with him proceeds the influence of his grace on those who are baptized.[60] (Emphasis is Wesley's.)

The real, vital union enjoyed by members of Christ's body is a strong theme within Wesley's work, inspiring the following observation from Harold Lindström:

For Christ does not give life to the soul separate from, but in and with himself....our perfection is not like that of a tree, which flourishes by the sap derived from its own root, but...like that of a branch which, united to the vine, bears fruit; but severed from it, is dried up and withered.[61]

An analysis of Wesley's Eucharistic theology led J. Ernest Rattenbury to state even more emphatically that the

---

[60] John Wesley, *On Baptism*, in Oulter, *John Wesley*, 322. Wesley held to the reality of grace mediated via baptism (i.e. baptismal regeneration) simultaneously with belief in the necessity of conscious acceptance of this grace—a position developed while arguing in favor of infant baptism and maintaining the central role of faith in the reception of grace. According to Wesley, the Christian must come to a conscious acceptance of the work begun in infant baptism if he or she is to experience the new birth. See Williams, 121; Borgen 139-40; Outler, *John Wesley*, 318. Wesley's sermon, *On Baptism*, places emphasis on sacramental grace and *The New Birth* emphasizes the need for conscious acceptance.

Methodists eventually adopted doctrines that differed somewhat from Wesley's, a33s stated in Williams, 121:

Apparently understanding only the second emphasis in Wesley [the need for conscious acceptance of grace], American Methodism has since reduced the service of Baptism to the point where it is little more than a dedication, and in British Methodism, while far more of the structure of the service has been kept, all references to regeneration were excluded in 1882.

[61] Lindström, 152.

unity enjoyed by members of Christ's mystical body is "organic, living, the oneness of Head and Body, of Vine and Branches."[62] He continues, "We are not a mere collection of individuals, but a collective body; one temple, one body, one vine."[63] Rattenbury's interpretation, considered in conjunction with the quotations from Lindström and Wesley above seem to indicate that Wesley's thought agreed with Catholic doctrine that acknowledges the Holy Spirit himself as the bond uniting the members of the Mystical Body of Christ with their Head *and* with each other.

In addition to this convergence, Wesley and the Catholic tradition share a strong sense of the community's involvement in the individual's way of sanctification. Wesley taught that Christianity "is essentially a social religion, I mean not only that it cannot subsist so well, but that it cannot subsist at all without society, without living and conversing with other men."[64] Works of mercy and piety, intercessory prayer, the practice of virtue and fraternal correction are vital components of the process of sanctification and all are contingent upon communal living.[65] Wesley considered intercessory prayer of particular importance for the Methodist community. For example, the 1744 edition of the Rules for the bands states "The design of our meeting is to obey that command of God,

---

[62] J. Ernest Rattenbury, *The Eucharistic Hymns of John and Charles Wesley* (London: The Epworth Press, 1948), 129. Hereafter Rattenbury, *Eucharistic Hymns.*

[63] Rattnebury, *Eucharistic Hymns*, 130.

[64] John Welsey, *Sermon on the Mount, IV*, bicentennial ed. 533-34. Wesley elaborates on the various ways in which virtue is practiced and built via human interaction throughout the sermon.

[65] Works of mercy and piety were also means of grace. See discussion in Borgen, 102-05.

'Confess your faults one to another, and pray one for another, that ye may be healed.'(Jas. 5:16)."[66]

These observations about Wesley's doctrine pertain specifically to the earthly communion of saints. However, if the members of Christ's Body are made one by the power of the Holy Spirit, is it not possible that these sentiments ought to extend to the saints in heaven? To answer this question, one must first ask whether or not Wesley thought that the eschatological Church was somehow present to historical reality. Several of Wesley's Methodist interpreters, particularly those who have focused on his Eucharistic theology, would answer the latter question in the affirmative. John Bowmer makes the following observation:

> [T]he Wesleys [John and Charles] thought of the
> Cross and the Eucharist as timeless. This leads us
> to consider the eschatological element in Wesleyan
> Eucharistic theology....They did not limit heaven
> to the place and time assigned to it in popular
> thought; to Wesley heaven was timeless, present as
> well as future.[67]

Similarly, the United Methodist general conference statement on the Lord's Supper asserts that when believers partake of the Sacrament,

> We commune not only with the faithful who are
> physically present but with the saints of the past
> who join us in the sacrament [Eucharist]....When

---

[66] From the 1744 edition of "Rules of the Bands" in Outler, *John Wesley*, 180.

[67] John C. Bowmer, *The Sacrament of the Lord's Supper in Early Methodism* (London:Dacre Press, 1951), 184. Also see Horton Davies, *Worship and Theology in England*, vol. 3, *From Watts and Wesley to Maurice, 1690-1850* (Princeton, NJ: Princeton University Press, 1961), 208; Borgen, 243; Rattenbury, *Eucharistic Hymns*, 121; Brevint, sect. 2, para. 7 in Rattenbury, *Eucharistic Hymns*, 178.

we eat and drink at the Table, we become partakers of the divine nature in this life and for life eternal....[68]

It is, of course, one thing to say that the eschatological Church is in some sense a present reality, and quite another to assert its awareness of the Church on earth and/or its interaction with the Church on earth. There are at least two documented instances in which John Wesley plainly asserts his belief that the eschatological Church is both aware of our presence on earth and serves God by serving our needs. The first instance is recorded in a private letter to Mary Bishop on May 9, 1773. The following is an excerpt:

> It has in all ages been allowed that the communion of saints extends to those in paradise as well as those upon earth as they are all one body united under one Head. And
>
> *Can death's interposing tide*
> *Spirits one in Christ divide?*
>
> But it is difficult to say either what kind or what degree of union may be between them. It is not improbable their fellowship with us is far more sensible than ours with them. Suppose any of them are present, they are hid from our eyes, but we are not hid from *their* sight. They no doubt clearly discern all our words and actions, if not all our thoughts too; for it is hard to think these walls of flesh and blood can intercept the view of an angelic being. But we have in general only a faint and indistinct perception of their presence, unless in some peculiar instances, where it may answer

---

[68] *This Holy Mystery*, 7.

some gracious ends of Divine Providence. [69]
(Emphasis is Wesley's.)

Nearly 20 years later, in his last sermon, *On Faith* (1791), Wesley not only confirms his belief in the interaction between heavenly and earthly Christians, he adds the notion that the saints in heaven are likely employed in the service of their earth-bound brothers and sisters:

> But we have no reason to think they [departed souls] are confined to this place [heaven]; or, indeed, to any other. May we not rather say that, as 'servants of his', as well as the holy angels, they 'do his pleasure', whether among the inhabitants of earth or in any other part of his dominions? [70]

In Summary

To summarize, there is ample reason to believe that Wesley's theology and the theology presented in *Lumen Gentium* converge on the following points:

• *Creaturely participation.* Wesley's Doctrine of Christian Perfection includes the notion that mankind participates (i.e. cooperates) in and with God's grace, contributing to its own sanctification. Furthermore, there is a corporate dimension to our participation, making social interaction vital to the process of sanctification.

• *Creaturely mediation.* Wesley's sacramental theology includes the concept of subordinate, creaturely mediation of Christ's grace. He extended the Anglican teaching about the

---

[69] Available online at The Wesley Center Online:
http://wesley.nnu.edu/john-wesley/the-letters-of-john-wesley/
John Telford, ed. *The Letters of the Rev. John Wesley, A.M.*, vol. VI (London: Epworth, 1931), 213.

[70] John Wesley, *On Faith, Hebrews 11:1*, in *The Works of John Wesley*, vol. 4, *Sermons IV 115-151*, bicentennial ed., 195.

means of grace so that it included, not only the two sacraments, but also such pious actions as prayer and scripture study. In this way, perhaps even more than in Catholic doctrine, the sacramental efficaciousness of human behavior is emphasized.[71]

• *The Holy Spirit as the bond uniting Christ's Body.* Wesley's theology includes doctrine concerning the bond shared by members of the Body of Christ, which is the Holy Spirit—a bond transcending time and space, holding the entire Body, past, present, and future in a vital, living communion. In this way, the eschatological Church is present to earthly, historical reality. In addition, Wesley's later work indicates a conviction in the interaction between the saints in heaven and Christians on earth. He clearly stated his belief that those who reside in heaven continue to serve God by serving God's children on earth and that it is quite likely that they can hear our words and perhaps, even our thoughts.

Consideration of all these convergences certainly supports the description of the Church as a sacramental communion as jointly expressed by Methodists and Catholics in formal dialogue statements. It also points toward the possibility of even greater convergences in the areas of mariology, doctrines about the communion of saints, and devotional practices—particularly that of invocation. In fact, Wesley's great emphasis on the social nature of Christianity would seem to add some amount of urgency to the development of Methodist doctrines and devotions concerning the eschatological Church. If the way of sanctification is communal and our community spans both heaven and earth, then the development of relationships with those who reside in heaven would be to our great benefit.

Implications for Ecumenical Dialogue

---

[71] I say "even more than in Catholic doctrine" because traditional Catholic teaching distinguishes between the objective presence of grace in a sacrament and the receptivity of grace by means of a sacramental. Pious practices such as prayer and scripture study would fall into the latter category. Wesley, however, places all on an equal footing.

The thoughts presented in this paper bear implications for Catholic-Methodist ecumenical dialogue on the levels of formal, doctrinal study and devotion. Because Catholic doctrines about Mary and the communion of saints are intimately connected with the Catholic understanding of the Church as a sacramental communion, scholarly reflection on one topic illuminates and clarifies understanding of the other. This is particularly true of Marian doctrines because they bring doctrines pertaining to the communion of saints into their sharpest focus.

Methodist mariology is a relatively new pursuit and has not, as yet, captured the attention of mainstream Methodist academics. If, however, the convergence between Methodist and Catholic ecclesiology on the subject of the Church as a sacramental communion as voiced in the dialogue statements is truly a convergence, then mariology— as well as scholarly study on the role of the eschatological Church in our everyday reality—would seem to be a logical pursuit for Methodist ecclesiologists. Furthermore, the apparent convergence would seem to carry with it devotional implications, for, if the saints in heaven are subordinate mediators/intercessors of God's grace, they are not irrelevant to Christian progress along the way of entire sanctification.

I close these reflections by asking Catholic and Methodist ecumenists to seriously consider the possibility of including mariological reflection on extra-Marian topics for scholarly purposes and to seriously explore the possibility of joining together in prayerful invocation of the Mother of Christ, asking her creaturely assistance as an instrument of grace in our pursuit of ecclesial unity. The history of Christianity has taught us that we can do nothing without prayer. It has also taught us about the reciprocal relationship between prayer and belief. Geoffrey Wainwright underscored the reality expressed in the phrase "*lex orandi, lex credendi*" when he recommended the ecumenical use of J. Neville Ward's book on the rosary, *Five for Sorrow, Ten for Joy*, asserting that "If

Methodists and Catholics met at *that* level [i.e., the level of prayer], then increased understanding at the doctrinal level might result."[72]

---

[72] Geoffrey Wainwright, *The Ecumenical Moment* (Grand Rapids, MI: William B. Eerdmans Publishing Company, 1983), 187.

7.

Making the Blessed Virgin Mary an Imperative in Our Protestant Church: A Reflection by a Methodist

Donald Charles Lacy

Our task as inspired Marian proponents and promoters in America and beyond is to bring our Mother Mary into the mainstream of Protestant worship, study, and witnessing. Our laity and clergy must become aware of her indispensability to the life of the one, holy, catholic, and apostolic Church of which we are all a part.

In my pastoral role and extensive ecumenical travels, over now more than fifty years, I have found that the time and space given to our Blessed Mother in Protestant churches is minimal; at least that is my experience, not only in the United Methodist Church but far beyond. Just a few of us, as indicated in the *TIME* magazine cover story of March 21, 2005, have sought to address and correct this serious problem. There is hope, and the Holy Spirit is abiding, providing, and guiding. Yet, there is an enormous amount of work to be done. I propose seven areas that I believe will go a long way in helping us achieve this imperative ministry.

First – We are called to put aside what, for many, is considered wearisome academia and dull theology. While those of us who provide leadership must be steeped in the magnificence of centuries of both academia and theology, their helpfulness among those needing to drink deeply of Marian ways may become virtually irrelevant to the task at hand. For example, I have discovered that such doctrines as her Immaculate Conception and Assumption almost immediately become roadblocks and will – in fact – serve as an impetus to move some Christians away from our precious goal. It is difficult enough to persuade some Protestants to believe in the virginal conception! Words and ideas that carry negative or confusing meanings indicate we are likely only frustrating a yearning we are seeking to uncover. Some of us are tempted to wax eloquently and intellectually about the Blessed Virgin Mary in the presence of those who have seen her simply as the Mother of Jesus and refuse to go beyond that. It takes restraint to get from where these believers find themselves to where we are called by the Holy Spirit to take them. An attitude of condescension, in particular, is hurtful and may close the door to any further dialogue. The great masses of United Methodists, Presbyterians, Baptists, Disciples of Christ, Lutherans, and others are not much interested and certainly not enthralled by being told what to believe by those who seem to pose themselves as infallible! However, I am convinced that with kindness, persistence, and patience we can experience and observe our brothers and sisters in Christ coming to terms with the imperative nature of Mary's special place in the Faith.

Second – It will take intentional ways to open the door for mainstream Protestant churches to catch more than a glimpse of her absolute importance in living the Christian Faith. Personal witnessing among those we call Protestants appears invariably the best means to guide them to an acceptance of a larger and indispensable role of the Blessed Virgin Mary in living a vital Christian life. At the same time reciting a simple "Hail Mary" in organized study and/or worship provides a positive approach. Smiles and frowns may come at first, but as they get acclimated to this majestic means of coming to her in mostly Biblical language they will find it more and more difficult to argue with this prayer. After all, who wants to argue with a woman who is unquestionably holy and very powerful? Granted such behavior may seem a bit rattling at first and obtrusive but the day can be carried by allowing the Holy Spirit to act. Our ministry to move toward a rightful place for Our Lady in Protestant churches is never optional, and if we persist, I firmly believe they will wonderfully accept our message that

Mary is someone all Christians can relate to. Can we avoid arguments? Probably not. This is where our insistence must be saturated with humility and self-control. We must be especially sensitive to the Holy Spirit providing opportunities. To be in harmony with the Holy Spirit is to be one of Christ's ambassadors. If you can sense that harmony, don't automatically assume all will be joy peace, contentment, and acceptance. A seriously fractured Church remains a fact of life and death.

Third – An effective way of placing our claims among fellow Protestants is to bring skilled laity and clergy from Anglican, Roman Catholic, and Orthodox Communions into our churches for presentations. This can be done, perhaps most legitimately, under the call of Christ for us to be one. Such an umbrella is basic to understanding what all of us are about. It is necessary even for those who insist their denominational way is "the" way! Such events are best done at first with a special group in mind, who are ecumenical in their thinking. From there we might benefit from a series, perhaps during Advent or Lent, which would lead to a church-wide prayer service. Lay participation in leadership roles is very important. Clergy tend to be "professionals" who are expected to be polished presenters and may not provide the "down to earth" approach many Protestant laity find more relational and comfortable. I believe we must especially approach the laity. Clergy can enjoy one another's company and affirm their ministry that is most rewarding for them without touching the hearts and minds of our lay people. In reality, Protestant clergy may be the most difficult of all to convince that our Blessed Virgin Mary rightly deserves to be seen in a much larger role in the life of their churches. In fact, they may strenuously labor against changing a stance that serves only to make mention of her as a historical figure mostly at the right place at the right time! We must not underestimate the magnitude of our ministry seeking to call full attention to her imperative place in the Christian Faith.

Fourth – In our day and time it is becoming more and more obvious Mary is the key to Christian Unity. The cultural and spiritual dynamics have come together in such a way as to bring the strongest female personage to the stage for Christ's people not only to rally around but "to be inspired by" in unique ways. A healthy and creative feminism is alive and well with what appears to be the Holy Spirit's guidance. We are called not to succumb to another questionable variety of feminism, rightly named "radical." Her lovely maternal and pure nature gives to the word "feminine" a model and image for both men and women. The drawing power is bold and fits a humanity needing the right kind of feminism at work in their spiritual lives. Who better to unite us than Jesus' Mother? She is "blessed among women" in all our Bibles and brings into all churches a rightful feminine power, transcending those who would deal only with equality in a legal sense. Christ's people, male or female – ordained or not, can relate to her as the Mother of our Savior and Lord, who calls us daily to be united in love for His purposes. Congregational or church gatherings elevating her in the scheme of things carry unlimited opportunity. More need to do a lot of this. Protestants may fight, flee, or freeze over a Marian theme but they cannot deny she is the Mother of Jesus Christ. Furthermore, those evangelically-oriented Christians are faced with a woman who is singularly significant to Him. Surely, His one and only Mother can bring us together! I can see Him watching approvingly.

Fifth – Ongoing study and meditative opportunities in Protestant church structures that elevate our Blessed Mother's significance will give permanence to the gains made. Such an approach avoids the temptation of making the Marian theme just another trendy event in the life of churches. We have a big job! Denominations have a way of regurgitating those issues some power brokers, lay and clergy, find not to their liking. Structures have built-in biases, often subtle, that get in the way of theological broadening. It may come under purely anti-Catholic prejudice or simply be a matter of not wanting to stir up something that likely leads to a loss in numbers. As we can quickly see, much depends on pastoral leadership with all the good and bad politics inherent in parish life. We must convince our pastors on Mary being much more than a sentimental personage during Advent and the Christmas season. How can this be done? Mostly through prayer with persistence and consistence that continually mentions her lofty place in key places and to persons of serious Christian commitment. Local and denominational boards and committees need to be confronted frequently in charity. Often our laity are the ones to do this task, simply because pastors always face the possibility of threats and/or intimidation coming from those who are far more interested in institutional stability. Risk taking is not an option; it is part of the job description for Christ's disciples - - demanding, gently or otherwise, His Mother be given her rightful place in the Faith. We are on a mission, which is guided by the Holy Spirit.

Sixth – An avenue, often overlooked, is the service and civic clubs to which many community leaders belong. Perhaps the most relevant aspect of such groups is the fact they are inherently ecumenical and even interreligious in nature. Having been a part of several different clubs over more than fifty years across Midwest America, I have never discovered a Rotary Club made up of all Presbyterians or a Kiwanis Club made up of all United Methodists! Furthermore, program opportunities enable pastors and priests to develop a commonality for service to the community at large. Yes, again we see risk enter the picture but who ever said our ordained people were to be free from this usually unpleasant experience? It is truly an ecumenical age and to think otherwise is to thwart spiritual growth for those of us in need of an ever broadening understanding of all of Christ's people. Our Faith emerges from a rich Judaism and finds itself becoming a world influence in the first century primarily through Roman Catholic and Orthodox witness. A program at a service or civic club may very well be the place for us to say these things. Obviously, not everyone will be thrilled by us talking about the indispensability of the Blessed Virgin Mary in the fabric of the Christian Faith. In fact, upon occasion someone may get up and walk out during your presentation! So be it. Are we not to be about our Father's business? Certainly, a lot depends on our attitudes in these situations. One's confidence, humility, and sincerity will carry the day. It is a time of testing but time is passing and there is just so much of it.

Seventh – Then, there is the matter of our own personhood, hopefully filled with the mission of bringing Mary into partnership in the Faith and the one who leads others to her Son. If she had not been the mother of Jesus the Christ, we would likely never have known her. That, alone, gives us and others a perspective necessary to the legitimacy of our mission. Who and what we are is so basic. If we do not feel the call to be her advocate, then we must rethink our spiritual journey. Manifestly, most among Protestants do not feel the call but there are those few who sense being chosen in a way that seems predetermined by God. Failure is not an option. It is who and what we are ultimately that gives credibility to our ministries in this area and otherwise. We are all witnesses for Christ and His Church. This is true wherever we are, with whomever we find ourselves, and whatever time it may be. Some will need lengthy sessions of prayer and meditation before embarking on mission. Others may have been on the road a long time. At whatever point you discover yourselves, remember God, Who made all of us, does not leave us to our own inadequate human strength and abilities. To be called or chosen is to know we shall be equipped. Millions of precious Protestants, who have not seen the light our Lord's Mother provides for us, need to understand their current Faith is not invalid but it is inadequate. She wants to come and be present with them, not because she is our Savior, but because her Son is.

So, inspired determination is built into the very fabric of our Faith and being. These are tumultuous times. Marian devotees and ambassadors must not fail. Under the guidance of the Holy Spirit we shall not fail! Praises be to the Father, the Son, and Holy Spirit – now and forevermore. Amen.

8.

Wilderness Transformed:
Revelation 12: 13-17

Jennifer Mary Kimball

Introduction

When the opportunity to present a paper at the First
International Congress of the Ecumenical Society of the
Blessed Virgin Mary first came my way, I was excited by the
possibilities, but also wondered what relevancy such work
would have for my ministry in a rural United Church of Christ
(UCC) congregation. For those unfamiliar with the UCC, it is a
theologically diverse Protestant denomination with a strong
emphasis on social justice. The United Church of Christ came
into being with the merger of the Congregational Christian
Churches and the Evangelical and Reformed Church. My
background and perspective has been predominantly shaped by
the Congregational heritage.

At first glance, apocalyptic writing, like that of the
Revelation to John, seems worlds away from the small,
Protestant church which I serve. As I read through the
dramatic battle of Revelation 12, familiar symbols began to
emerge. The wilderness, the flood, the earth, and the serpent
are not at all new to anyone who has any familiarity with the
Bible, particularly the Old Testament. But in Revelation 12:13-
17, these well-known and well-worn symbols are transformed.
Still, I wondered, what does this have to do with a little UCC
congregation in central New York? In the summer of 2008, I
embarked on a sermon series, preaching on one of these
symbols each Sunday. As I worked through my preparations, I
worried that the material was too academic and too far
removed from the people's experiences. To my surprise and

delight, the responses I received from churchgoers were enthusiastic. Week after week, the symbols continued to touch the congregation and I began to understand why. These symbols, each capturing in its own way the intertwining of death and life, represent the experiences of those striving to live the message of Jesus. I realized that the people to whom I minister know what it is to struggle to remain faithful through a wilderness time as they face a decline in church membership and resources. By "wilderness time," I am referring to the in-between periods of life when a person or community is in transition and the future looms uncertain. In June of 2006, devastating flooding hit the town and several neighboring communities. The historic church building, originally constructed in 1840 with an extensive addition added in the 1920s, was filled at one point with three to four feet of water destroying the whole lower level of the church, including the heating system, kitchen, gymnasium size community room, and two large classrooms. Having gone through this flood, the congregation knows what it is like, quite literally, to survive a flood. Living in a farming community, they know how life is linked to the earth. Being human, they know what it is to wrestle with the deception of the serpent. There is a good reason these symbols make repeated appearances in the beginning and last books of the Bible. They represent the deep struggles of those who try to live a life faithful to God and Jesus Christ.

An exegetical comparison of the wilderness, flood, earth, and serpent as they appear in Revelation 12:13-17 with Old Testament portrayals of the wilderness from Numbers 21:4-9, the flood from Genesis 7:17-24, the earth from Genesis 4:8-12, and the serpent from Genesis 3:1-13 illustrates how these symbols are transformed for one early Christian community. This transformation hinges on the life, death, and resurrection of Jesus Christ and the mysterious woman clothed with the sun. This paper will offer an examination and comparison of each symbol as found in the chosen Old Testament passages and in Revelation 12. It will conclude with a reflection on who this woman is and the various ways these symbols speak to one UCC congregation today.

Apocalyptic Literature

The Revelation to John is a particular genre of literature known as apocalyptic. Some background on this unusual type of writing is necessary in order to obtain any understanding of the book. Frederick Murphy in the introduction to his commentary on Revelation explains, "A work's literary form, its genre, alerts the reader to how the text should be read."[1] Misunderstandings regarding the type of literary form of Revelation have led to multiple misinterpretations of the book throughout the centuries. One example of such a misreading is to approach Revelation as a book of predictions for the future, particularly concerning the coming end of the world. M. Eugene Boring points out that this book has been used in practically every generation since its composition to predict the last days of the world in that time.[2] Since none of these predictions have yet come to pass, reading Revelation as a literal book of predictions is troublesome and limits the depth and richness of the writing.

The starting point for apocalyptic literature is the claim of the author that he or she has received "a direct revelation from the supernatural world."[3] The writing is the visionary's attempt to share with a particular audience what has been revealed to him or her. The message received in an apocalyptic vision often concerns God's coming plan for the end of the world as we know it. One common characteristic of apocalyptic literature is its dualistic nature. Things are seen "in terms of

---

[1] Frederick J. Murphy, *Fallen is Babylon: The Revelation to John* (Harrisburg, PA: Trinity Press International, 1998), 17.
[2] M. Eugene Boring, "Revelation" in *Interpretation: A Bible Commentary for Teaching and Preaching,* edited by James Luther Mays (Louisville, KY: John Knox Press, 1989), 4.
[3] Murphy, *Fallen*, 18.

binary opposites."[4] This dualism is apparent in the vision described in Revelation 12 where a battle is played out between the forces against God, represented by the serpent, and those for God, represented by the woman clothed with the sun.

Elisabeth Schüssler Fiorenza explains, "Apocalyptic language functions not as predictive-descriptive language but rather as mythological-imaginative language."[5] Recognizing apocalyptic literature as mythological and imaginative shapes the way it is to be read. According to commentator Christopher C. Rowland, the style of Revelation is like that of a metaphor, "it startles, questions, even disorients before pointing to a fresh view of reality by its extraordinary imagery and impertinent verbal juxtapositions."[6] Revelation challenges its readers to let go of linear thinking, a "this stands for that" approach so that its descriptive images are able to work on the reader's imagination. One way the book came to life for its early Christian readers was through its use of familiar Jewish symbols, such as the wilderness, flood, earth, and serpent, in new and surprising ways.

Context of the Revelation to John

Revelation is a piece of apocalyptic literature written for a specific audience in a certain time and place, under particular circumstances. Some understanding of the social and religious context of the book is necessary when considering its meaning both for its original audience and for today's readers. In recent times there has been some disagreement regarding the identity of the author and the conditions under which he wrote. Traditionally, it was believed the author of Revelation was John

---

[4] Murphy, *Fallen*, 22.

[5] Elisabeth Schüssler Fiorenza, *Revelation: Vision of a Just World* in *Proclamation Commentaries* edited by Gerhard Krodel (Minneapolis, MN: Fortress Press, 1991), 25.

[6] Christopher C. Rowland, "The Book of Revelation: Introduction, Commentary, and Reflections" in *The New Interpreter's Bible,* Vol. XII, edited by Leander E. Keck (Nashville, TN: Abingdon Press, 1998), 506.

the disciple and the same author as the Gospel of John and the Letters of John. Some modern scholars disagree with this assertion and conclude all that can be known of the author is that he is Palestinian Jew who immigrated to Asia Minor probably following the war of 66-70.[7] This theory ignores generations of Christian tradition that link John of the Gospel and Letters with the John who was banished to the Island of Patmos. For the sake of this paper, the author of the book will be referred to as John acknowledging the likelihood of some connection to John the Apostle. There is general agreement that the book was written towards the end of the first century, probably around the year 96.[8]

Christians living towards the end of the first century found themselves in a difficult situation. They were viewed with suspicion by both their Jewish and Gentile neighbors. They faced both social and economic discrimination. Boring describes the situation of the author and original audience of Revelation as an "identity crisis." As outsiders in their society, these early Christians would find it "difficult to endure without a strong sense of group and personal identity."[9] Traditionally it has been held that John wrote during a time of violent, systematic persecution of Christians by the Roman Empire. Some scholars propose that Revelation was written before Christians experienced such persecution.[10] Regardless of whether or not the persecution was widespread, these were frightening times and the threat of persecution was real and shaped the experiences and perceptions of John and his audience and must be taken into account when studying the book. Schüssler Fiorenza compares apocalyptic literature to science fiction literature in that it "constructs the future out of

---

[7] Susan R. Garrett, "Revelation" in *The Woman's Bible Commentary* edited by Carol A. Newsom and Sharon H. Ringe (Louisville, KY: Westminster John Knox Press, 1998), 470. See also Boring, *Revelation*, 34.
[8] Boring, *Revelation*, 10.
[9] Boring, *Revelation*, 11-12.
[10] Murphy, *Fallen*, 16.

the experiences and fears of people in the present."[11] John tries to make sense out of the experience of discrimination and the fear of persecution experienced by his Christian community, and in doing so gives the people a message of hope, encouragement, and comfort. What better way to do so, than to draw upon familiar symbols from his Jewish heritage? In doing so "John transforms the biblical material into something new in the light of his own historical and social situation and his own experiences, visionary or otherwise."[12] This "something new" in the form of biblical symbols spoke to John and his community and continues to have the power to speak to Christians today.

Numbers 21:4-9: The Wilderness Transformed

In the latter part of the first century, at the time of the writing of Revelation, Christians found themselves living in transition. They were no longer considered Jewish and therefore were not granted protection in being part of an established religion. Questions such as "Who are the People of God?" and "What is the meaning of belonging to the church?" demanded immediate attention.[13] These Christians, like the Israelites following their Exodus from Egypt, found themselves in the wilderness. By following Jesus, they left behind the known and familiar on their way to someplace new and uncertain. Stories of the Israelites' forty years of desert wandering would have held a particular relevancy for early Christians such as those addressed by Revelation.

One of the challenges and riches of apocalyptic literature is the complexity of the symbols. Schüssler Fiorenza describes it this way: "Revelation is not like a window to the world but is more like an onion or a rose with layers and layers of meaning."[14] These symbols have the power to capture the

---

[11] Schüssler Fiorenza, *Revelation*, 26.

[12] Murphy, *Fallen*, 28.

[13] Boring, *Revelation*, 13.

[14] Schüssler Fiorenza, *Revelation*, 19.

ambiguity of the human experience, enabling them to speak to generation after generation. The wilderness is no exception. Moses leads the people out of slavery in Egypt into the wilderness. In the beginning, the Israelites, like the woman from Revelation 12, find the wilderness to be a place of refuge. In the wilderness, they are safe from the Egyptians. In the wilderness, the people sing the Song of Miriam and the Song of Moses - playing instruments and dancing. Before long though, their triumphant songs turn into serious complaints.

In Numbers 21:4-9, the wilderness emerges as a place of danger and death. Repeatedly, the people complain to Moses, "Why have you brought us up out of Egypt to die here in the wilderness?"[15] As if life was not hard enough, God then sends deadly serpents making survival even more difficult. The people beg Moses to pray to God to remove the serpents. God does provide an answer to Moses' prayer on behalf of the people, but it is not the one for which they asked. Rather than removing the snakes, God gives them a remedy for the bites.[16] "Make a poisonous serpent, and set it upon a pole; and everyone who is bitten shall look at it and live."[17] The Israelites experience the transformation of the wilderness from a place of protection to one of danger and death. But the great paradox of the wilderness is that the way of death is also the way of life. A bronze serpent on a pole saves the life of those bitten by the fiery snakes. In the wilderness, life and death are intrinsically intertwined.

While the Israelites are plagued by deadly serpents in the wilderness, it is also the place to which the woman clothed with the sun escapes the serpent. When the serpent pursues

---

[15] Wayne A. Meeks, ed., *The HarperCollins Study Bible: New Revised Standard Version with the Apocryphal/Deuterocanonical Books* (New York, NY: HarperCollins Publishing, Inc., 1993), Numbers 21:5.
[16] Fred B. Craddock, John H. Hayes, Carl R. Holladay, and Gene M. Tucker, editors, *Preaching Through the Christian Year: Year B* (Harrisburg, PA: Trinity Press International, 1993), 508.
[17] Numbers 21:8.

the woman, she "was given the two wings of the great eagle, so that she could fly from the serpent into the wilderness."[18] Reading this passage through the lens of the Exodus motif, Boring writes, "The woman flees to the wilderness, as the People of God had found refuge from the dragon/Pharaoh in the exodus story John often uses as a model."[19] The difference is the woman continues to experience the wilderness as a sanctuary while for the Israelites the sense of protection eventually wears off.

In Revelation 12:15, the wilderness is called "her place." The woman dwells for a time in a place prepared for her by God.[20] The Israelites too dwell in a place prepared for them by God, but their experience is not as such. Barbara Brown Taylor provides an insightful description of what life was like in the wilderness for the people of Israel:

> When the people were still working six days a
> week making mud bricks for the Egyptians, the
> wilderness looked like heaven to them. Imagine!
> No work, no whips, no foreign masters with
> their foreign gods - just a clear, quiet
> passageway to the promised land. That was
> before they go into it, of course. That was
> before the sand coated them like a second skin,
> before their lips cracked from too much sun
> and too little water, before they began to dream
> of Egypt.[21]

In the wilderness, the Israelites find themselves homeless. They have left Egypt and there is no going back. The Promised Land remains just that, a promise. So they wander in an in-between place that is clearly not one which they can call their

---

[18] Revelation 12:14.
[19] Boring, *Revelation*, 158.
[20] Revelation 12:6.
[21] Barbara Brown Taylor, "Four Stops in the Wilderness," *Journal for Preachers* 24 no 2 (Lent 2001): 5.

own. The wilderness remains for them God's place, not theirs, and living under harsh conditions they find no comfort in this fact.

Again, the people of Israel complain: "For there is no food and no water, and we detest this miserable food."[22] Nourishment is a major issue in the wilderness. Without God's provision, the first part of the statement would be true: There is no food or water. Instead, it remains an exaggeration. God does provide for the people, making bitter water good to drink and delivering the gift of manna each morning. The problem is the people are sick of this limited menu. This complaint may also point to a deeper issue. The food and water situation in the wilderness serves to remind the people everyday that they are utterly dependent on God. If God did not provide them with water and manna, they would indeed die of dehydration and starvation. In the wilderness, the Israelites are constantly confronted with the truth that they are not in control of their lives. God is. In contrast, Revelation 12:14 describes the wilderness as the place where the woman is nourished.

The church I serve is living in wilderness time. The congregation, like many mainline Protestant churches, has experienced a significant decrease in membership in the last 20 years. The previous pastorate came to a rocky ending. The town itself has also undergone serious change and when wandering downtown, one sees empty storefronts on what was once a bustling street. Lack of employment drives many young people to leave town soon after graduation from high school, not to return. The church cannot be the church like it was in the 1980s and 1990s and survive, let alone thrive. Add to all the cultural changes, the widespread and very costly damages of the flood, and these indeed are uncertain, become wilderness times. Like the Israelites, the church is daily confronted with the possibility of death. Membership pledges do not cover the operating expenses of the church. There are few young people

---

[22] Numbers 21:5.

173

and fewer children in the congregation. Like the Israelites, we are well aware that the future is in God's hands, not ours. Following the flood, I continuously raise the question, "What is God calling the church to be and to do these days?"

It is becoming more and more obvious that death is the only way to new life. Recently, I stopped by to see the progress in our new church kitchen. All the major construction has been completed and the members are slowly but steadily chipping away at the finishing work such as painting. Recently, the church scheduled a celebration weekend, beginning with the traditional Fall Harvest Supper. This would be the first church supper since the flood. In a conversation with a dedicated member and deacon, the reality that the church may not be able to successfully manage a full dinner relying only on the current membership was acknowledged. We went on to discuss how the church may have to let go of all these old traditions and in a sense start anew. New life in the church may require breaking with the old in order to meet the changing needs of both the congregation and the community. But like the serpent on the pole demonstrates, death or the threat of death may be the very thing that delivers healing and new life. Wilderness time is filled with anxiety but if the center and heart of the congregation is Jesus and the gospel, then it also becomes a powerful time of transformation and renewal.

As Christians we have the great assurance that Jesus himself spent his time in the wilderness. After Jesus' baptism, "The Spirit immediately drove him out into the wilderness" where he remained for forty days.[23] Taylor explains, "As much as we might prefer to avoid it, the wilderness is where God is. The wilderness is where God does some of God's best work."[24] Whether we are aware of it or not, God is with us even in the wilderness. The wilderness remains a place of both death and life, often with death being the only route to new life. The

---

[23] Mark 1:12-13.
[24] Taylor, "Four Stops," 9.

wilderness is transformed when those who find themselves in this in-between time and place discover God is right there with them.

Genesis 7:17-24: The Flood: From Chaos to Life

The flood, both as a symbol and a human experience, represents a complex spectrum ranging from chaos and destruction to re-creation and new life. Reading the story of the flood as found in Genesis 6-9, with an emphasis on Genesis 7:17-24, alongside Revelation 12:15-16, highlights all these complexities. In Genesis, the flood is sent by God, the Creator. The creation God declared "good" in Genesis 1 is declared full of wickedness and evil. "And the LORD was sorry that he had made humankind on the earth, and it grieved him to his heart."[25] From very early on, the Bible interprets the flood as a reversal of creation and the bringing of a new beginning.[26] The flood is God's solution about what to do with a sinful generation. In Genesis, the story moves from chaos[27] to creation[28] to destruction and, therefore, back to chaos[29] to re-creation and new life.[30] Looking at the flood story as a whole in Genesis, Terence Fretheim offers the following conclusion: "The story reveals and resolves a fundamental tension within God, emphasizing finally, not a God who decides to destroy, but a God who wills to save, who is committed to change based on experience with the world, and who promises to stand by the creation."[31] God who breathed the breath of life into the first man is still intimately connected to God's creation.

---

[25] Genesis 6:6.
[26] Daniel R. Streett, "As It Was in the Days of Noah: The Prophets' Typological Interpretation of Noah's Flood," *Criswell Theological Review* 5 no. 1 (Fall 2007): 38.
[27] Genesis 1:2.
[28] Genesis 1-2.
[29] Genesis 7.
[30] Genesis 8-9.
[31] Terence Fretheim, "The Book of Genesis: Introduction, Commentary, and Reflections" in *The New Interpreters Bible*, Vol. I, edited by Leander E. Keck (Nashville, TN: Abingdon Press, 1994), 395.

The flood in Revelation 12 comes not from God, but from the serpent. Rather than rushing forth from God, the Creator, this flood comes forth from the serpent who "represents the primeval anti-creation forces of the watery abyss."[32] More discussion on the serpent is provided below. At this point, it is enough to recognize the contrast between forces of creation, God, and forces of anti-creation, the serpent. In the time between the writing of Genesis and Revelation, another and final new creation has been introduced through the life, death, and resurrection of Jesus Christ. Paul, in his Second Letter to the Corinthians writes, "So if anyone is in Christ, there is a new creation; everything old has passed away; see, everything has become new."[33] In Revelation the purpose of the flood is to wipe away God's new creation and return to the chaos. Both the floods in Genesis and Revelation seek to return to chaos, but in Genesis this is a step towards new life delivered by God while in Revelation chaos is the sought after goal of the evil serpent.

The goals and targets of the two floods are quite different. In Genesis, the flood hits the majority of the people, with Noah and his family and the rescued creatures being the few exceptions. "Now the earth was corrupt in God's sight, and the earth was filled with violence."[34] The Genesis flood aims to sweep away the violent and unrighteous people and in doing so bring an end to violence. In contrast, the flood in Revelation attempts to violently destroy the woman. The source of this flood is violent, previously seeking to destroy the woman's unborn child, then the woman herself; and then he "went off to make war on the rest of her children."[35] Although it is a challenge to recognize the God who sent the flood in Genesis as good and loving, the destructive portrayal is at least in part balanced by God's grief before the flood and God's new covenant with Noah following the flood. In Revelation, the

---

[32] Boring, *Revelation*, 160.
[33] 2 Corinthians 5:17.
[34] Genesis 6:11.
[35] Revelation 12:17.

serpent - following his failed attempt to wash the woman away - continues on in violence making war on her children, in a sense ushering in a flood of violence.

The flood, like the wilderness, bears witness to the difficult truth that new life and re-creation often come out of death and destruction. The original readers of Revelation would most likely have recognized themselves at this vulnerable point. In their case, the flood was not literal, but instead represented "deep, seemingly overwhelming troubles, which are not necessarily punishment from God but which provide an opportunity for God to rescue his people."[36] These early followers of Christ do not belong in their society and are struggling to define for themselves and others who they are. The threat of persecution makes these questions of identity a matter of life and death. They are going to be required to change, or experience a death of some sort, in a process to new life.

This is a journey well understood by my congregation since the flood of 2006. For several days, the town was divided by several impassible "rivers" and remained in a state of emergency for about a week. Blessedly, there were no casualties in the community, but the destruction to the town, including the church, was widespread. For a small, struggling congregation, many of whom also suffered damage to their homes, this was a death experience. Yet, out of the chaos and destruction new life has emerged. New leaders came forward to help with the rebuilding process. Community was fostered as the members came together with other churches and neighbors to clean up the damage. Once rebuilt, the destroyed space will be more usable than before, offering new opportunities for ministry and service to the town.

---

[36] Leland Ryken, James C. Wilhoit, and Tremper Longman III, eds., *Dictionary of Biblical Imagery* (Downers Grove, IL: Intervarsity Press, 1998), 293, column 2.

The church is on an intense journey from chaos and destruction to new life. On the year anniversary of the flood, we created a special altar to mark the occasion. Arranged in the front of the church were the items we will forever associate with the first days and weeks following the flood: Red Cross buckets, bleach, masks, crow bars, mops, shovels, and muddy boots. Arising out of this disarray was a single flower representing the new life bursting forth from the chaos. The floods of Genesis 3, Revelation 12, and June 2006 all demonstrate God's power over the forces of chaos and destruction. There is no destroying God's new creation.

Genesis 4:8-12: The Earth Rising

Violence, whether actual or anticipated, was a constant reality for the original audience of Revelation. They, like their Jewish ancestors, would draw strength from the assurance of an ally: the earth. From the beginning of creation when "The LORD God formed man from the dust of the ground, and breathed into his nostrils the breath of life,"[37] human beings, the earth, and God have been intrinsically linked in relationship. In both Genesis 4 and Revelation 12, the earth emerges as an active participant in the drama, or to use the language of literature, the earth is a character. As Boring explains, "The earth is not just the stage, the neutral scene where the human and angelic drama is played out, but an actor in the drama."[38] In both Genesis 4 and Revelation 12, the earth "opened its mouth."[39] While the effects of the action are different in the two stories, they both serve to highlight the ties that bind God, human beings, and the earth.

Genesis 4 is the story of the second generation of human beings. After Eve and Adam's expulsion from the Garden of Eden, the Bible tells that Eve gave birth to two sons, Cain and Abel. The story of the brothers continues when God

---

[37] Genesis 2:7.
[38] Boring, *Revelation*, 153.
[39] Genesis 4:11 and Revelation 12:12

178

accepts Abel's offering and disregards Cain's. Cain is so outraged by God's rejection of his offering that he murders his brother. In response to the tragedy, God says to Cain, "What have you done? Listen; your brother's blood is crying out to me from the ground!"[40] Here the earth is seen taking action in response to the first murder. The earth witnesses the injustice. "The earth has a voice; its mouth cries out as a witness and a judge of Cain's act."[41] Abel may be dead with no human witnesses, but he can be assured the earth will remember the injustice he suffered at the hands of his own brother. Job's desperate prayer could be Abel's: "O earth, do not cover my blood; let my outcry find no resting place."[42] In the Bible, the earth often stands on the side of those suffering violence and injustice, such as Abel, Job, and the woman from Revelation 12 and, therefore, against those seeking to destroy the victim. Once having witnessed Cain's act, the earth itself then rejects him. He is cursed from the ground and forced to live "a rootless life of wandering."[43] As Brigitte Kahl points out, "The earth does not remain a silent witness. It enters into solidarity with Abel and refuses solidarity with the human being who abused his strength and killed his brother."[44] When Cain murders Abel, not only are the relationships in the first family broken, but so is the connection between Cain and the earth.

Another act the earth takes on Abel's behalf is prayer. Carole Fontaine, a former professor of mine, says, "The first prayer to God in the whole Bible is earth giving voice to Abel's blood."[45] Even as the earth rejects Cain, it continues to be a

[40] Genesis 4:10.

[41] Paul S. Minear, "Far as the Curse is Found: The Point of Revelation 12:15-16" *Novum Testamentum* 33 no 1 (1991): 74.

[42] Job 16:18.

[43] Kristin M. Swenson, "Care and Keeping East of Eden: Gen 4:1-16 in Light of Gen 2-3," *Interpretation* 60 no. 4 (October 2006): 382.

[44] Brigitte Kahl, "Human Culture and the Integrity of Creation: Biblical Reflections on Genesis 1-11," *Ecumenical Review* 39 no 2 (April 1987):135.

[45] Material comes from notes taken at a lecture given by Dr. Carole Fontaine on January 1, 2004.

link between Abel and God, crying out to God on Abel's behalf. Since the moment of the creation of the first person out of earth and spirit, people, the earth, and God have been caught up in a "web of relationships."[46] In Genesis 4, the earth plays the role of witness and intercessor, connecting brother to brother and the brothers to God.

In Revelation 12 the earth continues to connect people to God by coming to the aid of the woman clothed with the sun. When the serpent attempts to wash the woman away with a flood, "the earth came to the help of the woman; it opened its mouth and swallowed the river that the dragon had poured from his mouth."[47] Instead of witnessing the violent act as in Genesis 4, the earth protects and rescues the woman in Revelation 12. Minear explains, "The act of drinking demonstrates the power of the earth to protect the woman and to provide for her a home in the wilderness."[48] In response to Abel's murder, the earth *receives* his blood demonstrating the earth's ability and willingness to stand by the victim. In response to the serpent, the earth *swallows* the flood showing its power to rise up and act on a potential victim's behalf. In Revelation 12, the earth once again stands as a link between God and the one suffering violence. By protecting and rescuing the woman, the earth serves God by standing between God and the forces against God. As both the story of Cain and Abel and the woman clothed with the sun demonstrate, "The future of humankind and the earth are profoundly bound together."[49]

The relationship between the earth and humankind is one well understood by the rural congregation I serve. While no active members of the church are farmers at this time, many of the people grew up working on family farms and they remain forever farmers at heart. They understand what it is to work

---

[46] Swenson, "Care and Keeping," 381.
[47] Revelation 12:16.
[48] Minear, "Revelation," 75.
[49] Ryken, *Dictionary*, 224.

the land and the frustration and satisfaction that come along with such a relationship. As I shared with the church the story of my grandmother and the "little people," as she referred to her plants, I could see many nods of recognition. I was talking to a group of people in a rural locale who know what it is to have a living relationship with the earth in which the earth is not just a thing available for human use, but rather it is alive and engaged in mutual give and take with its human partners.

One way my church is helping to care for the earth is through the making and selling of tote bags crocheted out of plastic shopping bags. At the time of the writing of this article the church has made approximately 95 tote bags. Each tote requires 65 plastic bags. This means over 6,000 plastic bags have been saved from being thrown into landfills! Not only does this project recycle plastic bags, it also prevents more from being used because they make excellent reusable grocery bags. The money raised from the tote bags goes towards the expense of flood restoration. Genesis 4 and Revelation 12 raise awareness of the different ways the earth takes action when people are abused. The tote bags are a small response to the abuse humankind has showered upon the earth.

Genesis 3:1-13: The Serpent and a New Creation

In the fall of 2007, I offered an adult education class at my church that looked at the biblical symbols in some of Nathaniel Hawthorne's short stories. Hawthorne, with his extensive reflection on New England Puritan life, brought us back to our early American roots. During our discussion of "Young Goodman Brown" we delved into the topic of the reality of evil in our lives and in the world. To our amazement the hour flew by and we left with a strong impression that there was much more to be said on the subject. Many mainline churches, such as the one I serve, often do not give much attention to the topic of evil. Perhaps this is part of the reason apocalyptic writings, like Revelation, seem irrelevant. In Revelation, the battle between good and evil is played out on a cosmic level. In trying to make sense of his own time, the author of Revelation relies on a timeless story with a power that still speaks to Christians.

> The old mythical story is retold in such a way
> that the events and institutions of John's own
> history shimmer through it. The mythical story
> reflects and evokes images and events of his
> hearer-readers' experience, allowing them to see
> their struggles in a transcendent context. The
> characters fall, not surprisingly, into two
> absolutely polarized groups with no middle
> ground.[50]

This struggle between God and evil is still at work in our lives whether we acknowledge it or not. Recognizing and naming the forces that work to convince people to turn away from God as evil empowers Christians to stand firm in their faith when confronting such temptation.

The correlation between the serpent, Satan, and evil is taken for granted by most Christians. Revelation 12, with its straightforward description of the serpent, clearly captures this identification. "The great dragon was thrown down, that ancient serpent, who is called the Devil and Satan, the deceiver of the whole world."[51] By the time of the writing of Revelation the serpent and Satan are one and the same. In this apocalyptic writing, the serpent stands for evil. Often this meaning is then read back into the story of Eve, Adam, and the serpent from Genesis 3, not taking into account that it took several generations for the these symbols to be equated. "At first no clear relation is seen between Satan and the serpent, but later the serpent is called an instrument of the devil, and then the

---

[50] Boring, *Revelation,* 152.
[51] Revelation 12:9.

two are equated."[52] A fresh look at the role of the serpent, Satan, and evil in Genesis 3 has much to say to Christians today, especially those who do not find the subject of evil to be relevant to their daily lives.

Evil is a complex subject and the story of the serpent in Genesis 3 captures its many dimensions. I define evil as the forces that human beings allow to come between themselves and God. Theories regarding what and who the serpent is range from neutral observer to Satan. The Bible tells us, "Now the serpent was more crafty than any other wild animal that the LORD God had made."[53] Crafty is a word play on "naked."[54] Scholars such as Wilma Ann Bailey comprise one side of the spectrum regarding the nature of the serpent. Bailey proposes the serpent is one of the living things made by God and is not to be identified with Satan. The serpent's concern in the Garden of Eden was the food supply. The serpent tries to get the humans to do something that will result in their death in order to protect its food source.[55] While this reading is interesting, it contributes to the denial of the reality of evil found in some churches today.

At the other end of the spectrum are commentators who equate the serpent with the Devil or Satan. Sidney Greidanus explains that because serpents do not speak, someone or something must have taken possession of this particular verbal serpent. Since the serpent questions God's command and calls God a liar, this someone or something must be Satan.[56] As discussed previously, there are problems

---

[52] Geoffrey W. Bromiley, *Theological Dictionary of the New Testament, Abridged in One Volume* (Grand Rapids, Michigan: William B. Eerdmans Publishing Company, 1985), 750.

[53] Genesis 3:1.

[54] Fretheim, "Genesis," 359.

[55] Wilma Ann Bailey, "Through the Eyes of a Serpent: A Political/Economic/Ecological Interpretation of Genesis 3," *Encounter* 67 no. 1 (Winter 2006): 82, 84.

[56] Sidney Greidanus, "Preaching Christ From the Narrative of the Fall," *Bibliotheca Sacra* 161 no 643 (July-September 2004): 267.

with this extreme reading also. The early Jewish understanding of Satan did not equate Satan with the Devil. For example, in the Book of Job, which postdates Genesis, the Satan is not the demon we think of today, but rather a job description of one who worked for God. The Satan in this context, according to Fontaine, is a "Persian Administrative District Attorney," a professional tattletale, who wanders the earth and reports back to God on the human condition.[57] The direct correlation between the serpent, Satan, and evil has yet to be made at the time of the writing of Genesis 3. The serpent as seen in Genesis 3 is a complex symbol and simplistic readings which describe it as innocent bystander or the Devil do not capture the depth of meaning of the symbol then and now.

The serpent, like evil, is a very tricky thing. Perhaps the best way to categorize it is as a trickster. Susan Niditch provides the following description of a trickster: "a character having the capacity to transform situations and overturn the status quo. The trickster has less power than the great gods but enough mischief and nerve to shake up the cosmos and alter it forever."[58] As a trickster, the serpent has subtle yet powerful tools at its disposal. To begin with, the serpent knows exactly when to strike. "The serpent responds (vv. 4-5) at precisely the point of exaggeration and vulnerability... ."[59] The serpent also knows how to strike. Under the guise of innocence the serpent asks a simple question, "Did God say, 'You shall not eat from any tree in the garden?'"[60] With this question, the serpent becomes a facilitator of temptation introducing the first woman and man to options that may lead them to turn away from God.[61] The woman and man now recognize that they have a

---

[57] Material comes from notes taken at a lecture given by Dr. Carole Fontaine on January 5, 2004.
[58] Susan Niditch, "Genesis," in *Women's Bible Commentary*, edited by Carol A. Newsom and Sharon H. Ringe (Louisville, KY: Westminster John Knox Press, 1998), 17.
[59] Fretheim, "Genesis," 360.
[60] Genesis 3:1.
[61] Fretheim, "Genesis," 360.

choice in whether or not they obey God. The serpent continues, "You will not die...."[62] Again, trickster seems to be a fitting description of the serpent for the serpent does not lie to the woman. Niditch and Fretheim both point out that the serpent speaks the truth.[63] The woman and man do not die when they eat the fruit of the tree.

The story of the serpent found in Genesis 3 is in no way a simple myth to be dismissed by sophisticated, educated readers, but rather a story that captures the complexities and subtleties of the reality of evil in our world and in each of our lives. Genesis 3 and Revelation 12 paint different, yet accurate portraits of how evil still is at work today. In Genesis 3, evil is slippery, striking at the woman's greatest weakness and using truth and fear to show her she has choices that do not include God. Often this is the way evil works in the lives of individuals. It takes a deep anxiety, such as the fear of financial ruin, which is a real threat, and then exaggerates it so a person puts making money above everything else, including God. In this example, money becomes the saving force in one's life, not Jesus Christ.

While the serpent in Genesis uses subtlety, fear, and truth twisting to convince Eve and Adam to turn from God, the serpent in Revelation uses brute force and violence. This serpent tries to devour the woman's newborn child[64] and when this fails he pursues or persecutes the woman.[65] Then he tries to sweep her away with a flood.[66] Although the serpent works quite differently in Revelation as compared to Genesis, there is truth in this portrayal as well. Here the chaotic nature of the serpent is clearly revealed. Evil, in whatever form it takes, works against God trying to undo the order of God's great creation, leaving in its wake chaos and disruption.

---

[62] Genesis 3:5.
[63] Niditch, "Genesis," 17 and Fretheim, "Genesis," 361.
[64] Revelation 12:4.
[65] Revelation 12:13.
[66] Revelation 12:15.

Taken together, Genesis 3 and Revelation 12 create a picture of evil that is quite accurate for Christians living in the United States today. This ancient myth and apocalyptic vision are still relevant and, as I preached on the existence of evil, I could tell I was expressing realities experienced by my UCC congregation for which they have not often been given language. These hardworking people who try hard to follow Jesus' way know what it is like to have fear, doubt, and exaggeration chip away at their faith. We struggle, both as individuals and as a church with the temptation to place money, status, power, and security above our commitment to Christ. In these ways, we have all experienced the serpent, as found in Genesis 3, trying to rupture our trust in God as it tempts us towards false gods. Genesis 3 offers a picture of what it is like to wrestle with evil on a personal level.

Revelation 12 provides a larger, institutional picture of evil. Many scholars, including Boring, Murphy, and Garrett identify the serpent as symbolizing the powers of the Roman Empire. Murphy explains the Roman Empire ruled and regulated local life through the use political and military force.[67] Seen in this light, Revelation 12 describes a battle between the earthly powers of the Roman Empire and God. Richard Horsley's *Jesus and the Empire* helps to link this experience of the early Christians to life today in the United States by comparing the U.S. to the Roman Empire. He writes, "Most remarkable are the many ways in which U.S. history resembles and repeats the history of Rome as a republic that built and ruled an empire."[68] The battle between good and evil as described by John reflects the early experience of Christian resistance to the attempts of the Roman government to come between them and Christ by forcing them to swear allegiance to Rome and its rulers and cults. This struggle is still experienced by Christians today as we live in a society that tries to get us to swear

---

[67] Murphy, *Fallen*, 1.
[68] Richard A. Horsley, *Jesus and the Empire: The Kingdom of God and the New World Disorder* (Minneapolis, MN: Augsburg Fortress, 2003), 137.

186

allegiance to political parties, militarism, and consumerism over loyalty to Jesus. The tension is largely felt in the United Church of Christ where there is a strong emphasis on social justice and working on behalf of the poor and the oppressed. My congregation feels the pressure of trying to be a church with limited human and financial resources and yet to be in service to the community and the larger world. We are Christians struggling together to resist the forces of evil that attempt to drive a wedge between us and God as individuals as we live in a larger overarching system that enforces worship of the gods of power, money, and class over the humble ways of Jesus Christ.

As this comparison between the serpent of Genesis 3 and Revelation 12 shows, evil is still at work in our world and continues to make war on the rest of the children of the woman clothed with the sun, "those who keep the commandments of God and hold the testimony of Jesus."[69] But for those who commit themselves to the life and ways of Jesus, the serpent and evil no longer have power over them. The serpent, like the wilderness, flood, and earth, is a complex symbol of both life and death. "Along with the snake's paradoxical combination of wisdom and evil, it represents not only death but also health and life. Perhaps its ability to administer death seemed to imply authority over life."[70] As Christians we follow the one who truly has power over death and therefore the serpent and the evil and chaos it represents has no power over us as long as we keep turning to Jesus and away from the powers of evil.

The Woman from Revelation 12

In Revelation 12, familiar Old Testament symbols, wilderness, flood, earth, and serpent, collide in a new and meaningful way through interaction with the woman clothed with the sun. Throughout the centuries, the identity of this

---

[69] Revelation 12:17.
[70] Ryken, *Dictionary*, 773.

woman has been debated. It has been proposed that she is Mary, the mother of Jesus, the church, the daughter of Zion, or the messianic community. It is a logical assumption to think this woman represents Mary, the mother of Jesus. She gives birth to a male child identified as the Messiah. It has also been proposed that she represents the church since the dragon goes off "to make war on the rest of her children." Others hear the echo of Isaiah 66:7-9: "Shall a land be born in one day? Shall a nation be delivered in one moment? Yet as soon as Zion was in labor she delivered her children." This allusion suggests the woman represents the people of Israel or daughter Zion who is about to give birth to a new nation.[71] Yet Boring describes why the woman is not to be correlated with just one of these identities: "Yet to interpret John's evocative symbolic language in this limited fashion would reduce it to a steno-symbol code. John the artist uses language more creatively. The woman is not Mary, nor Israel, nor the church but less and more of all of these."[72] The symbols in apocalyptic writings like Revelation are multi-layered. A "this means that" correlation oversimplifies the richness and depth of the message.

Murphy proposes the woman represents the messianic community both before and after the Messiah's birth.[73] As such, the woman is Zion awaiting its deliverance. She is Mary, struggling to deliver the Messiah. She is the early church trying to define itself and the modern church working to remain faithful to Jesus' message. She is all of us seeking to follow in the ways of Jesus Christ. Her struggle in the midst of the battle between God and evil is the fight with which we too struggle. For this reason, her encounter with the wilderness, the flood, the earth, and the serpent is one to which we all can relate, for where she is so are we … so we have been, are, or will be.

The woman clothed with the sun lives in the intersection of death and life. She flees to the wilderness, the

---

[71] Schüssler Fiorenza, *Revelation*, 81 and Garrett, "Revelation," 471.
[72] Boring, *Revelation*, 152.
[73] Murphy, *Fallen*, 283.

place of death and new life. She encounters the flood, which washes away the old creation making the ground fertile and ready for a new creation. She stands in solidarity with the earth, which season upon season moves from life to death to new life. She battles the serpent, an ultimate symbol of the interlocking of death and life. The transformation from death to life is the heart of the gospel, the good news of Jesus Christ. For this reason, the story of the woman of Revelation 12 is the story of all of us, even a little United Church of Christ congregation in rural New York. For day by day we live at the intersection of death and life, in the wilderness, amidst the flood, alongside the earth, and against the serpent. Through it all, we live, a new creation, in Jesus Christ.

Mary and the Syrian Tradition

9.

Theótokos the Theologian: A Syrian Appreciation of Mary's "Keeping things and pondering them in her heart"

Paul Snowden Russell III

Over the last 20 centuries, countless hours have been spent by Christians in pondering the life and example of the mother of Jesus of Nazareth. She has served as icon and inspiration to those who have longed for closeness to God; she has inspired many to use her as an example of steadfastness, courage, humility and obedience. Why, then, despite the fact that two of the most striking references to her in the gospels are to her independent religious reflections, do we so seldom imagine her as a theological thinker?

After the shepherds have visited the stable in Bethlehem and told their tale, we are told by St. Luke: "But Mary kept all these things, and pondered them in her heart." [1] After their visit to Jerusalem for Passover when Jesus was 12 years old and He so surprised His parents by calling the Temple "my Father's house," St. Luke reports "but his mother kept all these sayings in her heart." [2]

While western Christian authors have made comparatively little of these verses, they caught the attention of our brothers and sisters in Mesopotamia and beyond. Today, I would like to give you a taste of some of the things the Syrian Church has said about Our Lady as a theological thinker in her own right.

---

[1] 2:19
[2] 2:51b

Although the sad divisions in Syriac language Christianity have tended to spring directly from Christological roots, they have not manifested themselves very much in Mariology.[3] Thus, there is quite a bit of unity among the Syrians in the area in which we go to meet them. It is also true that the cultural background of these Christians provides them with a different array of assumptions to inform and direct their theological reflections in literature, art and abstract thought from those of Christians to their west. This background also gives rise to some unique elements in their approach to this particular area of Christian reflection. For these reasons, I think the Syriac language churches deserve a separate look in Mariology. Today, I will be trying to show you why I think it does.

Incarnation

The Syrian Christian Tradition emphasizes the doctrine of the Incarnation to a very high degree, even when considered among Christian groups. How can I make such a broad statement? Sometimes, it is the details of Christian practice that reveal the most about the convictions of those who engage in them. Here is Sebastian Brock's description of one of these details. He reports:

> ...a rather surprising text—a Syriac Orthodox calendar copied in North Iraq in 1689. Commenting on the feasts of March, the compiler states: "As for the feast of the Annunciation, the church celebrates it on whichever day of the week the 25th falls: even if it falls on Good Friday, we still celebrate the Liturgy, since the Annunciation is the beginning and source of all other feasts." [4]

---

[3] So says Sebastian Brock in his introduction to Hansbury, 2.
[4] This is found in Brock's introduction to Hansbury, 3.

As Brock points out, this practice clearly emphasizes the place and action of Our Lady in the working out of Salvation, as well as placing the Incarnation on the highest level of theological importance. It is clear from this that we are not looking at the Syrian Tradition in an area that it does not value.[5] We will find that their focus on the Incarnation has led them to reflect on it in creative ways that are not always known in the West.

Dialogue Hymns

Syrian Christianity draws from three main cultural sources: the Jewish, the Mesopotamian and the Greek.[6] Two of these are especially relevant to our topic: the Jewish tradition of Scripture study and the genre of Dispute Poems from early Mesopotamian literature.

The connection to Jewish exegesis means that the Syrian Christians were acquainted with a tradition that sought to clarify the Bible by creative expansion and reflection on the bare scriptural text.[7] The connection to the Mesopotamian tradition of literature means that their culture (and the

---

[5] When this paper was delivered, I was told by members of the audience that the Armenian Orthodox and, more broadly the Eastern Orthodox traditions, also celebrate the Annunciation in this manner; though Sister Nonna Harrison told me it is only among the Old Calendar groups that this kind of overlap is possible. This difference would then appear to be one between the Latin West and the rest of the Church. The point about the Syrian seriousness about the Annunciation is still accurate, I think, especially to one from the Latin side of that great, and sad divide.

[6] cf. Brock 2001. Dr. Brock has written extensively on the roots of Syrian culture. My remarks depend heavily on his writings.

[7] Upson-Saia discusses this connection in paragraphs 5 and 6, and provides some bibliography for modern study of it. Her term "Freeze-frame Exegesis" is an attempt to capture the quality of pausing on a moment or scene in Scripture to draw out its implications and interior more fully. A good example of this Jewish tenor and mixing of Scripture with reflection can be found in Hansbury, Homily 3, pp. 82-83, where Mary reflects on how various groups of women will rejoice at her Son's reversal of the effects of the sin of Eve.

imaginations of their audiences)[8] already knew a kind of work that used disputation as a tool to sketch out the strengths and weaknesses of divergent positions on important points of the day. Poems that focus on disputes between pairs of characters reach all the way back in time to Sumerian literature surviving on clay tablets written in cuneiform script. Their culture was accustomed to literature that advanced through the interaction of its characters. Syriac authors continued to use this genre in the Christian period for their own purposes.[9]

Materials for Study

There are 43 surviving Syriac Dispute Poems known to modern scholarship,[10] some six of which feature Our Lady. Their influence was felt in Syriac literature beyond the narrow bounds that modern scholars draw for their genre, so we

---

[8] I mean both "imagination" and "audience" in their literal senses when I use them in this paper. By "imagination" I mean the ability to make an image or picture of something or someone in the mind. It has no overtone of this image being fictional, as "imaginary" does when we commonly use the word. I mean "audience" as the group or groups of people who were expected to hear the works in question. The pieces we are going to examine were usually performed at liturgical worship, so their "audiences" would also have been worshipping congregations. I think the term "audience" is useful, though, because it carries, to me at least, more of a musical connotation than any other word that has occurred to me. The singing or chanting of these pieces was an important part of their life in the Church.

[9] See Brock 1999. Brock's evocation of the genre shows its potential for the Christian thinker, VII, 114-115:

> "In many cases, however, the biblical dispute poems retain the static quality of the genre in its original form; thus, for example in the case of the Angel and Mary we have an exploration, moving inwards, of Mary's psychological reaction to the Angel's extraordinary message. What we have here is, as it were, a still photograph extracted from a cinematographic sequence of the biblical narrative and then studied in detail."

The congruence of this picture with Upson-Saia's "Freeze-frame Exegesis" seems clear.

[10] As in the catalogue in Brock 1999, 116-119.

should not let their small number turn us away. We also have other material to study that shares much of its sensibility with the Dispute Poems. Jacob of Serug (ca 451-521) is the author of some metrical homilies concerning Our Lady that include passages of dialogue and characterization that owe much of their sensibility to the genre of the Dispute Poem. His works will provide the center of our picture. He is the author of the most useful material we have to work with whose authorship is known.

All these materials provide glimpses of ideas and images that were current among Syrians in Late Antiquity and, because of their continuing use, more recently. Their survival shows that they have been read and known in the Syrian churches. Their use in liturgical settings shows that they are not oddities but were deemed acceptable to the Syrian mainstream. For all these reasons, I will use them synthetically to try to pull together their scattered elements to achieve as rounded a picture of how Our Lady has looked to Syrian eyes as I can. Since my goal is to offer the riches of an aspect of the Syrian Tradition that is not echoed in the western churches (for the Greeks are "west" to the Syrians, just as we Latins are), I think I will be more successful if I try to make them speak with a unified voice. I also think this approach will better reflect how these works sound to the ears of Syrian Christians in our own day.

Mary in Unexpected Circumstances

Our treatment of Our Lady's life will begin with the Annunciation. The extra-canonical works dealing with Mary, such as *The Protevangelium of James* and *de Transitu Mariae* do survive in Syriac versions of relatively early date[11] but the canonical scriptural record is incomparably more influential and

---

[11] The end of the 5th century and the beginning of the 6th century, according to Ortiz de Urbina, *Patrologia* 93.

provides more material than we will need for our purposes, today. It does not make sense to stray beyond it.

Before we look at our first passage, we should remember the tendency, inherited from Jewish exegesis, to include the scriptural text in a writing while expanding it and commenting on it. This is characteristic of Oriental Christian traditions, so it is fitting that this technique appears in our first look at a Dialogue Poem. Listen to this creative offering of a possible conversational exchange that was not included in the gospel canon:

> The Watcher[12] spoke to the maiden,
> "Do not be upset, Mary; salutation to you,
> for you will conceive and give birth to the
> Wonderful; from your womb the Sun shall shine
> forth, and he will drive out the world's darkness."

> Mary says to the angel,
> "Explain to me, O fiery being[13], what you mean.
> Your appearance is weighty, your raiment is of
> flame, your lips are fire as they utter. Who is able
> to speak with you?

> "Your exalted manner of speech belongs
> elsewhere, why do you speak like us and with us?
> Your appearance is exalted and not of this earth;
> if there is some race of fiery beings then it is to it
> that you belong, O fearsome hero.

---

[12] This is a common Syriac term for one of the heavenly host who 'watches' because he stands before the face of God.
[13] Fire is a common Syriac symbol for spirit. Oriental icons frequently show the saints with flames over their heads when western Christians would use haloes. "Man of fire," "fiery being," or "offspring of flame" all mean "a spiritual being in human form" in the idiom of the West.

"O offspring of flame, explain to me the manner
concerning which you speak, for you have
announced a birth—yet I have known no man,
Your message is fearsome, like yourself:
your voice and your words are just like your
appearance.

"How can there be conception without a man?
How can a virgin give birth?
Who has ever beheld a crop without any seed?
Explain to me what it is you are saying,
how all this can possibly take place."

The Watcher replied, "It is the Holy Spirit who
will come to you and make holy your womb:
then the Power of the Most High shall descend
and reside in you; from your womb shall Riches
shine out --to pay all the debts of the world." [14]

This last stanza shows that Our Lady's unwillingness to accept the unexpected without reason is the central point of the piece. Mary knows how the created order conducts itself and crops do not appear without seeds. In order for her to allow that the world has behaved against its nature, she must be offered a supernatural cause as an explanation. This is why the Angel's declaration of God's coming personal involvement pulls her out of her confusion. It is perfectly natural for the Creation to act at the direction of its Creator. Her objection is not overborne so much as it is satisfied. This is why the Angel's introduction of the Holy Spirit ends the hymn and the discussion.

It is interesting that another Syriac hymn has the Angel offering the case of Elizabeth and John the Baptist as corroboration of his story.[15] In the context of a tale that

---

[14] Ibid., 88, stanzas 9-14.
[15] Bride of Light 45, 138, lines 90-103.

includes Mary expressing a desire for a reason to accede to Gabriel's announcement, this demonstration of a related miracle shows us God offering evidence for His divine actions that resides on the human level. It also allows for a theological motive for the Visitation of Mary to Elizabeth, above and beyond the natural desire of two expectant ladies to talk things over. This mixing of motives is a good example of how the Syrian Tradition views the biblical characters as real people living real lives. The purely human level of the drama is not down-played but is sensitively woven into the fabric of the whole. When, later in the same hymn, Mary is shown trying to make sense of her pregnancy after it has already begun, we see again this marshalling of evidence that she can grasp. She raises the possibility that she is suffering an hysterical pregnancy or that Satan has made use of her for his own purposes, which is unusual in a presentation of her thoughts and adds to the sense of urgency in her speech with her kinswoman.[16] Elizabeth's case offers a comprehensible piece of evidence to which she can have direct access. It is in search of that access that she sets off to see her cousin. The Son has already entered her and still she ponders. Until her mind is satisfied, she will not cease her reflections.

---

[16] Ibid. 139, lines 125-138:
> The blessed girl stood there,
> Pondering in her heart as follows,
> "Could it be that I am pregnant with wind,
> Just as can happen with others?
> Could it be that this was Satan
>
> Who has deceived me?
> I will go up and see this very day
> Whether it really is that Old Age has conceived:
> If it turn out that aged Elizabeth is not pregnant,
> Then it is Satan who has deluded me;
>
> But if Old Age has indeed conceived,
> Then it is with God that I am pregnant". Mary arose to go
> up, Bearing God himself.

In the Syrian imagination, Mary's questioning is the vehicle for her to learn things that lie beyond the bounds of her immediate present concern. We find her unusual opportunity to broaden her understanding acknowledged by Gabriel. In Jacob of Serug's *First Homily on the Nativity*, Mary's conversation draws from the Angel a confession of his own limits and an acknowledgement of the special knowledge and closeness to God that her status brings.

> The watcher said: "It is enough girl, conclude your discourse! My Lord is concealed and His place is hidden and his name is a secret.
>
> He is exalted above us and He is concealed from you and is hidden from all. He is distant with His Father, and He dwells with you, and how can you **investigate**?
>
> I have not seen Him, but to you who are His mother, behold He will be made manifest.
> He is concealed from our race and how I should speak of him, I do not know.
>
> His voice is heard by me but as for His appearance, I am not capable of (seeing it).
> His voice is in my ears while His place is alien to my eyes.
>
> That He is coming to you, I have heard from Him, and behold, I have announced it to you. Maybe He is in you; learn the truth from Him." [17]

We should notice that the Angel, himself, does not know how to speak about the Father. The message he passes along to Mary is all new to him and he does not claim to have special knowledge of it. This is an important point to keep in

---

[17] Kollamparampil 1, 51, lines 209-218.

mind. We should also notice the fact that the Angel was not, apparently, merely waiting for any opening to tell her all that he could. What he does know is drawn out of him by Mary's words.

Jacob goes on in the next lines of the hymn to show Mary over-riding the angel's speech "because she was sagacious." Jacob teaches that the manner and content of her speech are important aspects of her involvement in this process. Her response to this unprecedented communication from the Almighty draws approval from the hymnographer for its intelligence and effectiveness. In this passage, she is not only 'sagacious,' but she is also 'prudent,' 'not hasty,' 'not an infant'[18] and will not allow the Angel to leave 'unless [she] ha[s] learned the truth.'

> Mary became alarmed at the wonder that the
> watcher told of but she was not convinced that
> she should not ask a question, because she was
> sagacious.

> She pressed on prudently to learn from the angel
> so that the truth might not be hidden from her
> while it was being explained.

> "O fiery one, if you are not propounding any
> explanation in my ears the story that you are telling
> will not be accepted.

> Give me heed and I shall learn from you the truth;
> make manifest your word, do not speak to me by
> way of signs.

---

[18] The Syriac word translated here by 'infant' appears twice in the Syriac New Testament: in *Hebrews* 5:13 and *1 Peter* 2:2, both times as a term denoting a lack of advanced theological understanding.

I am not hasty as my mother Eve who was cajoled:
because she believed out of a single saying, she
tasted death.

She did not ask her messenger that [sic] how it
would happen that from the tree divinity should
reach her.

If she had asked she would have vanquished him;
therefore, allow me to approach you with a
question, do not be reluctant.

Not even the announcement of the serpent was
more terrible than yours if your explanation is not
more believable than his.

I am not an infant like her who became a snare to
her husband, for unless I have learned the truth,
you shall not depart.

Behold, she had wanted (to become) a goddess
which would be beyond (her) nature and you have
announced to me a conception without marital
union.

The purpose is the same; if the explanation does
not distinguish it; and without argumentation your
word will not be heard by me. [19]

Mary presses the Angel for more information and explicitly
refers to Eve who did not do as she should have done. So, the
hymn makes clear that her aggressiveness is not a sign of a
desire to pry into things she should let alone but comes from
her knowledge that her fore-mother strayed due, in part, to a
lack of knowledge and a lack of willingness to demand
explanations. Her pressing climaxes with these lines:

---

[19] Kollamparampil 1, 51-52, lines 219-240.

If you do not give me [an] explanation it is difficult
for me to be convinced and if you do not debate
with me unto the end, you are not true. [20]

This couplet is a demand for reasoned discourse as the *sine qua non* of Our Lady's involvement in the future the Angel is proposing. The voice of Jacob describing the Angel's reaction to this rather confrontational speech of Mary shows that, in his opinion at least, the Syrian believer was expected to approve of this sort of behavior. The angel has this unspoken evaluation of her in his mind before he begins his reply:

> The angel heard the disputation of the sagacious
> woman and wonder laid hold of him and the
> skilful teacher began explaining about the things to
> come.

> He wondered about the young girl who was subtle
> in her questions and his language floated over the
> explanation to demonstrate it to her.

> He saw that she was eager to **inquire** about the
> truth. He was prepared to demonstrate it to her
> exactly.

> He saw the young girl who was sharp in (her)
> replies, and he polished his word to speak with her
> the fearful things: [21]

Her high-level theological activity requires more from him than he might otherwise have offered. He is surprised at her able argumentation. Gabriel cannot just chat away with her; he finds he must "polish" his speech to bring it up to her level. It makes a difference to the conduct of the interview that she is so

---

[20] Ibid., 53, lines 255-256.
[21] Ibid., 53, lines 257-264.

canny. More information is forth-coming for Mary than would have been if she had been shy.

It is not only Mary, of course, who demonstrates a fully-developed grasp of the import of these events in Syriac literature. The Syrian tradition, itself, has a keen sense of Mary as being set apart by these meetings with unexpected visitors and by her taking on the burden of bearing the Word of God. We can see clear signs that the Syrians did not imagine Our Lady as fitting neatly into the Christian theological norm; she was a unique case. This is shown in the way that the Syrians used their own tradition to emphasize her singularity. When Jacob wants to stress Mary's active and aggressive behavior he employs the standard contrast with Eve but does so in a way that strikes directly against the tenor of his own theological tradition. Listen to this extended passage from one of Jacob's hymns.

"Hail, Mary, our Lord is with you," he was saying to her, "you will conceive and bear a son in your virginity."

She said to him: "How will this be as you say, Since I am a virgin and there is no fruit of virgins?"

In that moment it was very necessary to question, so that the mystery of the Son dwelling in her might be explained to her.

Mary **inquired** in order that we might learn from the angel concerning that conception which is a sublime matter beyond understanding.

Behold how most fair is Mary to the one who beholds her, and how loveable these things of hers to the ones who are capable of discerning.

This one **inquires** that she might learn from him about her conception, because it was hers and for the profit of the one who listens to her.

Eve had not questioned the serpent when he led her astray, she who by her will kept silent and firmly believed the treachery.

The latter maiden heard truth from the faithful one, nevertheless in this way she had sought out an explanation.

The former heard of becoming a goddess from a tree, but she did not say: "How will what you mention ever happen?"

The Watcher told this one that she would conceive the Son of God, but she did not accept it until she was well informed.

That she in her person would ascend to the divine rank, the virgin wife of Adam did not doubt the liar.

To this one who would bear the Son of God it was told, But she **inquired, sought, investigated, learned** and then kept silent.[22]

See now how much more beautiful is the latter than the former; because of her beauty, the Lord chose her and made her his Mother.

It was easy for her to keep silence and easy also to ask questions; by her discernment she learned the truth from the angel.

---

[22] The bold type face is my own emphasis.

As reprehensible as Eve was by her deed, so Mary was glorious, and as the folly of this one, so that one's wisdom is shown up. [23]

"Inquired, sought, investigated, learned" are all red-flag words that Ephraem the Syrian, the greatest name in the Syrian theological tradition, had spent much time debating.[24] By

[23] Hansbury, Homily 1, 31-33.

[24] Harvey 2001, 119, points out this fact. This line is very striking for a reader of Syriac theological works. These words and some of the theological difficulties that they give rise to in the mind of St. Ephraem are discussed in Russell 1994 and Russell 2000. Interested readers might look at hymns 55, 56, 65, 66, 67, 68 and 69 in the collection of St. Ephraem's works that we call *The Hymns on Faith* for an idea of how Ephraem speaks of these activities. These stanzas, 9-13, of hymn 55 give some idea of the mixture of futility and blasphemy that Ephraem thought was involved when creatures presumed to approach their Creator in this manner.

> 9. My beloved, who can handle or bind something which does not exist?
> That is how hard and difficult it is for you to inquire into His Being.
> Look, my son, at how restricted [you are] in the face of searching Him out,
> because a thing which does not exist testifies in this regard of something which does exist:
> investigation of Him cannot be altogether handled.
>
> 10. Let us learn from this and by this how much everything which gazes at the First Being goes astray
> because, when there was nothing, He was in existence and there is no explanation as to how.
> There is also another distraction, as many times as one approaches Him: how He ever begot has never been understood.
>
> 11. Let us speak from Him about Him: how great is the necessity that you should confess His Essence!
> [You are] constrained without persuasion, because a great persuasion comes from everything,
> (therefore there is indeed constraint) to magnify His Fatherhood without disputation or investigation,
> because a disputation arises from everything.

In order for you to inquire into His Fatherhood you have [already] inquired into His Essence.

12 Who would not honor the two in silence,
for they are concealed from everything and at the same time
mixed together, whether disputing or at once winning a victory?
His Fatherhood is good, His Essence is fearsome:
they help each other out in the way [a person's] hands do,
because their crown is one.

13 Who is there among those with speech whose power of
speech has the capability for him to express the Lord of All
Languages in all languages which had never expressed Him?
Something which can be completely expressed is [what] we are
also: its nature is our fellow.
There is One, though, Which is not a servant because His Father
is the Lord.

These opening stanzas of Hymn 66 may be even easier to grasp:

1 Whoever was insolent forgot himself
and wanted to define his Maker,
though he was a grain of dust.

Refrain: Glory to the Son!

2 Whoever has realized that he is dust
will acknowledge the finger which formed him
and established him.

3 Controversy fell in among the disputers
so that they might [try to] measure the great ocean
as [one would] a pond.

4 He removed them into a great mountain and, behold, they were
vexed to inquire into its size with a scale.

5 He provoked them with the hidden sun and put them in the
dark. It did not come to pass that they could see,
[but] only inquire.

6 [Those] who were cleansed by the Three,
behold, they have been defiled
in that they were divided with respect to Their names.

208

declaring that Mary "inquired, sought, investigated, learned" before she "kept silent," which "silence" Ephraem would see as a sign of high theological understanding and religious development, Jacob was turning these usually blasphemous activities into the core of Mary's contribution to the sum of Christian religious understanding. Mary's heroic and effective response to the entry of God into her life is a photographic negative of Eve's response to the snake but it is also exactly the sort of activity that the Syrian Tradition was teaching its members not to pursue. In this regard, Our Lady was not viewed as an example for all to follow but, rather, as a unique case that should not be imitated. This is very strong stuff for Jacob to be putting forward, since it risks a whiff of blasphemy as well as of theological incorrectness, but it is carefully chosen to show that Mary is unusual, a real boundary breaker in Theology, not just on the lesser level of gender roles.[25]

If one combines a sensitivity to his concerns about presumption with his approval of silence as an appropriate human stance in the face of the Divine (the subject of Russell 2000) one can appreciate how shocking and ground-breaking Jacob's picture of Mary as engaging in these forbidden things (and then keeping silence) would have seemed to the Syrian listener. Instead of them barring her way to that blessed state, these activities seem to be her ladder to it. Both Mary, and her hymner Jacob, are breaking down boundaries here!
There are many works on St. Ephraem that study this element in his thought. The fullest source for works on St. Ephraem can be found in den Biesen 2002.

[25] Harvey 2003, 49-51, points out this positive picture of Mary's active involvement in theological debate. Upson-Saia, on the other hand, paragraphs 28-30, reads the hesitation evinced by Mary in the Dialogue Poems as constituting a negative portrayal of her. I think this is exactly what the poems do not intend. Upson-Saia sees in *The Dialogue between Mary and the Angel* "a negative depiction of Mary's intelligence" and says "a concept such as the incarnation is simply too complicated for Mary's weak understanding." Of course, she is not including Jacob of Serug's hymns in her study, but I think that the slighting of Mary that she sees in these dialogues is not present in the text. I should note that Upson-Saia does, in par. 30, finally see approval of Mary's "persistence to find her Son and to understand the significance of His resurrection." Still, I

The Breadth of Mary's Understanding

It is interesting to see that the Syrian Tradition does not take all the expression of her place in the grand theological scheme on itself. That is, it does not only produce works in which the writer, himself, expresses a sense of theological and salvation history. It also imagines that this was something that was known to Mary and served as one of her motives for action. Reflecting on a gospel story that is very ready to depict its Christian characters as confused or ignorant, the Syrian Tradition produces a picture of Mary that is a portrait of a person who moves self-consciously forward as she responds to her religious and theological convictions.

Her knowledge is not limited to the aspects of the story that involve her most directly, either. The following lines, spoken by Mary to the infant Jesus, show that she has a grasp of soteriology and the proper role of God's Messiah in the world.

19. Let Eve, our aged mother, now hear and come
as I speak; let her head, once bowed in her naked
state in the Garden, be raised up.

20. Let her reveal her face and sing to You, for
shamefacedness has passed away in You;
let her hear the message full of peace,
for her daughter has repaid her debt.

---

think she has mistaken the meaning of the dramatic elements in the dialogues: rather than intending to slight Mary's intellect, I think that initial bewilderment is intended to highlight the unexpectedness of the situation, the uncomfortable nature of what is being proposed to her and the need for Mary to have great fortitude and intelligence to respond to that proposal with engagement rather than frozen uncertainty. In my opinion, we must grasp the over-turning of our own theological expectations along with Mary's personal and matrimonial expectations if we are to understand what these poems are trying to teach us.

21. The serpent that led her astray is trampled down in You, the Root that has shone forth from my womb.

The cherub and the sword are routed by You, and Adam, who was driven out, shall return.

22. Eve and Adam shall seek refuge in You

23. The banished servants shall return in You

24 .You shall shine out in Sheol over their dejected state

25. In You shall Sheol's prisoners come forth

26. In You all the hungry shall have their fill[26]

These lines are designed to show that Mary realizes the completeness of the salvation offered in Jesus Christ. One important part of this picture is Mary's realization that Jesus will repair the effects of the Fall. This is the reason for her to point out that Eve was both her mother and the mother of the Savior she holds in her arms. Our Lady realizes that her life's mirroring echo of Eve's life is necessary for the unbounded nature of the Divine actions she is participating in. Thus, Mary is not unwittingly providing a reworking of Eve's disastrous career; she is doing so in full awareness of it. The Syrian Tradition made much of Our Lady's understanding of the Incarnation and its effects.

The closeness of Mary to God, both physically and spiritually, is a common theme across the Christian Tradition. Her theological acumen is, perhaps, not so widely touted. It is especially interesting, then, to see that it becomes quite

---

[26] Bride of Light, 77-78, stanzas 19-26. Only selected lines are quoted, each is marked by its stanza number.

prominent in the Syrian imagination, even of her most human and maternal moments. We can see signs of it when she croons to her baby.

> Since You are my son, I will sing to You;
> since I have become Your mother, I will honour
> You. I gave birth to You, my Son, yet You are far
> older than I; I carry You, the Lord who carries me!
>
> My mind is distracted in awe at You; gather my
> thoughts so that I may praise You.
> I wonder at how still You are,
> for within You lies thunder concealed. [27]

Indeed, she is given so much credit for theological acumen that her knowledge is spoken of in the same breath as that of the Father. This following comment comes from Jacob of Serug as he describes the Visitation:

> The message of the Son had begun to reveal itself
> and it was proclaimed by angels and by men.
>
> No one but the Father perceived the mystery of
> the Son, and the Father sent it to the daughter of
> David by means of Gabriel.
>
> Only Mary learned that hidden mystery,
> but she did not reveal to anyone what was spoken
> to her by the angel. [28] [On mystery ...[29]]

[27] Bride of Light, 76, stanzas 6-7. Stanzas 14, 15 and 17 offer more paradoxes of the Incarnation.
[28] Hansbury, 52, Homily II.
[29] See Russell 2004 for a discussion of how two central Patristic writers, one of them Ephraem the Syrian, tried to make sense of how the Bible speaks of knowledge and of how knowledge reveals a person's essential nature. For an early Christian author to speak of Mary "learning" in that context is to credit her with being intimately acquainted with a primordial mystery.

It is important to understand that Mary's role in theological and soteriological matters is seen to be unique, but connective. It is true that her life and actions are not put forward as a model for general imitation and that her theological approach, while highly praised, lies far outside the bounds of what was thought to be appropriate for the general sort of Christian believer. Still, this does not mean that Our Lady was thought to be an isolated figure. Indeed, it is the fact that what she does and how she does it is understood to have universal consequences that is the spur to the Syrian interest in her. She performs a role that none other can undertake but it is one that has effects on all reasoning creatures. Jacob describes that aspect of her significance in this way:

> Blessed Mary, who by her question to Gabriel, taught the world this mystery which was concealed.
>
> For if she had not asked him how it would be, we would not have learned the explanation of the matter of the Son.
>
> The beauty of the matter which appeared openly is because of her; she was the reason that it was explained to us by the angel.
>
> By that question, the wise one became the mouth of the Church; she learned that interpretation for all Creation.
>
> For if Mary had not had sublime impulses, she would not have arrived to speak before the Watcher.
>
> If she had not possessed inner and outer beauty, Gabriel also would not have answered her with eloquence.

> She rose up to this measure on her own,
> until the Spirit, that perfecter of all came to her. [30]

So, our knowledge has been increased beyond its previous bounds by Mary's intelligent interaction with her angelic visitor. Jacob can call her "the wise one" because he has just been describing the way in which she earned that title. She is an archetype of the Church in that her speech is aided by the Holy Spirit and the Spirit enables her to engage in theological inquiry and proclamation. I think that the mention of her "inner and outer beauty" is not meant to convey an image of physical comeliness as much as to say that her theological acumen, which would be interior, was matched by appropriate behavior, visible to those around her. In other words, the result of the Holy Ghost coming upon her was to render her a rounded, complete religious being.

One of the most astounding aspects of the Syrian portrait of Mary is how fully it develops a depiction of her as a functioning theologian on the highest level. She is "the mouth of the Church," not just someone whose praises the Church should sing. That special quality comes not just from the content of her speech but from the heart of the one who spoke it, as this couplet makes clear. Jacob wants to say that Mary's speech is true Theology and is the fruit of loving faith rather than arid intellectualizing:

> Her utterance surpassed the joyful noise of the
> sons of heaven because she sang eagerly to her son
> lovingly. [31]

Mary, then, serves not only to sketch out some of the possibilities of human life through her own actions, but also to show how humans can engage in a proper approach to, and meditation on, God. Jacob seems to be saying that it is the love

---

[30] Hansbury, 38, Homily I.
[31] Kollamparampil, 88, Homily 1, lines 1029-1030.

with which His mother addresses Him that turns her words from blasphemous presumption into speech that surpasses the sons of heaven. Her maternal love makes presumption into praise.

See how even the manner of Gabriel's communication with her is affected by her manner of receiving it. A look back at the quote from above now shows us more about Mary, in light of these later lines.[32] We see that it is because her inquiry is sparked by a desire for "the truth" rather than presumption that the Angel responds openly to it. This connection between the manner and meaning of theological discourse is made even more explicit when, later in the same piece, Jacob shows her activity being met with a positive Divine response against a backdrop of others whose activities met with Divine disapproval.

> There are two aspects for the word when it is debated; one that of contention and the other of love among discerning ones.

> Because Mary questioned, she was not blamed by the angel. She was eager to learn; she was not given over to **investigate**.[33]

> Zachariah had been rebuked because he asked in the holy of holies, and the sentence of silence was given for the doubting speech.

> To the same instructor both have brought the same question but to both of them not the same aspect was shown in his discourse.
> The watcher blamed the priest because he asked: "How shall it happen?"

---

[32] Kollamparampil, 53, Homily I, lines 259-264.
[33] Note, again, the use of this red flag term.

But to the young girl he gave the crown of explanation, not blaming her.

Not having believed (at first), Thomas shone forth (later) in faith for that womb of doubt too gave birth to the truth.

But with regard to Eve the lack of doubt produced death for by the fact that she gave credence she was won over because she did not debate.

The aged Zachariah was convicted because he had questioned, for he was there where there was not even any need for questions.

Since Mary **inquired** she crushed **inquiry** from the audacious, and by her question she set down **silence** to the disputations.

If she had not stirred up a disputation with the watcher disputation would have increased in the world concerning her birth-giving.

If she had been **silent** when she had heard (the words), "Behold, the Lord is with you", iniquitous disputation would have choked the whole world.

Although the watcher explained to her the matter, there is (still) controversy and although the angel revealed to her the truth, disputation has increased.

If the girl has not **inquired**, "How it will happen?" the fiery one too might have neglected (giving) an explanation.

> Blessed is Mary who became an occasion for the
> hidden matter, so that it might be said clearly by
> the angel.

Without a question, explanation is mute and it is not told, and
without request not even the truth is able to demonstrate
itself.[34]

What a catalogue this is! Mary's speech has the right
manner and intention to make it pleasing to God. Zechariah's
speech was inappropriate and he was punished by being
condemned to silence. Eve did wrong because she did not enter
into debate at all when she should have (so error can be found
in both speech and silence). Mary's inquiry, though, was of a
sort to stamp down inquiry among "the audacious," who would
undertake inquiry in a destructive spirit. Her "disputation"
served to reduce the amount of disputation in the world. Her
drawing more of "the hidden matter" out of the angel was a
cause for her to be blessed.

One of the reasons that Our Lady's inquiry might have
received approval is that it does not seem to have set her
against the work of God in the world but to have served to ally
her with that work. The Syrians enjoy the freedom of
imagination on the topic of the relations between human free
will and divine action that comes from not having partaken in
the Latin agonies on that subject. This freedom allows them to
imagine the encounter between Mary and Gabriel as an
encounter between two rational creatures who had a lot of
things of extraordinary interest to talk about rather than of two
beings involved in an intricate dance whose steps remain
known to their Creator alone.

Listen to these remarkable lines from the pen of Jacob
of Serug:

---

[34] Ibid., 57-58, lines 331-360.

That moment was full of wonder when Mary was
standing, conversing in argument with Gabriel.
One humble daughter of poor folk and one angel
met each other and spoke of a wonderful tale.

A pure virgin and a fiery Watcher spoke with
wonder: a discourse which reconciled dwellers of
earth and heaven.

One woman and the prince of all the hosts
had made an agreement for the reconciliation of
the whole world.

The two had sat between heavenly beings and
earthly ones; they spoke, attended to and made
peace for those who were wroth.

Maiden and Watcher met each other and
conversed in argument on the matter until they
abolished the conflict between the Lord and
Adam.

That great strife which occurred amidst the trees
came up for discussion, and it all came to an end;
there was peace.

An earthly being and a heavenly one spoke with
love; The struggle between the two sides ceased,
and they were at peace. [35]

This scene emphasizes the reality of the two characters and the
importance of their actions. It stresses, again, the importance of
the fact that they spoke to each other "with love." The human
element in the working out of the Incarnation is also
emphasized by Jacob's pointing out that Mary not only acts as a
free agent in this scene, she also acts as a counterpart to "the

---

[35] Hansbury, 29, Homily I.

prince of all the hosts." Our Lady is an equal interlocutor with one of the greatest of creatures.

In another hymn, Jacob works to draw out the implications of this scene for his audience. His approving description of Our Lady's inquiry proceeds to a description of her preparation to receive her Lord, modeled on the preparation of a bride to receive her bridegroom. (She can be described as performing a number of tasks as a part of this preparation because Jacob has no grace/faith-faith/works sinkholes to avoid.) Mary, then, is being imagined as being her Son's physical mother and spiritual bride at one and the same time and both of these glorious roles come to her as a result of her appropriate theological engagement with the Angel.[36] Her humble obedience is an informed choice based on her earlier reasoning. She supports the Incarnation, both with her intellect and her heart.

This long passage is good evidence of the delicacy with which Jacob handles Mary's involvement in the Incarnation. While playing with the audience's expectations of what he would say about "inquiry" (that it is bad) and reverent silence (that it is the highest religious attitude), Jacob presents Mary as a faithful housewife, cleansing herself to receive the Divine Presence, but doing so in a completely unexpected way.

---

[36] This mixing of the multiple relations between Jesus and His mother had appeared earlier in Syriac literature in the works of the renowned Ephraem. Beggiani, 97, offers three delightful stanzas of this from the 16th of his *Hymns on the nativity*. The following shorter excerpt from the 11th of that collection that he also includes will give a taste of its flavor.

> She alone is Your mother, but she is Your sister with
> everyone else. She was Your mother, she was [Y]our
> sister, she was Your bride too along with all chaste souls.

The Syrians could play happily while remaining very serious about the message they were conveying.

- She cleanses her mouth by the "inquiries," as Isaiah's lips were purified in the Temple by the coal.
- She makes clear that this unusual behavior will not become habitual for her by giving her word that she will not again "inquire" in this way. (This tells the audience that "inquiry" is not for them, either.)
- She sprinkles her pure temple (that is, herself) "with love" to prepare for the Holy One. (This shows her in a very traditional role as the tabernacle or Temple that will contain the Word.[37])
- She pours out her good deeds as oil into her lamp, so she is a wise virgin, not a foolish one.
- She prepares the house with fragrant prayers and her praises are "sweet spices," so she is firmly in the Old Testament tradition of right worship.

This catalogue of religious housewifery culminates in a successful ending:

> And while the house was made radiant by these things in a holy manner, the Son of the King entered and dwelt in the shrine of virginity.

If we do not recall that all of this began with the cleansing of her mouth by her inquiries, we will miss Our Lady's unique response to the task of preparing for her unique arrival and will have lost the realization that these images describe an intellectual and religious process, not practical housekeeping. The length of the list of images, and even their homely flavor, are Jacob's response to the puzzle of how to domesticate (both literally and figuratively) the shockingly forward and intellectually adventurous lady he is describing. Mary ends by proclaiming herself "the handmaid of the Lord"

---

[37] Brock 1982, 186, notes the tendency of Syrian writers to use as images of Mary "objects that *contain* something holy." These lines referring to "her pure temple" and "her house" and going on to expand on those images fall into the heart of that kind of speech.

220

in good gospel fashion, but we should not overlook that the phrases "her will" and "free will" both appear in the final couplet of our passage. This is a description of a free agent taking her place in the economy of salvation and doing so with both her mind and her religious life fully engaged in the process.[38]

> See, the **inquiry** of the blessed woman, how beneficial it was!
> For, if she had kept **silent** this truth would not have shone forth.
>
> She asked, learned, and henceforth she did not doubt. The truth shone forth to her and after she saw it she did not **inquire** into it.
>
> She refined her senses and cleansed her mouth by the **inquiries**.
> She bound her word so that she might not again **inquire** into reverential matters.
>
> She heard the voice (saying) that the power of the Exalted One is coming to her,
> and again she did not **inquire** into the matter of how, or by whom or on what account.
>
> She gathered and removed all (such) reckonings from her mind.
> She sprinkled her pure temple with love before the Holy One.
>
> She swept her house with the holiness that was within her, and she embellished its inner walls with all kinds (of acts) of reverence.

---

[38] Kollamparampil, 59-60, *First Homily on the Nativity*, lines 383-418.

Again in it she set in order the good signets of
perfection.
She replenished it with the blossoms of all
manners of modesty.

She levelled its land with the choice implements of
virginity.
She hung up as ornaments, crowns of praises of
watchful care.

She took up and laced together veils out of
chastity;
She spread out and stretched out spacious
garments of watchfulness.

She poured out as oil, good deeds in her lamp
and her great flame has been inflamed in the
temple of her body.

She burned the fragrance of her prayers warmly
so that the pure fire of her faith should serve as
incense.

She threw, as sweet spices, the sounds of praise
into the fire of her love and from her thanksgiving
breathed the fragrance of choice incense.

Her words went out like guards from the royal
court so that the Royal Son might enter along with
them by the door of the ear.

And while the house was made radiant by these
things in a holy manner,
the Son of the King entered and dwelt in the
shrine of virginity.

She answered to the watcher with great love, "Let
your Lord come.

Behold, I am prepared so that according to His
will He might dwell within me.

Behold, I am the handmaid of the Lord as you are
His servant and if He has directed His will towards
me, I do not flee away."

Let it happen to me, according to your word sir,"
Mary said.
She gave her consent and henceforth she received
the fruit in her womb.

She by her will opened the door and then the King
entered, so that through free will the perfect seal
might be honoured.[39]

The reality of the human drama of the Incarnation (and
of the people involved) makes more prominent another aspect
of this picture of freedom. Even as Mary seems to be described
as more spiritually advanced, she never loses her firm anchoring
in the reality of her time and place. Thus, she continues to be
an individual human being despite her actions' universal effects.
This makes the Incarnation more immediate and tangible.

Conclusion

Where does all of that leave us? The first point to take
away from an examination of these small leavings of the Syriac
patrimony of the Church is that its teaching on the mother of
Jesus does include the main emphases of more western
Christians. For example, though we have not examined the
Syrian treatment of the trope of God's protective care of Mary,
it is not neglected by them. For example, in a piece handed
down in the Syriac Tradition,[40] Mary is being reviled in the
Temple for her unchaste life, as evidenced by her pregnancy

---

[39] Ibid.
[40] Bride of Light #47, 154, lines 250-271

before marriage. She prays "toward her womb" rather than toward Heaven (or the Temple altar) and asks for support in stilling the commotion. Her Son, from within her womb, makes her shine with glory, an Old Testament testimony of the presence and power of God that strikes all the priests dumb.[41] This sort of scene could be matched with many similar ones in Syriac works, but shows nothing peculiar to their picture of Our Lady.

The second point that comes to my mind is the effect that the close typological tie between Eve and Mary has on the Syrian understanding of Our Lady. Because it was Eve's actions, not her nature, that began the Fall in Eden, the Syrians were convinced that Our Lady must mirror those actions in order for the Salvation that comes through her to meet the case.[42]

- Where Eve does not bother to ask questions of the snake, Mary interrogates Gabriel.
- Where Eve brings labor to humans and discord between Creator and Creation, Mary brings peace and harmony.
- Where Eve reaches out for the forbidden fruit, Mary actively signs on to the Divine economy of salvation.

This is, in no way, a dismissal of the primacy or sole-sufficiency of grace to save us, in the Syrians' minds or in mine, but it is a claim that active and intelligent human acquiescence is necessary to rescind the earlier passive and unintelligent signing on to disobedience.

That leaves us, as a third point, the conclusion that, in the Syrian imagination, Our Lady did not serve as a static icon of virtue, whether maidenly or human, but as an example of

---

[41] cf, e.g., *Exodus* 34:29 where Moses' face shines when he descends from speaking to the Lord in the cloud on the mountain.
[42] This point has been made many times by Brock, Harvey et al.

right human action. Some of her actions seem to have been thought to be peculiar to herself (no Syrian author was likely to urge his listeners on aggressively to undertake inquisitive theological investigations) but some, surely, were seen as models to emulate:

- Mary's insistence on being given reasoned arguments before she would accept Gabriel's message,
- Her ready acquiescence once she had been given grounds for doing so,
- and her often-demonstrated sense of the coherence of God's actions in the world throughout history, and
- her loving approach to her Son that renders her every word and action pious rather than pushing
  must all have been held before the congregations as being worthy of any Christian believer.

Christianity is not a religion that expects, or desires, mindless obedience to its tenets from its adherents. It is, rather, a faith that desires both trust and thought, both humility and intelligent consideration. The gospels already, with their two mentions of Mary's quiet personal reflections in the midst of her suddenly surprising life,[43] as well as their striking evidence of her steadfast loyalty in following her Son all the way to Jerusalem, even to taking her stand at the foot of the Cross, had set the stage for this kind of dual portrait of her. It was the genius of the Syrian Christians to use their cultural armory to expound and deepen those elements in the picture of Mary so their liturgy could offer the people an opportunity to dwell on her life and reflect on her character. We are fortunate that Providence has allowed us enough of their writings so that we have the chance to stand alongside them as they reflect on that great source of Christian encouragement and insight: the Mother of Our Lord.

---

[43] *Luke* 2:19 + 51

Works Cited in Translation:

- Sebastian Brock (trans.), *Bride of Light Hymns on Mary from the Syriac Churches* Baker Hill, Kottayam, India: St. Ephrem Ecumenical Research Institute 1994 **(Bride of Light)**
- Mary Hansbury (trans.), *Jacob of Serug On the Mother of God.* Crestwood, N.Y.: St. Vladimir's Seminary Press 1998 **(Hansbury)**
- Thomas Kollamparampil, CMI, *Jacob of Serugh Select Festal Homilies* Bangalore: Dharamaram Publications (DP) and Rome: Centre for Indian and Inter-Religious Studies (CIIS) 1997 **(Kollamparampil)**

Secondary Works:

- Mar Aprem, *Nestorian Theology* Mar Narsai Press, Trichur 1980
- Paul Bedjan (ed.), *Homilies of Mar Jacob of Sarug* (6 vols.) Piscataway, N.J.: Gorgias Press 2006
- Msgr. Seely J. Beggiani, *Early Syriac Theology* University Press of America 1983 **(Beggiani)**
- Sebastian Brock, "Mary in Syriac Tradition", 182-191 in Alberic Stacpoole, O.S.B., (ed.), *Mary's Place in Christian Dialogue* Morehouse-Barlow Co., Inc.: Wilton, Connecticut 1982 **(Brock 1982)**
- Sebastian Brock, "Syriac Dispute Poems: The Various Types", VII in *From Ephrem to Romanos Interactions between Syriac and Greek in Late Antiquity* Aldershot: Ashgate 1999 **(Brock 1999)**
- Sebastian Brock, "The Dispute Poem: From Sumer to Syriac", 3-10 in *Journal of the Canadian Society for Syriac Studies* 1 (2001) **(Brock 2001)**
- Kees den Biesen, *Bibliography of Ephrem the Syrian* Giove in Umbria 2002 **(den Biesen 2002)**
- Angelo Di Bernardino (ed.), *The Eastern Fathers from the Council of Chalcedon (451) to John of Damascus* Cambridge: James Clarke & Co. Ltd. 2000
- Sidney H. Griffith, "Ephraem, the deacon of Edessa, and the Church of the Empire", 25-52 in T.P. Halton & J.P. Williman (ed.), *Diakonia: Studies in Honour of Robert T. Meyer* Washington, DC: CUA Press 1986 **(Griffith 1986)**
- Susan Ashbrook Harvey, "Spoken Words, Voiced Silence: Biblical Women in Syriac Tradition", 105-131 in *Journal of Early Christian Studies* 9.1 (Spring 2001) **(Harvey 2001)**
- Susan Ashbrook Harvey, "Women in Syriac Christian Tradition", 44-58 in *Journal of the Canadian Society for Syriac Studies* 3 (2003) **(Harvey 2003)**
- Susan Ashbrook Harvey, "Revisiting the Daughters of the Covenant: Women's Choirs and Sacred Song in Ancient Syriac Christianity" in *Hugoye: Journal of Syriac Studies* 8.2 (July 2005) http://syrcom.cua.edu/Hugoye/Vol8No2/HV8N2Harvey.html **(Harvey 2005)**
- Maxwell E. Johnson, "*Sub Tuum Praesidium:* The *Theotokos* in Christian Life and Worship before Ephesus", 52-75 in *Pro Ecclesia* 17.1 (Winter 2008)
- George Anton Kiraz, *A Computer-Generated Concordance to the Syriac New Testament* (6 vols.) Leiden/New York/Köln: E.J. Brill 1993 **(Kiraz)**

- Mar O'Dishoo Metropolitan, *The Book of Marganitha (The Pearl) On the Truth of Christianity* Mar Themotheus Memorial Printing & Publishing House Limited: Ernakulam, Kerala, India 1965 (**Marganitha**)
- John Panicker, "Mar Jacob of Serug on the Virginity of Mary", 45-54 in *The Harp A Review of Syriac and Oriental Ecumenical Studies* 18 (2005) (**Panicker**)
- Charles Payngot, "The Homily of Narsai on the Virgin Mary", 33-38 in *The Harp A Review of Syriac and Oriental Ecumenical Studies* 13 (2000)
- James Puthuparampil, "The Mariological Thought of Mar Jacob of Serugh (451-521)", 265-278 in *The Harp A Review of Syriac and Oriental Ecumenical Studies* 18 (2005) (**Puthuparampil 2005**)
- Johannes Quasten, *Music and Worship in Pagan & Christian Antiquity* Washington, DC: National Association of Pastoral Ministries 1983 (**Quasten**)
- Paul S. Russell, *St. Ephraem the Syrian and St. Gregory the Theologian Confront the Arians* St. Ephrem Ecumenical Research Center, Kottayam, Kerala, INDIA 1994 (**Russell 1994**)
- Paul S. Russell, "Ephraem the Syrian on the Utility of Language and the Place of Silence" *Journal of Early Christian Studies* (Spring 2000) 8.1, 21-37 (**Russell 2000**)
- Paul S. Russell, "Syriac Christianity: Yesterday, Today and Forever" *The Journal of Maronite Studies* 5, 1 (January-April 2001) www.mari.org (**Russell 2001**)
- Paul S. Russell, "Ephraem and Athanasius on the Knowledge of Christ: Two Anti-Arian treatments of *Mark* 13:32" *Gregorianum* 85, 3 (2004), 445-474 (**Russell 2004**)
- Solomon of Akhlat, *The Book of the Bee* (ed. by E.A.W. Budge) Oxford: The Clarendon Press 1886 Piscataway, N.J.: The Gorgias Press 2006 (reprint)
- Alberic Stacpoole, O.S.B., (ed.), *Mary's Place in Christian Dialogue* Morehouse-Barlow Co., Inc.: Wilton, Connecticut 1982 (**Stacpoole**)
- Alfred Stirnemann and Gerhard Wilflinger (ed.), *Syriac Dialogue First Non-Official Consultation on Dialogue Within the Syriac Tradition*
- George Thumpanirappel, *Christ in the East Syriac Tradition* Satna: Ephrem's Publications 2003 (**Thumpanirappel**)
- Samuel Thykoottam, *The Mother of God in the Syriac Tradition* *SEERI Correspondence Course (SCC) 4* St. Ephrem Ecumenical Research Institute: Kottayam, Kerala, India (no date) (**Thykoottam**)
- Kristi Upson-Saia, "Caught in a Compromising Position: The Biblical Exegesis and Characterization of Biblical Protagonists in the Syriac Dialogue Hymns" *Hugoye: Journal of Syriac Studies* 9.2 (July 2006) http://bethmardutho.cua.edu/Hugoye/Vol9No2/HV9N2UpsonSaia.html (**Upson-Saia**)
- Ignatius Ortiz De Urbina, S.I., *Patrologia Syriaca* Romae: Pont. Institutum Orientalium Studiorum 1965 (**Ortiz De Urbina**)

Mary and Byzantine Catholics

10.

The Intimate Role in Salvation of the Theotokos: Images of Mediation in Byzantine Liturgical Prayer

Barbara Jean Mihalchick, OSBM

Over the course of the past twenty years, I have been blessed to visit over 25 countries. No, this is not the typical life of a Catholic nun. These travels were a by-product of an international assignment with the Sisters of St. Basil the Great whose communities are scattered in more than a dozen countries. From Mexico City to Kiev, Ukraine to Buenos Aires - over the course of twelve years, I encountered people who had heartfelt trust in the Mother of God. I visited shrines built with the generous gratitude of those whose prayers Mary had answered. The Shrine of Our Lady of Guadalupe is always filled with families and an over-abundance of flowers. The shrines of Our Lady of Luhan in Argentina and Our Lady of Loreto in Italy exalt a Black Madonna. Our Lady of Mariapocs in Hungary and Our Lady of Perpetual Help in every country constantly attract the faithful seeking her aid. Perhaps some of you have visited shrines that I have not – such as Our Lady of Czestochowa in Poland or Our Lady of Fatima in Portugal. Hopefully, many of you also know the experience of begging and receiving through the maternal intercession of the Theotokos. It is this I want to center on as I speak.

The *Paraklesis* is a prayer of supplication to the Theotokos, the expression of a person or a people in desperate need of assistance. A crying out to the Mother of God for help in need, though so familiar among Catholics and Orthodox believers, is often not so ordinarily practiced among other Christians, perhaps. In fact such prayer may be held suspect. As a lifelong Byzantine Catholic having constant exposure to both Roman and Orthodox spirituality, trust in the intercession of the Virgin is quite integrated in my life of prayer and so necessary to it.

I could speak long and lovingly about the benefits received and the many intentions answered. I live on monastery grounds which house the Shrine of Our Lady of Perpetual Help. I frequently turn to her, in a place where thousands of pilgrims bring their concerns and petitions such as during our Labor Day weekend pilgrimage in her honor, soon to be celebrated for the 74th time. I go to the shrine to pray on numerous occasions to ask Our Lady to keep me safe when I travel or for guidance as I go to serve the Kingdom, or for any new and serious intention. I also pray there for the many who have brought their needs to her, the Source of Perpetual Help.

During the course of the past few months, I have been praying the *Paraklesis* daily in supplication to the Mother of God, for some very serious matters directly affecting my life. Among them is my plea for the healing of my best friend, Sister Dorothy, who began dialysis in April. She has experienced many complications adjusting to this new reality, which were made necessary by treatments that helped her survive cancer three times in the 1990s. More serious than her physical healing, is the continuation of her inner transfiguration in this latter stage of her life. Through these many weeks, I believe that through the intercession and blessing of the Theotokos, Sister is improving in body, mind and spirit.

Such is my faith, and in general, Eastern Christians the world over are known to be extremely devoted to the Theotokos. Some will accuse us of being extreme in what we say to her and about her. Frederica Matthewes-Green has written in her book *The Lost Gospel of Mary*,

> Many Western Christians are unfamiliar with Mary, and somewhat leery of her; they suspect that it's possible for devotion to her to get out of hand, and even eclipse the honor due to God. It is true that over time and in other lands, praise of the Virgin that had been intended as lovingly poetic

developed into something more literal, and consequently less healthy.[1]

The author later continues,

> We misunderstand if we hear these honors as precise theological assertions. The western Christian way of thinking about theology was powerfully shaped by the work of Saint Thomas Aquinas, who in the 10th century developed an approach that treats faith like a science.[2]

"Intended as lovingly poetic…," these words can be applied to many Byzantine Christian prayers, prayers which are identical in both the Eastern Catholic and Orthodox traditions.

I speak as the only Byzantine Catholic on the roster of this conference and in this ecumenical setting it may be wise to clarify just what this infers. Pope John Paul II made various efforts to reawaken Christians to the richness the Church has when using both its Eastern and Western "lungs" or dimensions, most notably in his Apostolic Letter, *The Light of the East*, published in 1995.

The church of Christ was born in what we call today the Middle East where Christ Himself lived. Wherever it spread, it reflected the character of the culture of the region while also continuing some of the ways of its origin, the Middle East. When missionaries went forth, they taught the truths of the Gospel of Jesus Christ, but the accents placed on these truths, and added as well in the style of worship, varied according to the missionaries' own experience and their ability to adapt to the culture they had entered. For instance, much of the style of prayer which existed in Jerusalem and in Antioch, continues to be used in eastern and western Christian churches

---

[1] Frederica Matthewes-Green, *The Lost Gospel of Mary* (Brewster, MA: Paraclete Press, 2007), xiii.
[2] Matthewes-Green, *Gospel,* 125.

233

today, representing early origins but quite different from cultural development in other areas of the world.

From Rome, missionaries went forth to lands occupied or invaded by barbarian groups. It served their purpose to bring a singular style of worship to these peoples, thus helping to bring about some stability through uniformity. This was not the case or the need in the eastern regions where the Church groups developed diverse forms of worship and traditions. In the East, local churches organized around the leading cities of a given area and took on the character we today would compare to an archdiocese. Ultimately five centers of Christianity developed. In the West there is Rome, a single Apostolic See with a uniform liturgical tradition. In the East there are Constantinople, Antioch, Alexandria, and Jerusalem. These patriarchates, known as the pentarchy, are all considered Apostolic Sees. Rome was considered the "first among equals."

The eastern and western Churches experienced different historical events, faced different heresies and threats, and developed differently in response to these conditions. This was true from the very time of the Apostles – think of the situation of St. Thomas, apostle to India, as opposed to the apostles who traveled north and west of Rome. With travel and communication being what they were in those times, we ought to marvel that the bishops were able to meet in "ecumenical" Councils several times to clarify and officially proclaim the basic truths of the faith.

Byzantine Christians, both Orthodox and Catholic, trace their beginnings either to the Eastern Mediterranean countries and Africa or to the missionary efforts which brought Christianity to Eastern Europe from these Greek-speaking lands which, of course, practiced Eastern Christian traditions. The name Byzantine comes from the ancient name for Constantinople, today's Istanbul. The Byzantine Empire existed for a full thousand years and the Byzantine Church's traditions, right down to the vestments used for worship, are greatly influenced even today by the Empire's ways.

It is necessary to say that not all of the Churches of the East developed under the Byzantine influence. The Coptic Church in North Africa, the Chaldean Church of Iraq, the Syro-Malabar and Syro- Malankar Churches of India are examples of the many Eastern Christian Churches which are not from the Byzantine Tradition. Taken together, there are 22 Eastern Catholic Churches or church traditions. In almost every case, there is a related Orthodox Church. This division resulted from the Great Schism of the 11th Century when representatives from the eastern and western Churches excommunicated each other. Since then, some members of each of these Churches formally reconnected with the Church of Rome, forming the various Eastern Catholic Churches. The reunion accords stated that the various eastern churches should maintain their traditions and styles of worship. However, the western church, larger in number and united in its uniform practices, often sought in unofficial ways to influence the Eastern Catholics to conform to its practices and beliefs. Eastern Catholics, frequently called "Uniates," are sometimes looked upon as a problem in regard to hoped-for reunion with the Orthodox Churches. There is a great need at this moment of history to pray for wisdom and courage for Church leaders to see the Body of Christ with new eyes and open hearts.

The various Eastern Catholic groups are referred to today as "Churches" or "particular Churches" not as "Rites." They have their own bishops, dioceses, often called eparchies, and a large department within the Vatican structure called the "Congregation for the Oriental Churches," second in size and influence only to the Vatican Secretariat of State.

The call of the Second Vatican Council to the Eastern Catholic Churches has been to reaffirm and reinstate their authentic eastern traditions wherever they have been lost and for whatever reason. This is the active mindset and practice of most of the Eastern Catholic churches today, including those of Eastern Europe since the fall of Communism. The differences in spirituality between the eastern and western Churches does not cause the Churches to be mutually exclusive, but instead are meant to be complementary; for instance the Divine Liturgy of the eastern tradition or the Mass in the western or Roman Church may be looked upon as the Last Supper whereas in the Byzantine Tradition it is considered the Heavenly Banquet. Both approaches can be traced to Scripture. Usually it is such a difference in emphasis which distinguishes them.

The particular Church to which I belong is the Byzantine Ruthenian Catholic Church. Its archbishop is here in Pittsburgh and it has three additional eparchies stretched across the United States. It is directly subject to the Pope of Rome, having no other church structure to connect with formally in another country, although its roots are in Eastern Europe. The Byzantine Ruthenian Church has had its own bishops and jurisdiction in the United States since 1924. Though a minority, it is one of the larger Eastern Catholic groups in this country; fourteen Eastern Catholic Churches exist in North America with their own bishops, eparchies and liturgical traditions; several parishes of other Eastern Catholic traditions exist here which are connected to local Roman or Eastern Catholic bishops.

Eastern Christians' prayer, most often, is a synthesis of theology expressed in poetic forms. It is not left to nor open to frequent reformulation. The liturgical prayers, our "official" prayers, if you will, have endured through the centuries. The words are consistent with the theology and the devotion of the Church, of the people. According to Father Meyendorff:

> There is no doubt that in the Byzantine Church the liturgical tradition, the liturgical texts and the continuous liturgical activities in which the entire society participated were seen as an essential witness of continuity and integrity... Eastern

Christianity visualized the liturgy as an independent authoritative source and criterion of faith and ethics.[3]

Referring to the Divine Liturgy of Saint John Chrysostom, Byzantine Catholic liturgist Father David Petras writes:

'Especially,' he (the priest, during the Divine Liturgy) continues, 'for our most holy, most pure, most blessed and glorious Lady, the Theotokos and Ever-virgin Mary.' Some might find it strange to offer the Liturgy 'for' the Mother of God and the saints, but this is not a real problem. The Liturgy, which is our participation in the death and resurrection of the Lord, is accomplished for all people, and Mary is the first and foremost among those people who are saved.[4]

The hymn, known as the *Axion Estin,* actually a combination of two hymns to the Theotokos, has been revered and sung throughout the centuries. "It is truly proper to glorify you, O Theotokos, the Ever-blessed, Immaculate, and the Mother of our God. More honorable than the Cherubim and beyond compare more glorious than the Seraphim, who a Virgin gave birth to God the Word, you truly the Theotokos, we magnify."[5] It is placed shortly after the Anaphora or Consecration of the Gifts and the *Epiklesis,* the supplication for the Holy Spirit to transform the gifts of bread and wine. This means the hymn and therefore the Theotokos has quite an exalted position in Byzantine theology.

---

[3] John Meyendorff, *The Byzantine Legacy in the Orthodox Church* (Crestwood, New York: St. Vladimir's Seminary Press, 1982), 123.
[4] David M. Petras, *Time for the Lord to Act* (Pittsburgh, PA: Byzantine Seminary Press, 2005), 118.
[5] The Byzantine Catholic Metropolitan Church *Sui Juris* of Pittsburgh, USA, *The Divine Liturgies of Our Holy Fathers John Chrysostom and Basil the Great* (Pittsburgh PA: The Byzantine Catholic Metropolitan Church *Sui Juris* of Pittsburgh, USA, 2006), 62.

Father Michael Polsky writes about the veneration of the Theotokos:

In the second, third and fourth centuries, the holy Church honored the All-holy *Theotokos* in exactly the same way as she does today. All the existing evidences of this veneration, data from the very first century, from the Apostles in the Gospels, reveals this as a most widespread and established practice. Saint Justin in the East, Tertullian in Africa, Saint Irenaeus in Gaul, Saint Methodius in Asia Minor, as well as Saint Ephraim on the banks of the Euphrates, speak of the [veneration of the] All-holy Virgin not as something new for their particular local church, but as something recognized and they speak of her as honored by all. They speak of what had been previous to them and the situation in their own time regarding their local confessions.[6]

Countless theologians, Fathers of the Church, saints, sinners and contemporary writers have continued to justify the praise of the Theotokos, to give thanks for her faithful intercession. Kyriaki Fitzgerald writes:

As first among all the saints, she not only is the human bridge between the Old and New Testaments, but, as well as the saints, she is alive in Christ now. The Orthodox uphold that through the life of the Church, she is close to us and

---

[6] Michael Polsky, "The Veneration of the Virgin Mary" Orthodox Christian Information Center, VII. The History of the Veneration of the Virgin Mary http://www.orthodoxinfo.com/general/veneration_mary.aspx August 4, 2008, September 23, 2008.

available to us as our helper and intercessor, through the love of the Triune God.[7]

Pope Benedict XVI , on the Feast of the Solemnity of Mary, January, 2008 said in his homily,

> [Mary, Mother of God], *Theotokos*, is the title that was officially attributed to Mary in the fifth century, to be exact, at the Council of Ephesus in 431, but which had already taken root in the devotion of the Christian people since the third century, in the context of the heated discussions on the Person of Christ in that period. This title highlights the fact that Christ is God and truly was born of Mary as a man: in this way his unity as true God and true man is preserved. Actually, however much the debate might seem to focus on Mary, it essentially concerned the Son. Desiring to safeguard the full humanity of Jesus, several Fathers suggested a weaker term: instead of the title Theotokos, they suggested Christotokos, Mother of Christ; however, this was rightly seen as a threat to the doctrine of the full unity of Christ's divinity with his humanity. On the one hand, therefore, after lengthy discussion at the Council of Ephesus in 431, as I said, the unity of the two natures – the divine and the human (cf. DS, n. 250) – in the Person of the Son of God was solemnly confirmed and, on the other, the legitimacy of the attribution of the title *Theotokos*, Mother of God, to the Virgin (ibid., n.251).[8]

---

[7] Kyriaki Karidoyanes Fitzgerald, "A Person in Communion: the Witness of Mary, the Mother of God" *Greek Orthodox Theological Review* 46 (2001) 229-253.
[8] Benedict XVI, "Mary, Mother of God" Libreria Editrice Vaticana, www.vatican.va/holy_father/benedict_xvi/audiences/2008/documents/ January 2, 2008.

Father Michael Polsky also points out:

The voice of the Œcumenical Church, at the Third
Œcumenical Council, only gave expression to the
veneration of the Mother of God, which had been
normative and established of old in the Church, by
defining the Virgin as *Theotokos*. But for this to be
said and for it to express the generally held
opinion, it was necessary that in all the preceding
centuries and in the life contemporary with the
Council, there should have been a corresponding
universally held confession. And it is just such a
confession in the greatness of the All-holy Virgin,
in her heavenly glory and in her prayerful and
grace-filled heavenly power that the Church has
always held, as the works of the holy Fathers of
the Church of the first centuries of Christianity
demonstrate.[9]

A text from Part One of the Byzantine Catholic
Catechism, *Light for Life*, which focuses on the Mysteries of our
faith, states:

Byzantine theology is even clearer about Mary's
role in the salvation of the human race. On the
feast of the Annunciation, Gabriel is described as
greeting Mary as the one 'through whom Adam is
called back to Paradise, Eve is freed from
bondage, and the world is filled with joy.' In her
womb, God is united with human flesh 'through
the good will of the Father and the operation of
the Holy Spirit' (Liti Stichera). On the feast of the
Dormition, the Church proclaims, 'Rejoice, O
Virgin, for you alone brought heaven and earth
together in giving birth to your Son (Stichera at
the Praises), and 'through her holy Dormition the

---

[9] Polsky, p.30.

world is given new life (Liti Stichera). As the one who gave birth to God in the flesh, Mary's choices had cosmic significance; and she is the first to participate in the complete salvation wrought through the incarnation of Christ, including the assumption of her body into the presence of God. Thus she has a unique role as intercessor for all humanity.[10]

Indeed, the Theotokos, uniquely privileged, plays an expansive role in the world. Opinions about this role today are sometimes taken arbitrarily to support personal views and goals. Paul Evdokimov in his book *Woman and the Salvation of the World* writes extensively to correct extreme views. Elizabeth Behr-Sigel likewise calls us to the traditional truths. She writes:

A woman, a human being, called to participate in a unique way in accomplishing God's plan for humanity, Mary, according to the fundamental Tradition of the Church, is not an archetype of 'woman' or of feminine holiness. She is rather a figure of the Church, of the body of Christ, of which men and women both are members, all of them called, as St. Ambrose said, to become 'mothers of Christ,' to bring to birth in each and every person, in themselves and in the world, the complete Christ, *totus Christus*. On the symbolic level, Mary is the anticipation of the new man, the new being and the new humanity, transfigured.[11]

When we talk about intercession, mediation by the Theotokos, no matter what our petition, are we not crying out

---

[10] Eastern Catholic Associates, *Light for Life, Part One: The Mystery Believed* (Pittsburgh PA: God With Us Publications, 1994), 93.
[11] Elisabeth Behr-Sigel, *Discerning the Signs of the Times: The Vision of Elisabeth Behr-Sigel* (Crestwood NY: St. Vladimir's Seminary Press, 2001), 112.

for the "transfiguration" of a given reality? We seek health in times of sickness, consolation in times of sorrow, protection in times of danger, strength in times of overwhelming trials. We desire that something be changed and we have confidence that, as our Mother, she cares. We most often do not see these situations of need and neediness as blessings and often enough we even forget to call out for our Mother's aid. As I was preparing this last month, a woman, an acquaintance, who is a lawyer working for the government called me. I had not spoken with her since last Fall. She was seeking prayers for a new job but continued to list many causes for intercessory prayer among her family members. That's fine – we Sisters of St. Basil welcome calls for our prayers every day. But, having the Theotokos very much in my mind as she called, I turned the petitions back to her. I said, "And who is your Advocate? You are a lawyer, you advocate for people. And who is your Advocate?" No answer for a moment. I said, "Is the Mother of God still your Advocate as you have told me in the past? Do you remember to seek herhelp?" "Oh my," she said, "This must be the reason I made this phone call today. I have been teaching my four-year old son to turn to Mother Mary, how could I have forgotten myself?"

At least this woman still does believe in calling out to the Theotokos when she remembers. It may be worth facing the unique realities of our times that form some of the personal challenges today to our growth, to our transfiguration. David R. Smith in his book on the *Paraklesis, Mary, Worthy of All Praise*, points out:

> There are two heretical tendencies in North American Christianity. One places Jesus Christ too far toward the human extreme, as did the ancient Arian heresy, and the other denies His humanity. 'Jesus' for this second extreme becomes a concept, a philosophy, a mantra, a tool distinct from the Person of Jesus Christ our Lord. In this way of thinking, we look to 'Jesus' for salvation the same

way we look to our car when we want to go shopping. There is no relationship with a person. And why? Because of arrogance and arrogance alone. Some folks refuse to call on the name of another human being for salvation, and so take our Lord's humanity away from Him. And for those in this group, the idea that we might call out to Jesus' Mother with the words, 'Save us!' seems almost unimaginable....We can enjoy the salvation that God sends us in Jesus Christ only by admitting our complete reliance on Him. We might neglect to honor the Theotokos because we think we can 'get to' Jesus without her, but we most certainly cannot enjoy salvation without the attitude of complete submission and dependence.[12]

In times of desperate need, those who do believe in the Theotokos' unique role of intercession for us, turn to her in prayer as Advocate, often praying communally. This service can also be prayed personally outside of a liturgical setting.

The best known devotion to the Mother of God in the Byzantine Churches is the service known as the *Paraklesis*, or 'Service of Consolation.' Modeled upon the office of Matins, it contains many elements of that service along with a special canon which focuses on the Mother of God as our consoler and protector. With its repeated intercessory litanies, it reflects a character of intense prayer uniting the worshippers in a concerned love for one another. The service concludes with a solemn veneration of the icon of

---

[12] David R. Smith, *Mary, Worthy of All Praise* (Ben Lomond, CA: Conciliar Press, 2004), 11-12.

the Theotokos, 'she who shows the way' to Christ (in Greek, Hodogitria).[13]

The *Paraklesis* is described as "a poem of the monk Theosterictus, but ascribed by others to Theophanes" by a Greek Orthodox Archdiocesan resource.[14] It was composed, it is believed, in the 9th Century.

By old tradition, during the two weeks of August preceding the Feast of the Dormition (or Assumption) of the Virgin, August 15, many churches and believers pray the *Paraklesis* daily as part of the Fast, the two week period which prepares for this great feast. When prayed in this season, certain prayers proper to the Dormition feast replace parts of the service.

This revered prayer service, very popular with the Greek Orthodox was less well known in the Byzantine Catholic Church until recently. We more often prayed the *Moleben* to the Mother of God, another shortened form of Matins. The *Moleben* contains many of the same prayers as the *Paraklesis*, but lacks a Canon, the eight-part mid-section of the *Paraklesis*. The service contains much that is penitential, in the sense of authentic repentance, that is, a cry to be restored in God's vision of one's reality. The "transfigured" element enters here again. The Byzantine Catechism reminds us:

> The celebration of this service (Paraklesis)
> heightens our awareness that troubles and
> temptations do not separate us from God's love.
> In Mary, a source of help and comfort, we gain a

---

[13] Eastern Catholic Associates, *Light for Life, Part Two: The Mystery Celebrated* (Pittsburgh, PA: God With Us Publications, 1996), 52.
[14] Demetri Kangelaris and Nicholas Kasemeotes, *The Service of the Small Paraklesis,* Revised 1997, Holy Cross Orthodox Press 1984, Greek Orthodox Archdiocese of America
www.goarch.org/en/Chapel/liturgical_texts/PARAKLESIS.asp, July 18, 2008.

further link with the divine through her intimate connection with God as his Mother. As the first saved by God, she already exemplifies that salvation means deification through the grace of our Lord Jesus Christ.[15]

The idea of "divinization" or "deification" or "transfiguration" as the meaning of salvation is shared by Eastern Orthodox and Eastern Catholics alike. St. Peter writes in his second epistle that we "may become participants of the divine nature" (2 Peter 1:4). Theologian Paul Evdokimov notes:

> The liturgical texts repeat ceaselessly that in the flesh she gave to Christ, all human beings have come to share in the divine nature of the Word. The Hodegitria Virgin (the one who shows the way) whose icon is venerated at the end of the Paraklesis service, traces the path of the Church in the human realm; she is 'the Gate.' As God-man, Christ calls Himself 'the Way and the Gate'; He is the only one. The Virgin is the first; she walks ahead of humanity, and all follow her. She gives birth to the Way. She is presented as 'the right direction,' as the 'pillar of fire' that leads to the New Jerusalem.[16]

These prayers celebrate the faithfulness of the Theotokos by expressing confidence, by giving praise, by allowing for a type of joy to enter the sorrow or neediness which brings the believer to pray these petitions.

As author Kyriaki Fitzgerald points out in an article:

[15] Eastern Catholic Associates, *Light for Life, Part Two: The Mystery Celebrated* (Pittsburgh, PA: God With Us Publications, 1996), 53.

[16] Paul Evdokimov, *Woman and the Salvation of the World: A Christian Anthropology on the Charisms of Women* (Crestwood NY: St. Vladimir's Seminary Press, 1994), 213-4.

Through true praise, not only is one directed to the object of praise, but also one surrenders oneself in the presence of the object of praise. At the same time, what we say through our doxology is of vital importance. Through praise and thanksgiving, one does not define that which is essentially beyond human understanding. Definitions presume equality, or more accurately, superiority to the subject of our attention. Therefore, there is an inseparable and living relationship between dogma and devotion in the consciousness of the Church. It is impossible to separate theological truth from worship on the one hand and the needs of people on the other. The words of our theology are meant not only to praise God but also to nurture others in their growth in life and holiness.[17]

What the author describes is the need to integrate, to be strengthened in our spiritual lives even as we pray for physical health or protection, emotional consolation or other helps. The lawyer who called me faithfully attends the Divine Liturgy on Sundays but has no practice during the week of praying with the Body and being reminded of the integration of faith and life, of using even one's neediness as a means to seek transfiguration in Christ.

David Smith's idea speaks further about this integration. He says:

In the same way the Theotokos walked, we must walk. We find the footprints of her passage in Scripture, in the great traditions of the Church, in

---

[17] Kyriaki Karidoyanes Fitzgerald, "A Person in Communion: the Witness of Mary, the Mother of God" *Greek Orthodox Theological Review* 46 (2001), 231.

our hearts. We must place our feet exactly into those prints. Sometimes the way is easy and joyful, and sometimes a sword pierces our hearts. In difficult times we need refuge and help, but where to find it? Where did the Mother of God find refuge and help? The scriptures tell us, 'Lord, Thou hast been our refuge and in generation and generation' (Psalm 89). The Theotokos continually sought shelter in God. And who was the defense of the Mother of God during her difficult years on earth? Again, the scriptures say, 'As for me, unto God have I cried, and the Lord hearkened unto me' (Psalm 54). The answer again is God himself. How often we seek to take onto ourselves the cares and responsibilities that belong to God alone! He provides us with shelter, and He defends us, and He has given us *the God-birth-giver and Virgin as pilot and author of good things.* The path of her steps leads us toward the comfort and peace that God has to give....This simple way of life, in which you leave to God the matters that belong to Him and only accept the cares that belong to yourself, is very difficult to sustain.[18]

While I prayed the *Paraklesis* this summer, as I mentioned for the intention of my sick friend but also for several other things that sadden me, I have been especially touched by the phrases in Ode 9 of the Canon which ask the Theotokos to restore things in God's way, to completely fill these life circumstances with her light.

> With gladness fill my heart,
> Most holy Virgin Lady,
> For you are she who received the abundant joy;
> Take the grief of my sinfulness,
> And make it disappear.

---

[18] Smith, 26-7.

"Most Holy Theotokos, save us.
A shelter and protection
And a wall unshaken,
Become, O Virgin, for those who flee to you,
A sheltered cover and refuge,
And a place of joy.
"Most Holy Theotokos, save us."
O Virgin, from the brightness
Of your light illumine
The ones who call you most piously Mother of God,
Take all the gloom of our ignorance
And banish it away.[19]

Doctor Virginia Kimball wisely points out, "Mediation is related to mission. The mission of the Theotokos is a consequence of Mary's role in the Incarnation. She is to bring mankind to her Son and to God's gifts of life."[20] This is the way Mary "saves us," by taking petitions of the faithful to her Son. Doctor Kimball writes about the Theotokos as "Advocate," "Mediatrix," and "Nurturer of the people of her Son," titles by which she is acclaimed in the prayers of the Akathist and the *Paraklesis.*

In her overview of the language of mediation present in these prayers, Doctor Kimball provides a listing of sixteen Greek words and fully describes their meanings in order to assist the reader and the one who prays to better appreciate the language of mediation. She writes, "They collectively point to life-giving graces originating from God that provide health,

---

[19] All quotes from "The Service of the Small Paraklesis (Intercessory Prayer) to the Most Holy Theotokos," Demetrios Kangelaris, and Nicholas Kasemeotes, translators, Greek Orthodox Archdiocese of America, www.goarch.org/en/Chapel/liturgical_texts/PARAKLESIS.asp July 18, 2008.

[20] Virginia M. Kimball, "The Language of Mediation in Eastern Liturgical Prayer: The Akathistos and Small Paraklesis" *Marian Studies* LII (2001): 193-4.

salvation, security, and fullness of Christian life. Each of the related words in Greek describes a particular aspect of 'salvation' and 'care,' which are components of mediation."[21] I am unable to handle the Greek language, but I refer you to her excellent article, "The Language of Mediation in Eastern Liturgical Prayer: The Akathistos and the Small Paraklesis" available in the journal *Marian Studies,* 2001, which can be accessed at the Marian Library at the University of Dayton, in Dayton, Ohio. In the English version which we will freely use the words Kimball has singled out, such as "deliver" and "refuge."

Canon, Ode 1 says :

> To God and the Savior you've given birth
> I ask you, O Virgin,
> From the dangers deliver me;
> For now I run to you for refuge
> With both my soul and my reasoning.

Words such as "protection," "shelter" and "port" are evident in Ode 3:

> A protection and shelter,
> I have with you in my life,
> You, the Theotokos and the Virgin,
> Pilot me towards your port;
> For you are the cause,
> The cause of that which is good,
> Support of the faithful,
> The only all-praised One.

"Salvation," "beseeching," "rescue" and "compassion" appear in Ode 4:

> As a hope and foundation,
> And a wall unshaken

---

[21] Kimball, 192-3.

Of our salvation;
Having you, the all-lauded One,
From afflictions do you rescue us.
Your depth of compassion
Grant unto me
As one beseeching you;
You have carried the Compassionate
The Savior of those praising you.

In writing about the compassion of the Theotokos expressed in the *Paraklesis,* Father Smith states:

Let us never forget to whom this great compassion is directed: The Theotokos was strong (on Golgotha) for you and me. Whereas we live our whole lives in a confused tangle of self-love, the Theotokos, and the compassionate Son she brought forth, bring salvation to the world through their self-sacrifice and giving. 'Behold your Mother!' (John 19:27) Behold your mother~! She is again sad – weeping for the one who is dying slowly – you! We live in a world where the avoidance of pain has become our first and last priority…
Behold your mother! Her compassion benefits you, and it calls you to a deeper place than any place you have ever been. The love of the Mother of God benefits us most when we make it our own.
Behold your mother and sing hymns. Allow her holiness to be written on your heart by words of devotion to her.[22]

David Smith also describes the Virgin Mother's powerful mediation in this way:

[22] Smith, 46.

Saints offer us two benefits, and the first is that
their lives teach us about the ways of God. When
we see their sacrifice, their holiness and wisdom,
we see what we might become...The life of the
Theotokos, more than that of any other saint,
gives us a model of the spiritual heights to which a
human can aspire....The second benefit of the
saints is their intercession for us. If we see the
saints as models, then we forget that they are alive
even now, standing eternally before the throne of
God, praying for those they love , for those who
love them and plead for their help...Whom could
we ask to pray for us with any more influence over
God than His Mother? Not only does she offer
prayers for us, but she does so fervently and with
strength. She longs above all things to make use
of her power for our benefit. 'Most Holy
Theotokos, save us!' we cry, and she hears us and
responds to our love for her and our belief that
she can do all things.[23]

The Theotokos' mediation is so needed in our times. The
role of prophets in every age is to properly name the signs of
the times, the present moment, and to show the finger of God
at work, consoling and also challenging. The age in which we
live presents us with temptations, with sufferings, with
innumerable occasions of sin all the while that humankind
makes incredible advances. I have been impressed with the
writings of Father Ronald Rolheiser of the Oblates of Mary
Immaculate. He and his international community invited
Catholic thinkers together to properly name the present and
show the finger of God at work in North American culture.
They produced the book *Secularity and the Gospel: Being
Missionaries to Our Children.*[24]

---

[23] Smith, pp. 35-6
[24] Ronald Rolheiser OMI, *Secularity and the Gospel: Being Missionaries
to Our Children* (New York, NY: The Crossroad Publishing Company,
2006).

With them we must read the signs of the times and prayerfully bring them to the Theotokos. In a presentation on this topic, Father Rolheiser spoke of these signs: First of all, a greater measure of freedom than has ever existed for humankind. Secondly, the everyday consciousness of society is often agnostic and atheistic. Formerly, the culture carried the faith for the people but this is no longer the case. Thirdly, western culture and its ways are intoxicating and overwhelming. It is not that it is all bad, for God is in much of the culture too, but one must carefully evaluate. Fourthly, excessive individuality is leading to the demise of public life and the sense of belonging to a community. Fifthly, people are experiencing an ever-increasing moral loneliness. And lastly, this is a time of bewildering pluralism. The culture is becoming multi-everything. This is not good because it can lead to either relativity - Pope Benedict calls it "the dictatorship of relativity," or to its other extreme- an attitude that believes that clarity trumps truth – in this mode, the stress is on dogmas, boundaries, imposition of beliefs – such as are visible in fundamentalist Islam or extreme Christian fundamentalism – any of which can turn militant. Our urgent need as we face these challenges is to develop a more powerful inner-directedness says Father Rolheiser.[25] Eastern Christian spirituality would say the same in different words.

We need first of all, to live a life "in Christ" as did the Theotokos. Eastern Christians have it right in this matter when they teach *theosis,* deification. They teach that only someone who is transfigured "in Christ" has attained personhood; the rest of life is about synergy, living up to that inward, precious gift, to let it transfigure all of our lives. We should often turn to

---

[25] Ronald Rolheiser, OMI "Religious Charism and the Spiritual Ritual," Tri-State Conference, Cincinnati, OH, DVD #101, North American Conference of Associates and Religious, June 3, 2006.

the Theotokos to ask her help to respond to the call of the Spirit, to live in faithful, loving relationship with her Son Jesus.

To live in this society as Christ-followers we need a faithful prayer life, with contemplation of Scripture. We need to dialogue with others, especially across generations in order to learn to integrate our faith with our everyday realities and challenges. The more we allow ourselves or our young people to keep God-stuff apart from every day's choices, the more we will be subject to anger, joylessness, polarization and godlessness. The Holy Spirit is not in these. The signs of the Spirit are still love, joy, peace, patience, kindness, gentleness, self-control, says Rolheiser.

Father Rolheiser goes on to offer us a powerful image. He says that living in these times is similar to the three young men in the furnace that was heated seven times more than normal and survived – saved by God [reference to the Book of Daniel]. We are hyper-stimulated and it is having its effect on us. Some of the flames are quite destructive – restlessness, greed, sex, money, fame, jealousy, anger – even within Church – and these can overwhelm us. He urges us to do as the three youths did in the fiery furnace – they sang their sacred songs! Ode 7 in the prayer of the *Paraklesis* notes this:

> Coming out of Judea,
> Once the young men did go to the land of Babylon;
> The flame of the furnace,
> They trampled down while chanting,
> With their faith in the Trinity:
> O the God of our Fathers, Blessed are you, our God.
> Most Holy Theotokos, save us!

This is just what we are about here –renewing our hearts to again and again sing the sacred songs. We sing out to the Theotokos, our Mother, whose whole mission is to mediate for us. I appreciate the expression used by Doctor Kimball in one of the titles in her article. She writes of "Mediation – The

Continuing Motherhood in the Plan of God."[26] Her continuing Motherhood! I experience this as continuing help as I turn to her. It is indeed the mission of the Theotokos. It is for me an everyday assurance in my own Christ-centered life.

We must remember that we are in flames heated seven times stronger than usual and we truly need an Advocate! We must remember that we too – through the overshadowing of the Holy Spirit – have the ability to become the "new creation," to have Christ live in us, so that we overcome the flames and continue to sing a hymn of gratitude. Like the Theotokos and through her mediation we are divinized, transfigured in our mode of relationship to the world. This is her mission.

So much more can be and has been written of the precious prayer, the *Paraklesis* that we will sing tonight. I hope these thoughts help you to approach the experience with a hope-filled confidence. I conclude with the words of David Smith:

> As we sing the *Paraklesis* we supplicate, but we also give thanks to the Theotokos, whom we know to be the Mother of our God. We recognize her delightful and thankful attitude, and in singing to her we desire to make that attitude our own. She has bestowed upon us many favors, even many of which we remain unaware, and will yet bestow many more.[27]

Today, tonight, Oakland, Pittsburgh becomes one more holy place. May we who have gathered to honor the Virgin Theotokos place our trust in her powerful mediation.

---

[26] Kimball, 188.
[27] Smith, 47.

Mary and Orthodoxy

11.

Mary as Exemplary Figure in Salvation History

Nonna Verna Harrison

In patristic homilies and Byzantine liturgical texts, the prodigious variety of images describing the Virgin Mary can be bewildering. She is daughter of Abraham and David, and the mother of the faithful. She is Wisdom, Pure One, lowly servant, and queen. She is city temple, tabernacle, table, candlestick, and censer. She is Bride of Christ and Mother of God, and many other things. Where do all these images and concepts come from? We know that the main theological title, Theotokos, which means Birthgiver of God, comes from the Council of Ephesus (431). But, what about all the others? The kaleidoscope of shifting images leads one to prayer and exultation: "Rejoice, Unwedded Bride!" as the Akathist Hymn says. But how do all these titles fit together theologically? What do they tell us about how to live as Christian women and men today? And what do they tell us about the church?

Many of them, or course, are drawn from the Hebrew Bible, the Scripture of Mary's ancestors, the people of Israel. Patristic Mariology, and Patristic Ecclesiology, to which it is closely related, is grounded in patristic Biblical interpretation. So this paper will seek to understand some of the titles of the Mother of God in terms of principles of early Christian exegesis. This approach will enable us to distinguish between different kinds of Marian titles and sort out some of the meanings.

Although the Church Fathers have different emphases in their interpretation of the Bible they have certain approaches in common.[1] They read the whole Bible as pointing to Jesus Christ. Many of them find him present throughout the Old and New Testaments. They find references to his incarnation and his church throughout the Bible, too. This means there are references to his Mother as well, since she brought him into the world as incarnate, and since she said "Yes" to God and is thus both a model for the church and its embodiment.

MAKING CONNECTIONS

The Christian Bible, with all the different books and literary genres it contains, has an overall narrative, the story of our world and its history. The creation (in Genesis) is at the beginning of the story, the age to come arrives at the end (in Revelation), and the middle is the incarnation, life, death and resurrection of Christ [Figure 1]. Early Christians mapped events in the Bible and events in their lives into this framework and sought to show how all the scriptures and all the events are connected to each other. Thus, in the first half of the Biblical story, Adam and Eve, Abraham and Sarah, Moses and Miriam, David and the prophets, and the rest of the ancient Israelites played formative roles in the history that led up to Jesus Christ. The second half of history leads from Christ's incarnation to the eschaton. Within this time we find the history of the church, all of its saints, all of future history, and the present community that reads the Scripture, hears it interpreted, and applies it to their lives (to *us*). If we choose, we can all be part of God's story that leads humankind to salvation.

All this is the horizontal dimension of the world of which the Bible speaks. According to early Christians, there is also a vertical dimension that connects earth to heaven. In Paradise, at the beginning, there was free communication between earth and heaven. The Hebrew bible then preserves the memory of repeated encounters of Israel with God. Then

---

[1] The literature on patristic exegesis is vast. A good starting point is James L. Kugel and Rowan A. Greer, *Early Biblical Interpretation* (Philadelphia, PA: Westminster Press, 1986).

the incarnation of Christ brings heaven to earth again, so that Christ, or his Mother, has become Jacob's ladder for the whole world, on which one can ascend and descend. Further communications occur in the church's history; and in the age to come, heaven and earth will finally be made one.

Early Christian interpreters of Scripture continually looked for connections between different points on this chart [Figure 1]. Adam, Abraham, David, the prophets, and many other Old Testament luminaries prefigured Christ and anticipated patterns in his life. Then they, Christ himself, and saints of the church became patterns for later Christians, such as ourselves, to imitate, not woodenly but creatively, in the context of our own life circumstances. Everything in our present story recalls the original events of creation, paradise, and the fall, and everything points forward to the eschaton. Events on earth also direct our attention upward to life with God and the angels in heaven.

The Mother of God, too, has her place in the world's history. She is found right at the center, with her Son [Figure 2]. She was instrumental in his incarnation; she stood beside him at the Cross; and she witnessed his resurrection. Orthodox icons show her present at his ascension. Israel's long history of struggle in relationship with God finds its fulfillment in her decision to say "Yes" to her Creator and receive him incarnate in her. Together with Christ, she thus becomes an example and a source of grace to all members of the church. It is as if all the holiness in Israel leads up to her and becomes concentrated in her. Then from her is born Christ, who brings into being the whole church. More members are added to it in each generation, until the end of history.

LEVELS OF BIBLICAL MEANING

Although the fathers interpret Scripture almost constantly in their innumerable sermons and theological treatises, and throughout their main writings, there are few places in which they reflect explicitly on the rules or methods of interpretation they follow. Two of the best places to look for such rules are Book 4 of Origen, *On First Principles*, and Augustine's discussion of the *Rules of Tyconius* in Book 3 of *On Christian Doctrine*. To be sure, Orthodox Christians would hesitate to call either Origen, Tyconius, or Augustine a central figure in their tradition, but the exegetical principles they identify are used by many, if not all, of the Greek fathers, and so we will use them in this essay.

Origen identifies three levels of meaning in Scripture, which he links with the three parts of the human person: body, soul, and spirit.[2] To be sure, a given Biblical passage may or may not have all three kinds of meaning. Yet it may have more than three, since there may be more than one kind of meaning in a given category, or there may be meanings that escape such categorization. The first level, associated with the body, is the literal level, which is concrete and historical. Thus, for example, Mary is the daughter of Abraham and the daughter of David, by concrete physical descent, and the Mother of Jesus Christ. Thus, she is a member of Israel, related to all other Israelites in one large family. She is a descendent of Abraham and has received his heritage and covenant with God. She has also inherited the royal blood of David's family. Her relationship with her Son, too, is bodily and concrete. It is not a function of moods that can come and go, nor does it risk being illusion; it is absolutely real and abides forever.

The other two levels of Biblical meaning are both allegorical. That is, they both point to different kinds of connections joining points on my chart [Figure 1]. The second level, that of the soul, makes connections of exemplarity, from anticipation to fulfillment and from model to authentic imitation. It is the level of moral interpretation, which is so dear to many preachers. Biblical characters come to represent certain virtues or vices that Scripture shows they embody, such as

---

[2] *On First Principles* 4.2.4.

Abraham's faith and hospitality, or David's meekness. The Mother of God has received all the virtues of her Israelite ancestors, and she sets an example for church members who come after her. She believed God and the angel, since she is full of faith. She is God's humble servant, and in purity of soul has contained God within her body. She shares the sorrow of Christ's Cross, but at his resurrection she emerges as one full of joy, radiant, always receiving that joy together with God's blessings and communicating it to others. And she is the figure of Wisdom in Proverbs, who builds a house, the church, and offers hospitality, bread and wine - that is, Christ in the Eucharist - to everyone who heeds her call and comes to her. She ponders God's mysteries in her heart, through prayer and contemplation, so that, quietly, her thoughts mature into wisdom. Finally, her unending love for her Son overflows, so that it spreads to everything he loves, to all his people, and to all of his creation.

The third level of Biblical meaning, that of the spirit, is usually about interpersonal relationships. In her birthgiving, Mary was given concrete relationships with the three persons of the Trinity. The Father gave her his Son. The Holy Spirit dwelt in her, made her womb fruitful, and made Christ present within her. And the Son of God became her Son. After he is born, these three relationships belong to her always. Her motherhood began as a physical event but grew as interpersonal, and grew even more to become spiritual. That is, she knew her Son first as a divine child become human with many physical needs, then as a man who is also divine, and then as God-man risen from the dead. Yet the earlier phases of her relationship with him remain in her and continue to define her identity. In ways that only she can comprehend, her earlier knowledge of him as a child and as a man must remain present within her later experiences of him as the glory of God. After his ascension, she relates to him through prayer; and in this, others can follow her example. Her relationship with God is so abundant that it includes the character of all kinds of human family love. She becomes at once the Daughter, Mother, and Bride of God.

Similarly, our relationship with Go grows into many kinds of love and interaction, as God comes to us in different ways, according to our needs-as Father, as Bridegroom, and, at Christmas, as Child.

Spiritual relationships also emerge between Mary and others. Because she shares in the relationship with God that Abraham founded, and in the community of his descendents, she is his daughter spiritually as well as physically, truly Jewish. She is also related to members of the Church, since she cares for them all as a Mother. Ultimately she represents the whole human race, and all of creation, since she is connected with all, in that she is herself human and created. She can draw other people, with whom she is connected, into her own relationship with God. So she fulfills the royal priesthood, a vocation given to all humans when they were created in God's image and likeness. She is the microcosm of creation and the mediator between God and the world, between the world and God. Through her, God became incarnate in the created world, and through her, all of creation says "Yes" to God and is offered to God, in order to receive him. On Christmas Eve, the Orthodox Church sings a hymn in which she is portrayed as humankind's best offering to God:

> What shall we offer you, O Christ who for our
> sakes has appeared on earth as man? Every
> creature made by you offers you thanks. The
> angels offer you a hymn; the heavens, a star; the
> Magi, gifs; the shepherds, their wonder; the
> earth, its cave; the wilderness, the manger: and
> we offer you a Virgin Mother. O Pre-Eternal
> God, have mercy on us.[3]

As a human person made in God's image, she appears at the center of creation. As she offers herself to God, she offers with

---

[3] Mother Mary and Archimandrite Kallistos Ware, trans., *The Festal Menaion* (London: Faber and Faber, 1969) 254, translation updated.

herself the whole universe of which she is a part, all of heaven and earth. In her, it is the created world that receives Christ incarnate.

Another form of Biblical interpretation specifically connected with the Mother of God involves things in the Hebrew bible that have come to represent her. All these things function as receptacles, and all of them contain either God or things that represent Christ; thus, she is the candlestick and Christ, the Light of the World, is the candle. This language still speaks of relationship with God so it is a sub-category of Origen's third, spiritual level of meaning. For example, she is the living temple of God. The temple, which played such an important role in the life of Israel, symbolized and foreshadowed her. But instead of being built of stone, she is a living human person. Of course, just as God dwelt in the temple, he dwells, even more fully and perfectly, in her. This temple imagery describes her holiness, as well. On a smaller scale, all the furniture and sacred vessels of the temple, and related things, which are lovingly described in the bible, likewise represent her. The Orthodox Church reverently applies all these images to the Mother of God. She is the tabernacle, table, censer, candlestick, priestly vestment, etc. By implication, Christ is God present in the tabernacle, the offering on the altar, the incense and light, the High Priest, etc. A related image is that of a table on which bread is set, or a cup in which wine is served, representing Christ as the Eucharist. On a larger scale, she is the city of God, which is personified in the Hebrew Bible as the Daughter of Jerusalem, the one who grieves in Lamentations and rejoices in Third Isaiah. Of course, she is the daughter of Israel, whose capital Jerusalem is, in a literal sense, too.

People sometimes wonder about the way she is symbolized by so many inanimate objects. Perhaps they worry that because she is a woman the tradition has depersonalized her and has portrayed her as having only instrumental value. Such objections are missing the point, particularly of the temple imagery, which plays a dominant role in the tradition. It really

263

points to her royal priesthood, and her profound contribution to the worship of God. Christ, of course, is the great High Priest, but she remains as close to him as the vestments and the sacred vessels that a priest uses in his priestly service. In other words, she has given him the human nature in which he is clothed and all the human tools he uses in his incarnate life. He needs this vestment and these implements to fulfill his priestly vocation on behalf of humankind and the whole world. In this way, she contributes to his priestly action. She is still serving as the mediator between God and creation. This is the vocation of royal priesthood God gave to every human person as made in his image. We have fallen, but Christ fulfills it, and his mother fulfills it with him. All Christians, then, are restored with them to this original vocation, this original responsibility.

In the Russian Orthodox tradition, before the Divine Liturgy, when a bishop is serving, he is ceremonially dressed in all his vestments in front of the congregation. He does not even put on his own episcopal robes. There are buttons on the back that he cannot reach himself. This shows that it is the whole community that makes a man a bishop and enables him to serve as one. During the vesting, the choir slowly and meditatively sings hymns to the Mother of God, such as this one:

> The prophets proclaimed you from on high, O Virgin: the jar, the staff, the tablets of the Law, the ark, the candlestick, the table, the mount uncloven, the golden censer, the tabernacle, the gate impassable, the palace and ladder, and the throne of kings.[4]

All this imagery comes from the Old Testament. Why is the Mother of God remembered in this context? If the bishop is a representative of Christ, his vestments represent the flesh the

_____

[4] Unpublished translation. Let me thank Fr. Timothy Sawchuk of Holy Trinity Church, Overland Park, Kansas, for sharing this text with me.

Lord took from his Mother. She is the summation of every place in the created world where God comes to dwell, including all of the temple's furniture, but also Jacob's ladder on which Christ came down to us. Her lap is his throne, and she is his palace.

THE RULES OF TYCONIUS

The *Rules of Tyconius*, which Augustine summarizes, are intended to explain the sudden shifts of subject that occur in Scripture, especially when it is being read typologically as a book about Christ. These rules may help us understand the shifts of reference that occur in Mariology and Ecclesiology. For example, who is the bride in the Song of Songs? Is she the Mother of God, or the whole Church, or the individual believer who is advancing toward perfection, or all of the above? Two of Tyconius' rules are relevant to our discussion here: the first, "Of the Lord and his body," and the fourth, "Of part and whole."[5]

Augustine explains that the Lord and his body are sometimes represented together as one person. He says that an example is the subject of the following: "as a bridegroom decked with a crown, and as a bride adorned with her jewels" [Is 61.10]. Who is that? Of course, the crowned bridegroom refers to Christ, and the bejeweled bride refers to the Church. Head and body together form a single person. This language suggests overlaps, sharing, and communion between Christ and the Church, since the body belongs to the head, and the head is part of the body. Paul applies this imagery to a marriage, in which husband and wife as it were, become parts of each other's being. Therefore, a husband must respect and care for his wife, as he does for his own body [Eph 5.25-33]. But a similar sharing occurs between Christ and his Mother, since he has received his body from her. So she has become his body in an immediate sense. Since she is at the heart of the church, of humankind, and of the creation, his body can therefore extend

---

[5] Augustine, *On Christian Doctrine*, 3.31.44 and 3.34.47-49.

through her to include all of these. A single church member is also his body. This is why metaphorical descriptions of Mary, the Church, and the faithful disciple have so much in common. The grace of Christ's headship extends to each of them. Each one, then, can become the bride in the Song of Songs.

This brings us to Tyconius' fourth rule, about the part and the whole. The Hebrew Bible often speaks of one person when referring to a whole community. For example, Jacob represents the whole people of Israel, and "Israel" is in fact another name for Jacob. Scripture often uses synecdoche, that is, it speaks of a part when it means the whole. The "daughter of Jerusalem" is said to weep at the time of the Babylonian exile, which means that the whole city is weeping. To be sure, there are connections between the exemplary individual and the community - ties of human fellowship, ties of bodily kinship, and spiritual ties. Because these ties are genuine, the exemplar - Jacob, the daughter of Jerusalem, or the Mother of God - in some way embodies the whole community. Likewise, the members of the community share in the character, or the grace, of their exemplary representative.

The greatest example of this phenomenon, of course, is Christ, who is a particular person, Jesus of Nazareth, yet theologians also speak of "the whole Christ,"[6] head and members. Christ acts through his members, that is, through his saints, or his Church throughout history. This grace of Christ, who is prophet, priest, and king, extends to his disciples in every generation, so that he can act through them as Savior of the world to carry out the works of his threefold ministry. In order for this to happen, his disciples need to let him work through them, and need to be willing to act in collaboration with him. This grace-filled collaboration, empowered by Christ himself, is what results in the imitation of Christ. In other words, participation brings imitation.

---

[6] Cf. Emile Mersch, *The Whole Christ: The Historical Development of the Doctrine of the Mystical Body in Scripture and Tradition,* trans. John R. Kelly, (Milwaukee, WS:Bruce Publishing Co., 1938), an excellent study.

Because Christ is risen from the dead, death no longer divides his body. This means that the saints, who are in communion with him, remain in communion with us. The virtues they have practiced and the good deeds they have done in Christ therefore become examples for Christians today. In imitating the saints, ultimately we are imitating Christ. So then we are doubly blessed, because we receive grace directly from Christ and also indirectly through his faithful servants. The Lord blesses us, and the saint prays for us, since they both love us. In this way, Christ's grace multiplies in the church.

As an exemplar, the Mother of God has a special place, since she is at the heart, or at the root, of the Church. In responding to God, she sums up the life of Israel and comes first in the church, which follows her. We are called to share in her faithful response, in her true discipleship. The Church is a community that is jointed to her in responding to Christ, like the maidens who accompany the bride in the Song of Songs. According to interpretive tradition, the maidens learn from the bride and follow her example, so that they too become brides of Christ. In her response, Mary embodies the whole church in herself. All Christians, therefore, can hope to participate in her discipleship.

BODY OF CHRIST AND BRIDE OF CHRIST

Each saint walks a unique path to God's kingdom, each offers a unique example of virtues to imitate yet each mediates Christ's grace, which draws others to accompany him or her. So we have many examples to follow, and we can select those who are best suited to our own character and circumstances. We inevitably follow more than one.

The church is both the Body of Christ and the Bride of Christ. So, each of us is called to be Christ's body, to let him act through us for the benefit of others. Each of us is also Christ's bride, like the Mother of God, called to find him everywhere and respond to him with love. For example, in an act of charity, the donor is the body of Christ in giving to the poor but is also Christ's bride, seeing Christ in the face of the poor. Likewise, the recipient is Christ's body through his poverty, but is also Christ's bride, finding him in a benefactor who comes like divine providence. As members of the church, we are always interacting with each other. So, in our community life, we each have the task of building each other up, of being body of Christ and bride of Christ for others, in many ways, again and again. In so doing, we have plenty of opportunities to imitate Christ *and* to imitate the Mother of God.

This means that, on Origen's third, symbolic level, every church member is both masculine and feminine. The worship of Jesus Christ, who became incarnate as a man, does not privilege the masculine exclusively; nor does the identification of our creaturehood with the Mother of God privilege the feminine exclusively. This allegorical androgyny follows from the fact that each of us is called to practice all the virtues, in order to arrive at human wholeness. We each begin with one virtue that is congenial to us, and as we work on learning it, we finally have to practice all the others in order to reach its perfection. Human culture divides virtues by gender, so we think of nurturing as feminine and courage as masculine. In the end, however, each of us needs all the virtues in order to be fully human.

FINDING WHAT IS PASTORALLY APPLICABLE

Each saint hears or reads the Gospel message in a personal way and becomes a unique embodiment of the message of Scripture. Just as there are many saints, Scripture has multiple levels of meaning, as we said earlier. How, then, can the Church decide which possible meanings of Scripture to adopt, and which to lay aside? Are there some paths we had better not follow? Here again, patristic methods of interpretation are a good guide.

First, it is important to pay attention to the *aim* of Scripture, which is to glorify Jesus Christ and bring the church community to wholeness and salvation. So if a certain verse is being used to beat people over the head, or is harmful to a group of people in the church, such as women, its interpretation is missing the mark. It is a good idea to look for another interpretation. The church fathers usually provide several possibilities among which we can choose.

Early Christians had several criteria for excluding certain interpretations as misguided. If it appears that something in Scripture conflicts with the message of the Bible as a whole, if it undermines church teaching - the Creed or the Rule of Faith, if it is morally unworthy of God, or if it is obscure and incomprehensible, then it is time to look for a different interpretation. The idea of excluding things that are morally unworthy of God is particularly important. When the Afrikaaner church in South Africa used the Bible to justify Apartheid, for example, this criterion can clearly be applied.

Since the symbolism of the Mother of God is based on Biblical interpretation and therefore has multiple levels of meaning, the same criteria apply here that apply to Scripture. So we need not think of Mary as oppressive to women because some think her imitation would demand an impossible feminine ideal, combining virginity with motherhood and total submissiveness. Again, we must not interpret the parallel between Christ and Mary as meaning that he is not divine, or that she is not a creature. Let us honor her by quietly discarding, or reinterpreting, symbols we cannot apply pastorally today, and celebrate the many symbols that we can apply.

Figure 1: EARLY CHRISTIAN BIBLICAL INTERPRETATION
Making Connections

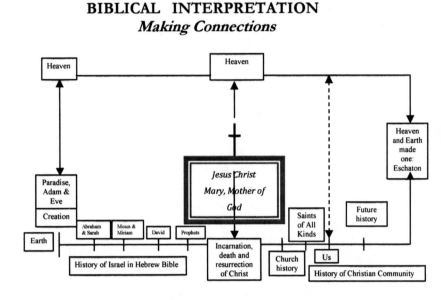

Figure 2: FROM HEBREW SCRIPTURE TO THE CHURCH

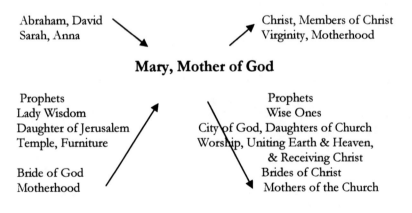

Abraham, David
Sarah, Anna

Christ, Members of Christ
Virginity, Motherhood

Mary, Mother of God

Prophets
Lady Wisdom
Daughter of Jerusalem
Temple, Furniture

Bride of God
Motherhood

Prophets
Wise Ones
City of God, Daughters of Church
Worship, Uniting Earth & Heaven,
      & Receiving Christ
Brides of Christ
Mothers of the Church

270

CPSIA information can be obtained at www.ICGtesting.com
Printed in the USA
LVOW12s1054150115

422860LV00001B/111/P